Action Research
and
Organizational Development

Action Research
and
Organizational Development

J. BARTON CUNNINGHAM

Foreword by A. W. McEachern

Westport, Connecticut
London

0376940

Library of Congress Cataloging-in-Publication Data

Cunningham, J. Barton.
    Action research and organizational development / J. Barton
Cunningham ; foreword by A. W. McEachern.
        p.   cm.
    Includes bibliographical references and index.
    ISBN 0-275-94265-1 (alk. paper)
    1. Social sciences—Research. 2. Action research.
3. Organizational change. I. Title.
H62.C813 1993
300'.72—dc20   92-1744

British Library Cataloguing in Publication Data is available.

Library of Congress Catalog Card Number: 92-1744
ISBN: 0-275-94265-1

First published in 1993

Praeger Publishers, 88 Post Road West, Westport, CT 06881
An imprint of Greenwood Publishing Group, Inc.

Printed in the United States of America

The paper used in this book complies with the
Permanent Paper Standard issued by the National
Information Standards Organization (Z39.48-1984).
P

In order to keep this title in print and available to the academic community, this edition
was produced using digital reprint technology in a relatively short print run. This would
not have been attainable using traditional methods. Although the cover has been changed
from its original appearance, the text remains the same and all materials and methods
used still conform to the highest book-making standards.

Contents

Foreword

Over a year ago Dr. Cunningham asked if I would write a foreword to this book, which was then inchoate and untitled. I suggested that I was probably the wrong person for this since I was, and more or less continue to be, one of those old fashioned, positively and behaviorally inclined scientists whose orientation and methods have received such a drubbing lately at the hands of a "new" breed of epistemologists and ontologists. Despite this caveat, Bart, who had been my student and a rare fellow Canadian in our school about twenty years ago, sent me a copy of his manuscript and repeated his request.

The difficulties I've had over the years understanding those with a "qualitative," intuitive orientation to research on the complexities with which humans embroil themselves in organizations is simply this: I can't tell the difference between what they say they do and what "normal" scientists say they do. Some time ago, in a research methods seminar, doctoral students reviewed a number of descriptions of studies purporting to represent a participative, involved and committed approach. Each of these was by a different author, with different objectives, different skills, and experiences and dealing with different problems, communities, and organizations. It soon became clear that the fundamental "methods" were the same as those described by "conventional," social scientists: the participative authors reported making observations on the basis of their own preconceptions (which "normal" scientists call theories or working hypotheses), adjusting the observational techniques to the peculiar circumstances of those things or people being studied, and then trying to make sense of what had been observed by elaborating, modifying or drastically revising their preconceptions. What's so different about that?

Nothing, so far as the basic observational or empirical approach is concerned. As I see it, the differences are not so much methodological as contextual: The people doing the research are different, they have different preconceptions or theories, different objectives, skills and habits, and they observe different objects, however much they were liked, identified with, or even, god forbid, depersonalized. Furthermore, there are similar differences among "hard" scientists. How else could a pair of paragons of the non-intuitive variety have thought they had discovered and demonstrated cold fusion?

That these differences in objectives, in approaches, in habits and sensitivities are important is the main methodological message of this book. It is a difference between those whose primary objective is to find out things that will help people, and those whose primary objective (they sometimes say, though I doubt it) is just to find out things, period. It is a difference between the engineers and the physicists and chemists, between the medical practitioners and the biologists, the policy analysts and the economists, the campaign managers and the political scientists, the clinical and experimental psychologists, and so on. To be sure, there are fashions with respect to the adulation attached to different professions with different objectives. Even in my own school of public administration, a title of the utmost practicality, there have been phases during which some faculty have eschewed the engineering implications of their professional identity, and pretended to be pure scientists with Truth as their only objective. I've never been able to understand that either.

This book unashamedly adopts a practical orientation with a view to providing organizational practitioners (scientists, managers, developers, consultants, and workers) with an approach to understanding and *doing something about* the aspects, practices, and problems of organizations that they don't like. Based on his wide experience with different organizations, Bart offers suggestions for systematic problem identification, evaluative analysis and review, invention of alternatives to old bad habits, and ways in which these inventions can be put to good use. When he adds the necessary skepticism, the need to question anything and everything that is going on, including old methodological conventions, he sounds much like a working scientists with humane objectives.

Organizations may be necessary for complex cooperative actions, but as they're put together nowadays they're certainly a mess. Given the limited sensory and perceptual tools with which humans are equipped, they need all the help they can get as they approach such self-created imbroglios. Most people know there is a blind spot in their visual field corresponding to the juncture of the optic nerve and the retina. It usually doesn't affect visual perception because we habitually fill in the blanks by adding old information to the physical sensation, which may be a kind of mechanical intuition. Many people have similar holes in their hearing at frequency ranges corresponding to damaged areas in their cochlea, caused perhaps by over exposure to industrial noise or what passes for music in some circles. They may or may not fill in the blanks, as Beethoven probably did, as a function of training and experience and interest in interpreting sounds. These are some of our grosser and relatively easily identified imperfections as observers of the world around us. What you see and hear may be what you get, but it may be unrelated to what other people see and hear. To complicate things even more, we then try to communicate with others, using abstractions from what we think we've seen and heard. Words are abstractions, as are numbers and drawings, graphs and impressionistic paintings. Which leads me to conclude that the precision of science, action oriented or not, is an illusion. Recognizing that we are all afflicted with the same imperfections should lead to the kind of skeptical modesty that Bart displays as he offers detailed practical advice for those who want to find out what's wrong with organizations in order to do something to improve them.

A. W. McEachern

Acknowledgments

This book has undergone many changes based on comments from colleagues and my practice in the field. My thinking will continue to evolve over the next number of years from the continuing act of carrying out research in field settings and from the comments of those I have worked with.

In any such endeavor, there is the tendency for one to think that his creation is of tremendous importance. There are several people whose ideas are indirectly or directly a main thrust of this work. The spirit of this book owes much to continuing association with Alex MacEachern. It grew from the practices and ideas of professors and colleagues I was associated with over twenty years ago at the University of Southern California including Wesley Bjur, Ross Clayton, Neely Gardner, Shan Martin, Alberto-Guerrio Ramos, and Gilbert Siegel. Credit is obviously due to many of the people I associated with when I was at the Tavistock Institute in 1981 and 1982. More recently, there are other people who contributed significantly in my development. I have had long discussions with Eric Trist about the action research practices that represent the Tavistock tradition. I have also had several opportunities to piece together an appreciation of the Lewinian action research practices through a close working relationship with Jim MacGregor, one of Alex Bavelas' students. John Farquharson and Joe Lischeron continue to be the source of ideas and inspiration. Most of all, I would like to thank my wife Donna for helping me prepare this draft for publication.

Part I

The Need

1

A Definition
of Action Research

There appears to be a growing recognition of the difficulties involved in using the traditional scientific research paradigm for practical organizational development. The traditional scientist is becoming more and more sophisticated while the users of the research are demanding more practical, clear, and timely solutions. The procedures do not seem to recognize the dynamic nature of organizational problems.

A major concern for managers and researchers is that many organizations are linked to events where the surrounding organizational environments are changing at an dynamic rate. These environments might be characterized as complex and "turbulent." These are situations where goals are continually adjusting to new demands, and where the organization's growth is increasingly dependent on what is happening in the society at large. What becomes precarious in these situations is that individual organizations cannot expect to adapt successfully through their own actions. Rationality and science cannot solve many of the problems these organizations face.

Over the next decade or so, we can still expect to observe a number of researchers operating within the narrow limits of their own fields of science, receiving funding from long-established funding agencies. They will use conventional notions of research, relying on experimental canons--quantification, experimental control, replication, reductionism, and the like. They will write articles for academic journals based on controlled research settings, such as laboratory or simulated environments.

This book is about action-related research and organizational change, and attempts to summarize many of the developments over the last twenty-five years. Action research is a brand of research originating after World War II to solve problems in applied settings. Action research was never in the mainstream of the social sciences, as its tools and techniques were viewed as inadequate by the traditional scientist. It never got off the ground and was condemned to a sort of orphan's role in the social sciences shortly after World War II. The early optimism that some had held toward the potentials of action research disappeared when many of the originators retired.[1]

This book is based on the belief that an action science can offer a blueprint for scientific and organizational development activities in applied settings. Its success depends on our ability to define its place in science, its rules and assumptions, and its activities and procedures. Over the last three decades, there have been several developments making it easier to carry out action research. This book illustrates the place of an action research and the research practices guiding it.

WHAT IS ACTION RESEARCH?

This book outlines how managers and researchers can use action research procedures to carry out organizational studies. It provides a perspective on the developments in action research and bridges the Tavistock experiences and those of Lewin's Center for Group Dynamics. It illustrates a model of research focusing on knowledge creation and discovery rather than replication and verification.

"Action research" is a term for describing a spectrum of activities that focus on research, planning, theorizing, learning, and development. It describes a continuous process of research and learning in the researcher's long-term relationship with a problem.

Many people have contributed to the body of knowledge on action research. Some action researchers have emphasized experimentation, others have been concerned with feedback, planning, or learning and theory building. For example, the staff at the Tavistock Institute of Human Relations emphasized collaborative problem-solving and joint learning. Lewin and his associates at the Center for Group Dynamics were more concerned with theory building and experimentation. That is probably why people at the Tavistock never really "mated" with the Center for Group Dynamics, even though many in the field say they did. Lewin's people were not interested in analyzing unconscious processes. They were experimentalists. Lewin's brand of research was quite different from that at the Tavistock.

An action researcher is a person with a scientific attitude, an understanding of qualitative research principles, an understanding of the dynamics of change, and a commitment to studying problems that are relevant in real settings. This process is as much an act of scientific research as an act of engagement with people experiencing the problem. It deals with conscious and unconscious data. It involves theorizing, experimenting, and implementing, being extremely rigorous with some steps, and very flexible with others. In practicing action research, the social scientist is "engaged" within an organization or group undergoing a change. The word "engagement" comes from the existentialist literature--*engager*--and means being committed to or engaged as the problem evolves. Engagement in a research process is an opportunity to pool the resources and ideas of both clients and researchers.

Action research encourages the researcher to experience the problem as it evolves. This is the act of "engaging" in real-life problem-solving, and getting legitimization from real organization. The researcher must be able to access real-life data in "real" time. It is an act of being engaged in the universe where the problem is occurring. This requires the commitment and interest of those who are experiencing the problems. Tommy Wilson, the founding director of the Tavistock Institute was fond of saying, "You can't stop a man in the street and ask him to let you open up his abdomen in the interest of pure science. He won't let you." Because it will never resolve all organizational problems, action research is not a replacement for conventional experimental science. Traditional science encourages the testing of ideas in controlled settings, while controlling extraneous variables to gain a better understanding of the effects of the experimental variables. In this context, an action science is an important supplement for experimental science. Each must be carried out at the appropriate time.

For the maximum benefit, action research activities can supplement other scientific activities. Each type of research has its place. It may become appropriate to carry out conventional research to verify conclusions and interpretations, but it is also necessary to apply these results in unique situations. These applications may provoke further ideas and problems. The action researcher is not looking for something to experiment upon, but responds to the provocations in the field.[2]

This book illustrates the usefulness of an action research process in enhancing organizational change and development. The book is organized so that the reader can gain an understanding of a sequence of activities to assist research and change. Part I illustrates the need for an action research approach. Chapters 2 and 3 provide an overview and early history leading to the development of action research. Part II includes chapters on the action research process. Chapter 4 illustrates how some very creative discoveries emerged from non-conventional research practices. Chapter 5 outlines a number of action research principles and Chapter 6 is an overview of the action research and organizational process.

In Part III, the research approach is described with chapters on interviewing, developing questionnaires and other measures, and analyzing qualitative data. Parts IV and V summarize certain principles and practises for focusing and implementing organizational change.

NOTES

1. N. Sanford, "Whatever Happened to Action Research," *Journal of Social Issues,* vol. 26, 1970, pp. 3-23;   See also M. Foster, "The Theory and Practice of Action Research in Work Organizations," *Human Relations*, vol. 25, 1972, pp. 529-556.

2. This chapter expresses the views of Eric Trist. It was written based on interviews with him when he visited my home during the summers of 1985, 1988, 1989, and 1990.

2

The Need for
an Action Research

Most scientific pundits claim that research exists to further the cause of science, answering questions with reliable and unbiased information.

This scientific activity can consume enormous amounts of time. Like a sail boat, it is also expensive. This research is also detailed, meticulous, and demands sometimes boring tabulations and observations. Further, the technical skills using mathematics, statistics, and computer programs must be integrated and allied with a scientific attitude and attention to detail.

Traditions which assist the evaluation and prediction process anchor scientific research. These traditions include establishing experimental controls, replication, and precise measurements, while also guarding against invalidity and unreliability. The goal is to discover new facts, verify old facts, and to analyze their sequences, causal explanations, and the natural laws governing the data gathered.

Traditional science has achieved modes of success in trying to explain and solve societal and organizational problems. There is much that can be measured in society, and traditional science has done very well in accomplishing this task. It has been particularly relevant in chemistry, physics, biology and other fields some call the "hard" sciences.

Apparently, recognition is growing of the difficulties involved in using this traditional scientific research paradigm for practical organizational development problems. That is, "there may be an inherent incompatibility between practical problem-solving and "scientific research," and maximizing one may minimize the other."[1] Scientific research practices are often accused of being unfortunate impediments to effective action. Paradoxically, the traditional scientists are becoming more and more sophisticated, while the research users are demanding material which is simple, clear, and timely. Thus, there have been several suggestions that research procedures should recognize the dynamic nature of organizational problems.[2]

Practicing managers and lay people have had some difficulties using and understanding the applications of traditional science rules in organizations. Managers hold to their "intuitive" methods of change. They have learned to accept that science is rather impractical; that theory and practice have nothing to do with one another; and that the scientific methods of categorization are impediments to good logic and reason.

We are witnessing an increased need for research tools to assist in solving practical problems, as many organizations grow in size and many societal problems become more apparent. One has only to look at a daily newspaper to find illustrations of problems needing research and organizational development--such as health care, social welfare, policing, and community needs. The Nobel prize winner Alexis Carrel wrote:

> In fact, our ignorance is profound. Most of the questions. . .remain without an answer. . . . How is the mind influenced by the state of the organs? In what manner can the organic and mental characteristics, which each individual inherits, be changed by the mode of life, the chemical substances contained in food, the climate, and the physiological and moral disciples. . . . As yet, we do not know what environment is the most favorable for the optimum development of civilized (people). Is it possible to suppress struggle, effort, and suffering from our physiological and spiritual formation? How can we prevent the degeneracy of (human nature) in modern civilization? Many other questions could be asked on subjects which are to us of the utmost interest. They would remain unanswered. It is evident that. . . our knowledge of ourselves is still most rudimentary.[3]

The range of problems confronting organizations may require a shift in the way we think about research and problem-solving. In fact, many of these problems are systemic and connected with other problems, since the problems of the work system may be related to those in society.

Many social scientists have recognized that they cannot answer timely organizational questions with experimental scientific practices. There is no longer a privileged access to organizations where the internal and external environments could be controlled for research purposes. As one manager in a public sector organization remarked: "Academic research has probably got its place. But it's not very helpful for the problems we face in organizations." Such comments have stirred leading management theorists to suggest that we should revise our concepts of management.[4]

Users of the traditional research paradigm are aware of some of its difficulties in applied settings. Most of the studies in field settings are convenience samples which cannot be generalized. At best, these studies achieve internal rather than external validity; they are explicit about what they are measuring, although the measures may not coincide describe field setting concepts.

Unfortunately, the growth of professionalism or a set of practical research canons has not united the field of practical researchers.[5] Organizational development practitioners or researchers are accused of producing "mushy" theories, devoid of useful concepts for describing human behavior.[6] Consequently, the research outcomes of leading practitioners of any non-experimental style of research remain both difficult to de-code and largely unavailable to the growing number of graduate social scientists.

There is probably a need for an action oriented research process, one which is based on rigorous standards of problem-solving. This would be a research process which allows the practitioner to guarantee the methodological "rightness" of the research, especially where one researcher's conclusions can be verified with those of another. Such a view of science focuses on action-related science rather than a laboratory type. Alex Carrel provides a statement of the need for such a science of society.

> In order to endure, society as well as individuals, should conform to the laws of life. We cannot erect a house without a knowledge of the law of gravity. "In order to be commanded, nature must be obeyed," said Bacon. The essential needs of the human being, the characteristics of (the) mind and organs, (the) relations with (the) environment, are easily subjected to scientific observation. The jurisdiction of science extends to all observable phenomena--the spiritual as well as the intellectual and physiological. (Human nature) in (the) entirety can be apprehended by the scientific method. But the science of (human nature) differs from other sciences. It must be synthetic as well as analytic, since (the human being) is simultaneously unity and multiplicity. This science alone is capable of giving birth to a technique for the construction of society.[7]

There are many researchers who have worked toward the goal of a more rigorous action research.[8] They experience the difficulty of constructing an action science.

Whatever happened to action research? Nevitt Sanford responded to this question in the early 1970s, and suggested that the several action related programs--true action research, evaluation research, and applied research--were not undertaking the study of action as a means of advancing science. Problem analysis, conceptualization, execution, evaluation, and training are often carried out by several people. There are experts in conceptualization, theoretical model building, research design, experimentation, and so on. We have dehumanized our research subjects and have called them respondents, and given them no benefits to the research done on them.[9]

Action research is a process of systematically collecting research data about an ongoing system. Its purpose, as defined here, is to develop or discover aspects of the system's operation which can lead to improvement and change. The process involves understanding the system, defining solutions or discoveries, applying and modifying these solutions, and assessing the results of the actions. This book describes the characteristics of an action research process for carrying out research and implementing changes.

Action research is a unique scientific process in its concerns for accepting the values inherent in the client system[10] and differs from traditional scientific inquiry because of the researcher's involvement with people's expectations and values. It relies on the researcher's ability to select good information from poor information, especially as it concerns the behaviors and perceptions of individuals and groups. Judgements of the reliability and validity of action research data might be based on factors and interrelationships creating the problem for the client.[11]

NOTES

1. S.E. Seashore, "Field Experiments with Formal Organizations," *Human Organization*, vol. 23, 1964, pp. 164-170.

2. C. Argyris, *Intervention Theory and Method* (Reading, Mass: Addison-Wesley, 1970); S. E. Seashore, "Field Experiments with Formal Organizations"; G. I. Susman and R. D. Evered, "An Assessment of the Scientific Merits of Action Research," *Administrative Science Quarterly*, vol. 23, 1978, pp. 582-603.

3. A. Carrel, *Man, The Unknown* (New York: MacFadden Publications, 1961), pp. 7-8. The words in brackets are substitutes for the word "man."

4. See for example H. Mintzberg, "Managerial Work: Analysis from Observation," *Management Science*, vol. 2, 1971, pp. 97-100.

5. C. Argyris, *Intervention Theory and Method*.

6. A. W. Gouldner, *The Coming Crisis of Western Sociology* (New York: Avon, 1971).

7. A. Carrel, *Man, The Unknown*, pp. 7-8.

8. C. Argyris, *Intervention Theory and Method*; E. L. Trist,"Engaging with Large-scale Systems: Some Concepts and Methods Based on Experience Gained in Field Projects at the Tavistock Institute," Paper contributed to the McGregor Conference on Organization Development, (Endicott House, Endicott, New York, 1967); K. Lewin, *Field Theory in Social Science*, D Cartwright, (ed.), (New York: Harper, 1951).

9. N. Sanford, "Whatever Happened to Action Research," *Journal of Social Issues*, vol. 26, 1970.

10. C. Sofer, *The Organization from Within: A Comparative Study of Social Institutions Based on a Socio-therapeutic Approach* (London: Tavistock Publications, 1961).

11. C. Argyris, *Intervention Theory and Method*.

3

The Early History
of Action Research

The early history of action research can be attributed to contributions of experimental researchers, psychoanalysts, educators, operational researchers, medical researchers, and practitioners.[1] This chapter reviews the early history of action research and the key events and individuals associated with it.

Two traditions are associated with the early history of action research. The work of Kurt Lewin and his associates at the Center for Group Dynamics at the Massachusetts Institute of Technology became know for its group dynamics work. Another tradition grew from the work of a group of war-time researchers who later formed the Tavistock Institute of Human Relations in London, Great Britain. The group dynamics stream sought to carry out experimental research and theory building, while the Tavistock stream used psychoanalytical skills in developing a social science. Both streams placed an emphasis on laboratory training and developing knowledge of group life in field settings. An off-shoot of these efforts were researchers who sought to develop approaches to action training and learning.

This chapter describes the early history of action research with the goal of illustrating the cases and research experiences that might be used to guide us.

ACTION RESEARCH IN THE UNITED STATES

Kurt Lewin is associated with an action research emphasis which began in the United States. The underlying theme was to work collaboratively with managers and workers to understand and study the problems affecting them. Lewin felt that psychology needed to do more than just explain behavior. "We must be equally concerned," he said, "with discovering how people change so that they learn to behave better."[2] He had the conviction that any psychological problem could be examined in an experiment, and he was intrigued with the challenge of devising experiments in laboratory or field settings.[3]

Kurt Lewin's personal theories and history cannot be detached from the origins of action research in the United States. His ideas also had an enormous impact on certain developments at the Tavistock Institute of Human Relations, and especially on the thinking of Eric Trist.[4]

In the fall of 1933, Kurt Lewin began a new life in the United States, forced to leave Germany because the Nazi grip was tightening. He first held a two-year appointment at Cornell and then appointments at the University of Iowa until 1945. Lewin's interest in the psychological study of social issues resulted in his paying much attention to building a "bridge between social theory and social action." His work describes the challenges confronting minority groups everywhere.[5] He pointed out that every individual had a base for life--a life space--and the group is one of the most important components. The group is all important; it is the source of social status and feelings of security.[6]

Lewin was also concerned with the social problems of workers in industrial settings. An excellent example of an action research type of collaborative problem-solving was illustrated in his long association with the Harwood Manufacturing Corporation. In 1939, Lewin was invited to meet with the company's staff to discuss problems of training people from the mountains of Virginia to meet standards of production used in industrialized areas of the north. The local workers produced only about one-half as much as others in the northern plants after a customary twelve weeks of training.[7]

In a problem-solving session that lasted a full morning, Lewin suggested that the employees' failure might be due to feelings that the production goal was impossible to attain, possibly so unrealistic that employees felt no feelings of failure from not reaching it at all. Suggested changes included:

1. Eliminating the pressure put on the employees.
2. Dealing with workers as members of small groups rather than individuals.
3. Finding some method to give workers the feelings that their standards were realistic.

The production improved slightly, but many employees still did not reach the company standard. Finally, management decided to take a step previously rejected. They hiring experienced workers from other northern communities.

The newcomers (approximately sixty people) soon began attaining management's production standards. The other employees initially remained at their previous production levels, but began to change after about two weeks. They could see that the apparently unattainable goal could be reached. "What the experienced newcomers could do, the original trainees could also do."[8]

The collaborative relationship at Harwood lasted for eight years, until 1947. Lewin made a number of visits to the plant and encouraged the management to start a program of research to employ Alex Bavelas[9] to plan a series of small group studies. The earliest study sought to discover the effect of giving employees greater control over their output and an opportunity to participate in setting goals. Bavelas[10] attempted to change the informal norms of work groups regarding productivity in a garment factory. The experimental group members were invited to discuss the problem of production standards and were encouraged to make their own decisions. The control groups were not required to come up with a group decision about a solution. The results illustrated that the group who participated in decision-making also increased their productivity.

In the same factory, another team of researchers employed group discussion methods to gain acceptance for changes in work methods.[11] In this experiment, a control group of employees was introduced to the job changes in the conventional manner while two experimental groups were allowed varying degrees of participation regarding the changes. The increases in productivity were spectacular in that learning was more rapid and the productivity was higher in the experimental group. Other effects were increased morale and commitment and reduced labor turnover and grievances. These changes were similar when the control groups were reassigned to new jobs after thirty-two days of the older treatment. The dramatic results of the Coch-French experiment were replicated when French and some Scandinavian colleagues attempted a similar experiment in the footwear department of a Norwegian factory. The Norwegian experiment suggested that the effect of group discussion on the norms of behavior is conditioned by the larger organizational structure. The power of the group to influence its members in the organizational context seems to depend on the significance of the issues with which it is permitted to deal and its freedom and authority to act on these issues.[12]

The idea for these studies came from an earlier study examining the changing of food habits using different styles of decision-making. These were investigations of problems related to war-time shortages, and the use of group decisions as a means of changing habits. In attempting to change these food habits, the experimental groups participated in discussions about the "right" foods to eat; the discussion was facilitated by Alex Bavelas who worked with the assistance of an expert in nutrition. The control groups participated in a lecture by a nutritionist. The follow-up illustrated that a greater positive change in eating habits had occurred through group discussions. The resulting conclusion seemed to be that active participation was a more effective change tactic than passive participation (e.g. lecture). This suggested that the way to research a social system is for the researcher to participate in changing it.[13] These experiments were often interrupted by the needs of production. However, many of these experiments are still looked upon as examples of good experimental research in field settings.

Lewin had been at Iowa for nearly a decade by the time the war ended. His time there was often interspersed with visits to other universities and industrial settings, which were criticized by his academic colleagues. During his years in

Berlin and in Iowa, Lewin continued to be a vigorous advocate of the use of mathematical models in psychology. He was convinced that in order to raise psychology to a higher level of science, there was a need for a formal system of concepts, coordinating definitions, and laws. However, Lewin's attention centered more and more on group dynamics, experimental social psychology, and the process he termed action research.[14] He began to search for funds for an institute which was loosely attached to a university. With the help of Douglas McGregor, the Center for Group Dynamics gradually emerged at the Massachusetts Institute of Technology.

The action research approach is often associated with this center, originally at the Massachusetts Institute of Technology, and then at the University of Michigan. The Research Center for Group Dynamics was initially staffed by people who worked with Lewin at Iowa.[15] The researchers associated with the Center carried out work in a number of program areas: group productivity, communication, social perception, intergroup relations, group membership and individual adjustment, and the training of leaders and the improvement of group functioning.[16] The chief methodology was that of group experimentation, especially experiments of change carried out both in the laboratory and in the field.

A primary premise of the work of the Center for Group Dynamics was that methods of science can be employed in the study of groups. The researchers sought to develop a field of group dynamics dedicated to advancing knowledge about the nature of groups, the laws of their development, and their interrelations with individuals, other groups, and larger institutions. They used techniques of experimental psychology, controlled observations of behavior, and methods of social group work. The goal was to construct a coherent body of knowledge about the nature of group life. Thus, Lewin envisioned a general theory of groups for diverse matters as: family life, work groups, classrooms, committees, military units, and the community. He saw such specific problems as leadership, status, communication, social norms, groups atmosphere and intergroup relations as part of the general problem of understanding the nature of group dynamics.[17]

The group dynamics research taking place during the 1940s and 1950s offered a description of the properties of groups, their origins and consequences, and a general framework, possibly best recorded in a book by Cartwright and Zander.[18] Group dynamics was a growing discipline concerned with the positive and negative forces at work in groups. The essence of the theory of groups is summarized as follows:

> A (person) who joins a group is significantly changed thereby. His relations with his fellow members alter both (the person and others). A highly attractive group can bring great pressure to bear upon its members; a weak group will not have as much moulding power. To effect any sort of change in the goals or outlook of a group, a change in its equilibrium is necessary. To try to do this by appealing to members

individually is seldom effective, as was learned by those of Lewin's associates who in 1940 began their experiments in industry. They discovered, for instance, that if a group sets the range or level of productivity in a factory, any attempt on the part of any single employee to deviate from that standard heightens the normal social pressure of his co-workers to push (him/her) back into line. The further (the person) deviates from the norm, the stronger the pressure on (the person) to conform to it.[19]

Rather than disturb a relationship with the group, the individual will as a rule take considerable risk to conform. Thus, the behavior of the whole group might be more easily changed than that of an individual.

In a 1945 article, Lewin described the objectives of the Center for Group Dynamics. Its task was to educate research workers in theoretical and applied fields of group life and to train practitioners.[20] The plan was to have the "research center use qualitative and quantitative psychological, sociological, or anthropological methods. . . . " The main methodology continued to be group experimentation in the laboratory and in the field.[21] The work at the Commission on Community Relations (C.C.I.) was an important contribution to the many research efforts carried out at the Research Center for Group Dynamics. The goal of the C.C.I was to concentrate on problems people confronted in fighting prejudice. They recognized there was much to be learned but there was little time to carry out experiments to find out ways of overcoming prejudice. There was the hope that their actions would lead to more learning. "Such action would lead to more reliable knowledge. Action would become research, and research action."[22]

Working with Lewin's guidance, Cook, Chein, and Harding outlined four varieties of action research to carry out C.C.I.'s objectives. These were named:

1.   Diagnostic
2.   Participant
3.   Empirical
4.   Experimental

Diagnostic action research is "research designed to lead to action." The goal is to diagnose a problem or need for change, and seek cures which are "feasible, effective, and acceptable to the people involved. Research is really a process of becoming aware of the problems and offering solutions to them.

Participant action research assumes the participants will help in effecting the cure, and thereby be more keenly interested. This action research seeks to gather and present data in such a way that the participants can analyze them and develop recommendations for responding to the results.

Empirical action research is a way of record keeping and accumulating experiences in day-to-day work, ideally with a succession of similar groups. The goal is to gradually develop generally valid principles in recurring experiences.

Experimental action research calls for a controlled study of relative effectiveness of various techniques in identical situations. The goal is to encourage the development of scientific knowledge.[23]

Action Research at the University of Michigan

The action research efforts after Lewin's death are partially represented by some of the practices of the Institute for Social Research at the University of Michigan.[24] After Lewin's death, a number of senior staff members moved to the University of Michigan as part of the Institute for Social Research.[25] Much of their work in organizations became known under the term "survey feedback." This feedback approach is illustrated in a study at the Detroit Edison Company in 1948, where researchers began systematic feedback of data from a company-wide employee attitude survey.[26] The method of feedback, to "organizational families," proved to be more effective in producing change. The concept of the organizational family refers to a supervisor at any hierarchical level and the employees reporting directly to him/her (any supervisor would be a member of two organizational families-the group he/she supervises and the group in which he/she is a subordinate).[27] The feedback technique, utilizing group discussion and group involvement, proved to be more effective in increasing understanding and communication as well as changing supervisory behavior. Similar results were obtained in a study[28] involving twenty three organizations and approximately 14,000 people; there was some evidence of diffusion to groups not participating in the feedback process.

Survey feedback is a way of understanding the capabilities and needs of the organization's membership; it is based on the assumption that employees have needs for personal growth and development and that an effective organization (especially one that allows individuals to satisfy their needs in a supportive and challenging environment) can better encourage individuals to take on greater responsibilities. Groups are highly important and most people satisfy their needs through groups. Groups can encourage greater responsibility, reduce alienation, and provide powerful supervisorial forces.

This survey feedback emphasis suggested that employees are more productive when their jobs are designed to utilize the employee's total capability-his/her total knowledge, interests, and commitments.[29] The individual is a product of his/her environment, and parts of that environment are the individuals and groups he/she interacts with. Effective problem solving and decision-making does not naturally occur as a result of participation; an important variable in the choice of the appropriate mix of individuals and groups, chosen because of their particular skills, knowledge, information, or personality.

ACTION RESEARCH IN GREAT BRITAIN

Another stream of action research can be found in the experiences of a number of psychologists, social psychologists, and social anthropologists in Great Britain. These research efforts grew out of the developments in the war-time army, by a group most of whom were at the pre-war Tavistock Clinic. The original organization, the Tavistock Institute of Medical Psychology, was brought into existence in 1920 to respond to the need that neurotic disabilities were not just a war-time phenomena. It was composed of key doctors who were concerned with neurosis during World War I. Although the quality of their work varied, it had developed by the beginning of the war.[30]

The group who entered the Directorate of Army Psychiatry took a novel approach of going out into the field to find out from commanding officers what they saw as the pressing problems. They would listen to their troubled military clients as a psychoanalyst would to a patient. There was the belief that constructive ideas for problem-solving would emerge in these discussions. The concept of "command" psychiatrist arose to describe this approach. A psychiatrist with a roving commission was attached to each of the five army commanders in home forces.[31]

Toward the end of the war, a number of psychiatrists and social scientists undertook a large number of projects using an action oriented philosophy of relating psychiatry and the social sciences to society. This was labelled "Operation Phoenix" and sought to define the new post-war role. The democratic tradition in the Tavistock made possible the election of an interim planning committee made up of those who had led the work in the army.[32]

During and immediately following the war, this group of researchers conducted a number of successful action programs in personnel selection and treatment and rehabilitation of war-time neurosis casualties of returning prisoners of war.[33] The work in this period was the basis for the formation of the Tavistock Institute of Human Relations. The general approach was to gear the collaboration of members of an organization while attempting to solve their problems.[34] Unlike the emphasis at the Center for Group Dynamics, the Tavistock research method or process for carrying out action research was not used for constructing a general theory of groups. Rather, it was intended as a type of social science not described in conventional academic journals.

The research process usually began by forming a study or steering committee (made up of key actors-who had some knowledge and influence to bear on the problem) to monitor the study. The steering committee would usually be involved in developing a strategy to carry out the research and implement the study's findings.[35] The researchers usually obtains data from interviews and unobtrusive measures (e.g., of absenteeism, turnover, and other organizational records). The findings of the research are usually implemented in a test area of the organization, and under protected conditions. The steering committee is usually quite active in advising and monitoring the research and implementation from start to finish.

The Tavistock researchers attached a fair degree of importance to Lewin's work, and some of it undoubtedly influenced the ways of carrying out research in large-scale organizations. Actual examples of how Lewin influenced the Tavistock research are difficult to pinpoint, as there are significant differences in the paradigms. The Institute and the Center for Group Dynamics created a new international journal, *Human Relations*, which was an outlet to manifest the connection between field theory and object relations psychoanalysis. It sought to further the integration of psychology and the social sciences and relate theory to practice. This journal encouraged the publishing of the results of field research which would have little chance to become published in traditional scientific journals.

The Tavistock researchers recognized the relevance of psychoanalysis in carrying out work in the society at large. They highlighted the researcher's (or research team's) general ability to describe and aggregate various levels of evidence on the nature of the problem and its solutions.

By 1948, the British government was forced to react to conditions of the devalued pound and low productivity in industry. They established the Industrial Productivity Committee, and its Human Factors Panel, with grant money for projects. Three projects were proposed and accepted by the Tavistock: (1) a project at the Glacier metal company seeking to improve cooperation between management and labor within a single company, (2) a project in the Yorkshire coal mines on organizational innovations to raise productivity, and (3) post-graduate education for field workers interested in applied social research.

The Glacier project sought to use a form of process consultation place in observing and resolving conflicts. It was a very serious and practical attempt to explore the relationship between industrial efficiency and industrial democracy. The experiments highlighted the value of defining and role relationships, the importance of avoiding confusion arising from conflicting definitions, and the necessity to clear up misunderstandings about words and symbols. The experiments sought to devise efficient formal systems of authority, responsibility and function, and patterns of communication, and to seek equitable ways of deciding differential rewards for work done.

It came to be believed that relationships in the firm would become much more harmonious and effective if the making of rules governing behavior were jointly done by committees representing all grades and skills--a legislative system. Once the rules were made, managers were entirely responsible to the legislators for administering them effectively--the executive system.

The goal was to extend the system of democratic management throughout the company. The system allowed individuals to participate in matters affecting their work; it provided channels where people could learn the consequences of decisions and take appropriate action; it affirmed managerial authority; and it created an atmosphere where people felt free to express themselves. In all, it removed some of the inequalities and injustices generating tension, uneasiness, and distrust, making it possible for people to work effectively in roles that were clearly defined and equitably rewarded.

Glacier Metal was an example of a collaboration of a rather unusual kind between social scientists and managers over many years. It illustrated that the task of management is not just a technical one. Management also has a job of creating a social organization in which everyone may participate to the greatest possible degree and with which everyone may feel a sense of close identification.

Jacque's book, *The Changing Culture of the Factory*, was the first major publication of the Institute, and was reprinted several times.[36] While the book enjoyed immense success, there were no requests for Tavistock to continue this work.

A second program in the Yorkshire coal mines is probably the most renowned illustration of the Tavistock action research process, and is to be credited with the discovery of self-regulating work groups in a coal mine. It is known for the theory of organizations as sociotechnical systems.[37]

The observations of the Tavistock researchers on the functioning of longwall methods of mining (organizing groups around task specialities) and their analysis of the superiority of the composite system were put to test by factual comparison of the two systems. Absenteeism and productivity were used for logically explaining how changes in the technology affected the social system. Another project which continued this work was in the Calico textile mills in Ahmedabad, India. The general objective of these projects was to encourage a style of decision-making in changing work and managerial practices. In spite of the general difference in cultures between India and western societies, the action research process produced similar findings.

The third initiative was a training program for industrial fellows was an opportunity to gain experience in other settings. Each of the six fellows had a tutor. After working with institute staff for one year, they were to return to their industries. The experiential learning approach of the program was not viewed favorably at the time.

ACTION RESEARCH AND OPERATIONAL RESEARCH

Another development which began at about this time led to the setting up of an Institute for Operational Research.[38] The activity called operational research arose from the specific need felt by R.A.F. officers for making better use of a new technical development-radar. The engineers developing the radar had been collaborating with the proposed users.[39] Thus, it seemed natural to have a group of scientists and technologists, who were called staff officers, to work with the people in charge of and responsible for the higher command. The operational research (O.R.)-group was expected to watch and study these operations and their degree of success, as well as observe the wider consequences of the new equipment. Similar groups were soon formed elsewhere, and by the time the war ended, they could be found around the world, attached to commands in all services of Great Britain and some allied countries.

The people who started O.R. in Great Britain were engineers and scientists who took for granted the study of operations. The ideas of studying the performance of operations and the use of mixed teams can be traced to Taylor.[40] Operational research methods, at the time, depended on first hand observation of what was going on, while carrying out experiments to complement their observations. Researchers were personally involved in the collection of the data; consequently, they knew and understood how the recorded data available to them were gathered and what they meant, or did not mean.

Soon after operational research began in Great Britain, an independent development began in the United States under the name of "operations research." In the United States the development came from the need to prepare for active involvement in a war to be fought some thousands of miles away. Mathematicians felt that by applying their expertise to the analysis of tactics, logistics and strategy, they could make a contribution. The research approach in the United States was different, in that it was much more theoretical than in Great Britian; it was mainly based on written sources of information rather than on direct observation; it had a longer time horizon and less contact with detailed considerations arising from practical situations. The success of the small-scale but organized efforts in Great Britain provided the impetus to the growth of an activity where scientists solved problems that might ordinarily be thought of as lying outside their proper domain.

Wartime O.R. in Great Britain had been almost wholly secret, often concerned with matters carrying high security classification. The practical approach to operational research was difficult to conceal because many people in important positions had contact with it during the war years. Leading scientists were involved when the government took action to channel scientific effort to the needs of post-war construction. The first international conference of operational research in Oxford in 1957 provided a number of examples of operational research. The English and Americans were not speaking the same language. It appeared that the English approach was more practical for problem-solving but much less technically sophisticated. This probably marked the period when operational research in Great Britain became more technically sophisticated.[41]

The practical approach to O.R. did not die in Great Britain and it managed to stay alive and took a renewed emphasis when the Institute for Operational Research (I.O.R.) was established in 1963, with a mission of carrying forth the practice of operational research. This was broadly defined as the application of scientific method to the making of complex decisions in industrial and other organizational settings.[42] The birth of I.O.R. was conceived by Russell Ackoff and Eric Trist, and found its home within the administrative framework of the Tavistock Institute of Human Relations. The period when I.O.R. was founded had been paralleled by a growing tendency for O.R. to become identified with a well-defined range of mathematical techniques. However, the appointment of the first director, Neil Jessop, was significant in that it marked the opposite trend of bringing O.R. into close contact with the social sciences, in order to broaden its scope and increase its relevance to problems of wider significance to society.

The revival of the practical version of O.R. in Great Britain was partially exemplified at the Operational Research Society conference in 1964 on "O.R. and the Social Sciences." The event and the papers presented are often referred to in the appraisal of the direction and emphasis of O.R. It marked the need to move back from the highly specialized techniques toward less sophisticated attention to the various aspects of practical problems. The swing appears to be reviving interest in the relevance of the social sciences. Papers in the *Journal of the Operational Research Society*[43] are a few examples of papers appraising the direction of O.R. However, there does not seem to be any research organization or academic department that is taking the lead in the fight for a revival of practical O.R. The practical approach seems to be most alive in O.R. branches of government and industry.

ACTION RESEARCH AND TRAINING

There are several action researchers who have provided ideas about training, and their applications ranged from laboratory training to data based training. Laboratory training involved group participants receiving feedback about their own behavior and using that feedback as data for learning about themselves. The group was a "laboratory" where data were generated. Today, laboratory training bears little resemblance to earlier forms. However, in 1946, it constituted an important breakthrough from traditional training which was often not associated with individual needs or organizational problems.

The birth of laboratory training is associated with a workshop at the State Teacher's College in New Britain, Connecticut (1946). In particular, a workshop sponsored by the Connecticut State Interracial Commission and the Research Center for Group Dynamics of M.I.T. was important in the emergence.

The workshop sought to address the need of the Connecticut State Interracial Commission to assist staff in translating their good will to overcome various forms of bias. It sought to train the delegates and provide research data on what might produce change in the individuals. It began with a program that encouraged discussions with a group of forty-one hand-picked students. During the evenings, some of the students who were in residence asked to sit in on the discussions of trainers. While part of the research team was inclined to dismiss this appeal on the grounds that it violated the canons of the scientific approach, Kurt Lewin held that the participants had a right to attend these sessions. Based on this argument, a meeting of the staff, participants and observers was held.

This first meeting lasted from 9:00 p.m. to 6:00 a.m. in the morning. The length of this meeting impressed on the researcher the importance of persons working through their own data-learning from observations on their own behavior. The discussion proved valuable, and more students appeared the next evening.[44]

A three-week session was later organized during the summer of 1947 at Bethel, Maine, under the auspices of an organization created for that purpose, the National Training Laboratory for Group Development.[45] Because there was limited knowledge about the nature of groups, the teachers relied on having students learn from their experiences in small discussion groups. Such person-centered interaction may have reduced the concern for the study of groups.[46]

Proponents of the laboratory method sought and won support for further experiments. The work of that summer was to evolve into the National Training Laboratory in Group Development in 1949, under the directorship of Leland Bradford. The name was later shortened to National Training Laboratory or N.T.L.

The laboratory training approach altered its name over the years--from basic skill training groups to T-groups and sensitivity groups. This reflected the shift in emphasis from group skills training to interpersonal and intrapersonal learning. There were also shifts to include training approaches to enrich individuals in organizations. Typically, top-and middle-level managers left their organizations to receive training at an off-site location. These training events could last from three days to two weeks. The "trained" managers were then returned to the work site to practice their new skills.

Managers returning to their work setting often had difficulty applying the results of these methods, and there were even cases where their effectiveness might have declined. The managers found themselves either opposing their supervisors or resuming previous practices. On recognizing this difficulty, practicing managers and trainers began to realize that effective training had to be linked with organizational problems.

There were numerous other training designs and programs which attempted to maximize the effectiveness of organizational training activities by integrating data about people or organizations with training designs. One such program was carried out at the Training Division of the California State Personnel Board in 1954. The training emphasis sought to develop a climate for facilitating the use of results of training in the organization.[47] The program sought to give managers practice in interpersonal management skills, so that they could boost their confidence and ability to improve their effectiveness. The training division used the word "organizational development" to describe its activities which emphasized individual training to alter attitudes and behaviors. This was different from the practices of organizational development which sought to change the organization's culture.

The Laboratory Emphasis in Great Britain

A development in Great Britain matched the laboratory emphasis with the creation of Group Relations Conferences (G.R.C.). The training integrated the psychoanalytic theory of the British object relations school as characterized by the work of Melanie Klein and Wilfred Bion with the sociotechnical approach to open systems. The approach provides a view of the psychological dynamics of individuals and groups within the context of social and political realities. It focuses on the boundary between the individual and the group or organization.

The conference a temporary learning institution or laboratory is formed. Participants are free to experience and discuss the covert dynamics within groups. They discuss the political mechanisms between groups and the impact of authority and its exercise on the individual, the group, and the institution.

The conferences include two types of exercises: (1) "here and now" exercises, and (2) conventional discussions of the experiences. The "here and now" exercises are experimental events where participants are faced with the task of learning about group dynamics as they unfold. These include small face-to-face groups, large groups, and intergroup exercises. In these events, the staff function in a consultative role and will comment on the unfolding process. However, they do not teach or lead in a conventional way by providing content or structure. And, participants often experience frustrations towards the conference organizers. In this way, the conference encourages people to take responsibility for the group dynamics in which they find themselves.

Other events are more traditional and include reviews, plenary sessions, application groups, role analysis groups, and lectures. These events are also controversial. The shift from "here and now" experiences to a more cognitive mode of discussion is usually quite difficult and a provocative learning.[48]

An important aspect of the G.R.C. model suggests that the culture of a group evolves through various stages of work, conflict, and avoidance. The conferences assist individuals to examine their own experience in the group--one's intentions, feelings, beliefs, impressions, anxieties--and relate them to real life. As a result of the experience, the participant is:

1. Developing a habit of attention to his (her) ongoing experience.
2. Learning to recognize fantasy as a mode of experience, and to distinguish between fantasy and reality.
3. Learning to recognize the influence of shared fantasy in groups and organizations.

4. Becoming alert to the influence of fantasy in relations between leaders and
    followers.
5. Gaining facility in using some key theoretical concepts for describing the
    unconscious structuring and conscious organization of working groups.[49]

The group relations experience illustrates that the excitement of discovering
the power of group processes may create unrealistic expectations. The Group
Relations Conference is essentially a mode of learning about groups, and their
primary work tasks. It illustrates the difficulties of normal groups under
conditions of inadequate structure, poorly defined tasks, and inadequate
leadership. And, there is more to leadership than just setting an agenda, managing
the boundaries, and delegating tasks. Ultimately, it includes creating a vision and
sense of purpose which followers can identify with.

Action Learning

Action learning is a strand of training which is philosophically connected to
the action research tradition. It is based on a training process which is
experienced based, and highlights a process of learning by doing. It includes
learning by posing fresh questions rather than by copying what others have
already shown to be useful-perhaps in conditions that are unlikely to recur.[50]

Action learning was developed by Professor R. W. Revans in response to
post-war problems. It was developed to respond to these management needs by
establishing programs which encourage colleagues to meet and work together, in
groups, for the purpose of solving organizational problems within the British coal
industry. These action learning groups or "sets" are described as "the heart of the
action learning process."

Sets are comprised of managers who have the authority and responsibility
for action within their organizations and who, by working together, are able to
learn with and from each other. In action learning, they are used because the
dynamics in small groups help to change the behavior of the participants rather
than to reinforce habitual behavior patterns and attitudes.[51]

The goal of this process, like the learning process, is to change the behavior
of the participants while solving or attempting to solve real-life problems. In this
way action learning is also a social process whereby those who try it learn with
and from each other. Although action learning was initially developed for
problem-solving within the British coal industry, its uses have evolved to include
training for managers and for solving community problems.[52]

SUMMARY

Action research was never meant to be anti-theoretical. Indeed, Lewin's term "there is nothing so practical as a good theory" was often used to describe an approach to theory construction that was based on organizational problems. Such theories are aimed at responding to problems by dealing with them in real settings. Thus, organizational actions are best understood by understanding the relationship of various activities as they interact.

The difficulty with any definition of action research is that the term can be used to summarize many activities which have the "veneer" of research and action. Two researchers attempting to solve the same problem could inevitably reach different conclusions and still meet the criteria of action research within some paradigm or another.

The action research carried out at the Center for Group Dynamics was very different from that at the Tavistock. The field experiments by Lewin and the operational field methods at the Tavistock Institute of Human Relations (from 1945-1965) are illustrations of attempts to change behavior. Lewin's action research emphasis is also recognized for some of the developments in organizational development, namely, the formation of N.T.L. and emphasis on survey research and feedback.[53]

The various streams of action related research represent some of the past practices and "role models" that have guided the field's development. Many of the practices grew as a group of researchers, associated with the Center for Group Dynamics and the Tavistock Institute of Human Relations, worked together on specific problems. These practices do not exist in pure form in their original institutions, nor have they inspired action research practices which are based on uniform canons or principles of action. Present day action researchers usually do not fall clearly into one stream of application or another, although the original role models, writings, and practices are there to guide them. Many of the people who have been associated with these original institutions have continued their work in other settings.[54]

Most present day action researchers refer to Lewin's original works,[55] point out that theory needs to be amalgamated with practice, and that action research is a process of diagnosing, theorizing or planning, acting, and evaluating. Most are problem-solving and analytical, and derive their insights from empirical examples. Most are specialized applications that pay attention to diagnosis, action, or evaluation; few action researchers engage in a process of theorizing about organizations.

There is probably no "canonized" Tavistock procedure for carrying out action research, although several have been discussed.[56] These generally describe a process where there is initially a period of defining the critical problems facing the client system, and then forming a study or steering committee (made up of key actors who had some knowledge and influence to bear on the problem) to monitor the study. The definition of the problem, variables, hypotheses, and methods undergo modification as interim results are validated or invalidated.[57] The methods of gathering data include actual observations of behavior, perceptions, unobtrusive measures, interpretations derived from interviews, intuition, brain-storming, group discussions, and decision-making. In responding to organizational problems, good research is determined by the degree to which the results are used in improving organizational practices.

NOTES

1. This short historical sketch merely highlights some of the people who illustrate the different orientations which unfolded in the United States and Great Britain.

2. A. J. Marrow, *The Action Theorist* (New York: Basic Books, 1958), p. 158.

3. A. J. Marrow, *The Action Theorist*, p. 156.

4. Trist acknowledged this impact. See: A. J. Marrow, *The Practical Theorist* (New York: Basic Books, 1969), p. 69; Trist, 1988 (personal communications).

5. A. J. Marrow, *The Practical Theorist*, p. 108.

6. K. Lewin, "Psycho-sociological Problems of a Minority Group," *Character and Personality*, vol. 3, 1935, pp. 175-187.

7. A. J. Marrow, *The Practical Theorist*, p. 141.

8. A. J. Marrow, *The Practical Theorist*, pp. 141-142.

9. Alex Bavelas was then at the University of Iowa; (W. French later joined Bavelas in some of the later experiments).

10. K. Lewin, "Group Decision and Social Change," in T. M. Newcombe and E. L. Hartley, (eds.), *Readings in Social Psychology* (New York: Holt, Rinehart & Winston, 1947).

11. L. Coch and J.R.P. French, Jr., "Overcoming Resistance to Change," *Human Relations*, vol. 34, 1948, pp. 555-566.

12. J. R. P. French, Jr., J. Israel, D. Aas, "An Experiment on Participation in a Norwegian Factory," *Human Relations*, vol. 13, 1960, pp. 3-9.

13. K. Lewin, *Focus Behind Food Habits and Methods of Change*, Washington, D.C.: National Research Council, Bulletin 108, 1943; K. Lewin, "Group Decision and Social Change."; K. Lewin, R. Lippitt, and R. White, "Patterns of Aggressive Behavior in Experimentally Created 'Social Climates'," *Journal of Social Psychology*, vol. 10, 1939, pp. 271-299; K. Lewin, "Action Research and Minority Problems," *Journal of Social Issues*, vol. 2, 1946, pp. 34-46; K. Lewin, *Dynamic Theory of Personality* (New York: McGraw-Hill, 1931); K. Lewin, *Field Theory and Social Science* (New York: Harper and Brothers, 1951); K. Lewin, "Frontiers in Group Dynamics: Part I, Concept, Method and Reality in Social Science; Social Equilibria and Social Change," *Human Relations*, vol. I1, pp. 5-40; K. Lewin, "Frontiers in Group Dynamics: Part II, Channels in Group Life, Social Planning, Action Research," *Human Relations*, vol. 12, 1947, pp. 143-153.

14. A. J. Marrow, *The Practical Theorist*, pp. 156-157.

15. Marian Radke, Leon Festinger, Ronald Lippitt and Dorwin Cartwright were the

first staff members at the Center for Group Dynamics at M.I.T. All had worked for Lewin at the University of Iowa. Others joined after. See. A. J. Marrow, *The Practical Theorist*, pp. 180-190.

16. A. J. Marrow, *The Action Theorist*, p. 156.

17. D. Cartwright, and A. Zander, (eds.), *Group Dynamics: Research and Theory*, 2nd ed. (Evanston, Ill: Row McNally, 1960), pp. 3-32; See also: D. Cartwright, *Field Theory in Social Science*, Papers by K. Lewin, (ed.), (London: Tavistock Publications, 1952).

18. D. Cartwright, and A. Zander, *Group Dynamics: Research and Theory*. There were several very influential studies that occurred during Lewin's time and could be attributed to these pioneering years. See: A. Zander, "The Study of Group Behavior During Four Decades," *Journal of Applied Behavioral Science,* vol. 15, 1979, pp. 272-282. There were investigations of group climate of inter-group conflict and styles of leadership. K. Lewin, R. Lippitt, and R. White, "Patterns of Aggressive Behavior in Experimentally Created 'Social Climates,'" pp. 271-299. Other experiments on different aspects of group life included: social pressures within groups, see: L. Festinger, S. Schachter, and K. Back, *Social Pressures in Informal Groups* (New York: Harper, 1950); communication networks, see Alex Bavelas, "Communication Patterns in Task-oriented Groups," *Journal of Acoustical Society of America*, vol. 22, 1950, pp. 725-730, behavior in cooperative and competitive groups, see M. Deutsch, "A Theory of Cooperation and Competition," *Human Relations*, vol. 2, 1950, pp. 129-152.

19. A. J. Marrow, *The Action Theorist*, p. 169.

20. As quoted in A. J. Marrow, *The Action Theorist,* pp. 171-172; See: K. Lewin, "The Research Center for Group Dynamics at Massachusetts Institute of Technology," *Sociometry*, vol. 2, 1945, pp. 126-136.

21. See A. J. Marrow, *The Action Theorist*, p. 169; Lewin also planned to link some of the work of the Research Center for Group Dynamics with work at the Commission on Community Relations (C.C.I) of the American Jewish Congress.

22. A. J. Marrow, *The Action Theorist,* p. 197.

23. I. Chein, S. W. Cook, and J. Harding, "The Field of Action Research," *American Psychologist*, vol. 3, 1948, p. 45; As is true in many fields, central areas of research are replaced by seemingly more pertinent topics, possibly because the results had not lived up to previous expectations. The gradual dissolution of the network at the Center for Group Dynamics may have been a contributing factor to the decreasing interest and activity. A. Zander," The Study Group Behavior during Four Decades," pp. 272-282.

24. Persons such as Rensis Likert, Floyd Mann, Stanley Seashore, Ronald Katz, Howard Baumgartel, and others were associated with the survey feedback approach developed at the Institute of Social Research; R. Likert, *New Patterns of Management* (New York: McGraw Hill, 1961), v-vi; R. Likert, *The Human Organization* (New York: McGraw Hill, 1967), vi-vii.

25. Three centers were part of the Institute for Social Research: The Survey Research Center, the Research Center for Group Dynamics, and the Center for Research and the Utilization of Scientific Knowledge.

26. F. C. Mann, and L. R. Hoffman, *Automation and the Worker: A Study of Social Change in two Power Plants* (New York: Holt, Rinehart and Winston, 1960).

27. F. C. Mann, and J. Dent, "The Supervisor: Member of Two Organizational Families," *Harvard Business Review*, vol. 32, 1954, pp. 103-112.

28. D. G. Bowers, "O.D. Techniques and their Results in 23 Organizations: the Michigan ICL study," *Journal of Applied Behavioral Science*, vol. 9, 1973, pp. 21-43.

29. W. L. French and C. H. Bell, Jr., *Organizational Development* (Englewood Cliffs, N. J.: Prentice-Hall, 1973), p. 36; E. L. Trist and H. Murray, *The Social Engagement of Social Science: Selected Writings*, by members of the Tavistock Institute, 1989.

30. E. L. Trist and H. Murray, *The Social Engagement of Social Science: Selected Writings, Volume II* .

31. E. L. Trist and H. Murray, *The Social Engagement of Social Science: Selected Writings*.

32. It consisted of J. R. Rees, Leonard Browne, Henry Dicks, Ronald Hargreaves, Mary Luff, and Tommy Wilson. They co-opted two war-time associates to join this Tavistock group: Jock Sutherland and Eric Trist; E. L. Trist and H. Murray, *The Social Engagement of Social Science: Selected Writings* by members of the Tavistock Institute, 1989.

33. W. R. Bion, *Experiences in Groups and Other Papers* (London: Tavistock Publications, 1961); W. R. Bion, *Learning From Experience* (Heinemann, 1962); W. R. Bion, and J. Rickman, "Intra-group Tensions in Therapy," *Lancet*, 2, 1943, pp. 678-681; H. Bridger, "The Northfield Experiment," *Bulletin of the Menninger Clinic*, vol. 6, 1946, pp. 71-76.

34. The I.P.C. made a decision to create: (1) a clinic to enter the National Health Service to focus on outpatient psychiatry, and (2) the Tavistock Institute of Human Relations to study wider societal problems. The decision to construct a clinic was made in anticipation of the Labour government's plans to construct a national health service. A Rockerfeller Foundation grant provided some financial support for the initial projects. The Tavistock Institute of Human Relations was formed in September 1947. See: E. L. Trist and H. Murray, *The Social Engagement of Social Science: Selected Writings*

35. Alfred W. Clark, (ed.), *Experimenting with Organizational Life: The Action Research Approach* (New York: Plenum Press, 1976).

36. E. Jaques, *The Changing Culture of the Factory* (London: Tavistock Publications, 1951).

37. E. L. Trist and K. W. Bamforth, "Some Social and Psychological Consequences of the Longwall Method of Coal-getting," *Human Relations*, vol. 4, 1951, pp. 1-38.

38. Operational research is the British description of the American version of operations research. To the British, operations research is incorrect English (using a noun as an adjective). O.R. is a form of action-related research developing from work at the Bawdsey Research Station, where the term was coined in mid-1938.

39. T. Burns and G. M. Stalker, *The Management of Innovation* (London: Tavistock, 1961).

40. F. W. Taylor, *The Principles of Scientific Management* (New York: Harper & Row, 1911).

41. J. Stringer "Operational Research for Multi-organizations," *Operational Research Quarterly*, vol. 18, 1967, pp. 105-120.

42. J. K. Friend and W. N. Jessop, *Local Government and Strategic Choice* (London: Tavistock, 1969); J. K. Freind and A. Hickling, *Planning Under Pressure: The Strategic Choice Approach* (Oxford: Pergamon Press, 1987).

43. R. L. Ackoff, "Resurrecting the Future of Operational Research," *Journal of*

Operational Research Society, vol. 30, 1979, pp. 189-199.

44. Some historians suggest that, during this project, observers were secretly placed in each of the groups. By some means, the group members found out about the role of the "secret" observers in their groups. Group members insisted that they be allowed to sit in when the observers made their reports to the staff.

45. The workshop was sponsored by the Connecticut Interracial Commission and the Research Center for Group Dynamics, then at the Massachusetts Institute of Technology. The team consisted of Kurt Lewin, Ronald Lippitt, Kenneth Benne, Leland Bradford, and Ronald Leavitt.

46. D. Katz and R. L. Kahn, *The Social Psychology of Organizations* (New York: John Wiley and Sons, Inc., 1965, 1978), pp. 671-674. This was initially financed by the Office of Naval Research and sponsored by the National Education Association and the Research Center for Group Dynamics.

47. N. Gardner, "Training as a Framework for Action," *Public Personnel Review*, January 1957, pp. 39-44.

48. M. E. Correa, K. B. Klein, S. R. Howe, and W. N. Stone, "A Bridge Between Training and Practise: Mental Health Professionals' Learning in Group Relations Conferences," *Social Psychiatry*, vol.16, 1981, pp. 137-142.

49. R. W. Menninger, "A Retrospective View of a Hospital-Wide Group Relations Training Program: Costs, Consequences, and Conclusion," *Human Relations*. vol. 38, no. 4, 1958, pp. 323-339.

50. R. Revans, "Action Learning: Its Origins and Nature," in *Action Learning in Practice*, (ed.) Mike Pedler (Aldershot, England: Gower, 1983), p. 14.

51. M. MacNamara, and W. H. Weekes, "The Action Learning Model of Experiential Learning for Developing Managers," *Human Relations*, vol. 35, no. 10, 1982, p. 880.

52. N. Foy, "Action Learning Comes to Industry," *Harvard Business Review*, Sept.-Oct. 1977, p. 161.

53. K. Lewin, "Group Decision and Social Change," in T.M. Newcombe and E.L. Hartley, (eds.) *Readings in Social Psychology*, (New York: Holt, Rinehart & Winston, 1947).

54. W. L. French and C. H. Bell, *Organizational Development* (Englewood Cliffs, N. J. : Prentice-Hall, 1973).

55. More recently, there is a special issue on sociotechnical systems in: W. Barko and W. Pasmore, "Special Issue: Sociotechnical Systems: Innovations in Designing High-performing systems," *Journal of Applied Behavioral Science*, vol. 22, 1968, pp. 195-360. A more recent assessment of sociotechnical interventions is presented in R. I. Beekun, "Assessing the Effectiveness of Sociotechnical Interventions: Antidote or Fad?" *Human Relations*, vol. 42, 1989, pp. 877-897. One of the best historical accounts of sociotechnical theory is contained in E. L. Trist, *The Evolution of Socio-Technical Systems* (Toronto, Ontario: Ontario Quality of Working Life Center, 1981).

56. K. Lewin, "Action Research and Minority Problems," *Journal of Social Issues*, vol. 2, 1946, pp. 34-36.

57. A. W. Clark, (ed.) *Experimenting with Organizational Life: The Action Research Approach* (New York: Plenum Press, 1976).

Part II

The Process and Principles

4

The Emerging
Action Sciences

The affirmation of knowledge through a traditional or a positive science has provided fundamental changes to our society. Since the sixteenth century, scientific research findings have refuted theological dogmatism and conventional wisdom. Church doctrine has yielded and has been readjusted so that it did not clash glaringly with scientific evidence. Conventional wisdoms on many subjects--such as eating habits, sex, child rearing and education, have been constantly challenged with scientific facts. The prestige of positive science has grown in these triumphs. The procedures were used largely to test social dogmas, and were not developed to make discoveries or solve problems.

In recent years, there has been a growing concern regarding the long standing debate on the adequacy of positive science research methods in field settings.[1] There appears to be a growing recognition of the difficulties of applying the positivistic research paradigm for carrying out research and change in real-life settings. That is, there may be an inherent incompatibility between action and research. Maximizing one may minimize the other.

It would seem that the positive science paradigm is, for all scientific purposes, unchallengeable for providing generalizable scientific evidence. Until a new paradigm is articulated and accepted as useful for tasks of discovery or invention, we may continue to recognize the more accepted scientific paradigm. Sometimes, more important discoveries have occurred when positive science failed, or because there were efforts to challenge the conventional research ideals. This chapter describes some discoveries which occurred in both the physical and social sciences that illustrate, at least partially, some action scientific practices.

ACTS OF DISCOVERY IN THE PHYSICAL SCIENCES

The act of discovery and creation may be difficult to achieve within the rules of a positive science. Many discoveries have been made because positive scientists have gone astray and made mistakes. Arbitrariness has had an important effect on scientific discovery in providing the novelty and provocative questions to be confronted by the scientific community. A piece of equipment, designed and constructed for the purpose of positive research, may have failed to perform in the anticipated manner, revealing an anomaly that cannot, despite repeated effort, be aligned with professional expectations. When the profession can no longer evade anomalies that subvert the existing tradition of scientific practice, there is then an extraordinary investigation that leads to questions or difficulties with conventional methods. These episodes are called scientific revolutions, as they are traditional-shattering complements to the tradition-bound activity of positive science.[2]

Thomas S. Kuhn has argued that, as paradigms change, scientists adopt new instruments and see the world in different ways. "Insofar as their only recourse to the world is through what they see and do, we may want to say that after a revolution scientists are responding to a different world."[3] If they were left to their own initiative, the scientist would have to make observations based on experience, just like the layperson. However, the scientist collects an array of experiences and develops conceptual categories to aid observations. Thus, when something is observed, he/she had certain expectations about what will happen. The questions and operational definitions are tuned to collect data to fulfil these expectations. If something else occurred in observing, the scientist may not have the questions or categories to measure it. "In a sense such questions are parts of positive science, for they depend upon the existence of a paradigm and they receive different answers as a result of paradigm change."[4]

Several physical scientific discoveries have emerged from chance, from mistakes in the use of science, or from the ability of scientists to recognize unique data. The scientific discovery of oxygen, electricity, cyclosporine, insulin, and DNA illustrate these dynamics.

The Discovery of Oxygen

At least three different individuals have a legitimate claim to the discovery of oxygen--C. W. Scheele, Joseph Priestley, and Lavoisier. Scheele, in Sweden in the early 1770s, discovered an enriched gas. Priestley, in 1774, identified a gas released from heated red oxide of mercury. Lavoisier in 1775, possibly as a result of a hint from Priestley, reported that the gas obtained by heating the red oxide of mercury was air itself purer. In 1777, Lavoisier identified the gas more clearly, but he never really understood its composition.[5]

The Discovery of Electricity

The discovery of electricity illustrates some of the difficulties of scientists working within conventionally accepted theories. At the time, there were several competing schools interpreting a variety of electrical phenomena. One school suggested that electricity was a fluid; scientists would attempt bottling the fluid by holding a water-filled glass vial and touching it to a conductor suspended from an active electrostatic generator. The scientists would experience a shock when removing the jar from the machine and touching it to the water.

The first experiments did not provide electrians with the Leydan jar. The initial attempts to store electrical fluid worked only because investigations held the vial in their hand while standing on the ground. Electricians had still to understand that the jar required a conductive coating and that fluid is not really stored in the jar at all. This required a drastic revision of the fluid theory.[6] Scientists grew to accept the Leyden jar, with its inner and outer conducting coating, as a way of illustrating that electricity was not really a fluid and was not really stored in the jar at all. Many of the experiments which led to the emergence of the Leyden jar were performed by Benjamin Franklin and were the basis for the theory of electricity.

The Discovery of Cyclosporine

In 1976, a pharmaceutical breakthrough occurred that reversed the bleak record of transplant surgery. It happened when Swiss researchers were examining soil samples in search of a new antibiotic. By chance, they found a fungus that produced a powerful immunosuppressant, a substance that blocks the body's defence mechanisms from rejecting foreign tissues. The new discovery, now known as cyclosporine, received its first clinical trials in London, Ontario, in 1980. A surge of transplants followed, increasing the chances of survival to better than even odds of a successful graft. These advances signify dramatic improvements since South Africa's Barnard first performed the first heart transplant in 1967, when his patient died only eighteen days after receiving his new heart.

The Discovery of Insulin

Frederick Banting's history and experiences in the discovery of insulin began on October 30, 1920, as he was preparing a talk for physiology students on carbohydrate metabolism. In fact, diabetes was a subject in which he had little particular interest. He had never treated a diabetic patient and had no interest in the dietary treatment of diabetes. But, as he prepared his talk, he was naturally interested in a leading article of the November issue of *Surgery, Gynaecology and Obstetrics*. It was entitled, "The Relation of the Islets of Langerhans to Diabetes with Special Reference to Cases of Pancreatic Lithiasis," by Moses Barron. The sole importance of the study was that Banting happened to be using it for bedtime reading when he was thinking about carbohydrate metabolism.

The night after the lecture, Banting could not sleep. In his 1940 memoirs, he wrote: "It was one of those nights when I was disturbed and could not sleep. I thought about the lecture and about the article and I thought about my miseries and how I would like to get out of debt and away from worry."

Finally, at about two in the morning, an idea occurred to him. He might obtain an internal secretion by the experimental ligation of the duct and the subsequent degeneration of a portion of the pancreas. He got up and wrote down the idea and spent most of the night thinking about it.[7]

There are several imprecise statements about the history of insulin and, in some cases, Banting added to the misinterpretations. In one very authoritative statement of the discovery of insulin, Banting recalled, "I arose and wrote in my note-book the following words, ligate pancreatic ducts of dogs. Wait six weeks for the degeneration. Remove the residue and extract."[8]

In fact, in the note book in the archives of the Academy of Medicine in Toronto, Banting wrote these words:

Diabetus
Ligate pancreatic ducts of dogs.
Keep dogs alive till acini degenerate leaving Islets.
Try to isolate the internal secretion of these to relieve glycosurea.[9]

Banting received some obvious criticism for not spelling "diabetes" and "glycosuria" correctly. The stories suggest that "he could not even spell diabetes, let alone treat the disease."[10]

The history of the discovery of insulin has become well known as an example of a newcomer to the field coming up with a novel idea. Through persistence and trial and error, Banting came up with a fresh approach, even when there was little encouragement from friends and colleagues.

Banting consulted others at the University of Western Ontario and received comments that "surely someone had tried it before." He even tried going to the library and found nothing, which is surprising even allowing for the deficiencies of this university's medical library. Many commentators suggested that this was really an indication of either bad memory or an inability to carry out a literature search.

Banting was in Toronto for a wedding of one of C. L. Starr's daughters during the weekend. He stayed over to see Professor Macleod at the University of Toronto on November 7. Banting recalls that Macleod was tolerant at first, but apparently "my subject was not well presented for he commenced to read the letters on his desk." Macleod remembers that Banting had only a superficial textbook knowledge of the work that had been done on the effects of pancreatic extracts in diabetes. To Macleod, Banting was a young surgeon who had virtually walked in off the street. And the research would take much time and expense.

Before returning to London, Banting explained the whole situation to Dr. Starr, who was a "father-like advisor." In December, Starr talked with Macleod and apparently told him that Banting was a well-known surgeon. Both Starr and Macleod advised him not to give up his work in London, but that he might come to Toronto during the summer for a month or two.

It was only by circumstance that Banting finally ended up at the University of Toronto doing research. He had decided to leave London and had hoped for a job as a doctor on an oil expedition. When the company finally decided not to take a doctor, Banting turned to the University of Toronto.

The laboratory work, which Banting and his research assistant Best carried out, was marked by mistaken applications. They had not done a pancreatectomy before and they had much to learn. The biggest problem was to produce a diabetic condition in the dogs. However, many of the dogs they experimented on died from infections, overdoses of the anaesthetic, blood loss, excessive heat, dirty equipment, and mistakes during the operations. In some cases, the experimenters lost track of the dogs they experimented on, and there were times that they were buying dogs off the streets to experiment on. In fact, the whole research program was not far from failure at times.

When they finally began introducing the extract to counteract the diabetes, the first dog died. But there was no attempt to do an autopsy to find out why. The second dog which they did their experiment on was in a dying condition, so it was not written up. Two injections in a dying dog would certainly be questioned. After many mistaken applications, it must have been impressive for Banting and Best to see a dog come out of a coma, stand, and walk after the injection of an extract.

The Discovery of DNA

The account of the events which led to finding the structure of DNA, the fundamental genetical material, is an illustration of creative thinking and constant "trial and error" detective work. It illustrates the different styles of two scientists, Francis Crick and James Watson. The scientific style of Francis Crick was one of molecular model building. James Watson, from his own admission, spent many hours playing tennis, having sherry at Pop's, watching films, and dreaming, thinking, or doodling. The chemical composition of DNA had already been produced, and it was compatible with data from other scientists which they had "come upon." Thus, what was needed was to define the backbone configuration.

> Suddenly I realized the potentially profound implications of a DNA structure in which the adenine residue formed hydrogen bonds similar to those found in crystals of pure adenine. . . . each adenine residue would form two hydrogen bonds. . . . two symmetrical hydrogen bonds could also hold together pairs of guanine, cytosine, and thymine. I thus started wondering whether each DNA molecule consisted of two chains with identical base sequences held together by hydrogen bonds between pairs of identical bases.[11]

As he continued to work, he became more and more impressed with his idea, and had only brief thoughts that an idea this good might be wrong. His scheme was in "threads" by the following noon.

The next day Watson began again.

> Though I initially went back to my like-with-like prejudices, I saw all too well that they led nowhere. . . . and began shifting the bases in and out of various other pairing possibilities. Suddenly I became aware that an adenine-thymine pair held together by two hydrogen bonds was identical in shape to a guanine-cytosine pair held together by at least two hydrogen bonds. All the hydrogen bonds seemed to form naturally, no fudging was required to make the two types of base pairs identical in shape.[12]

This was the break that they needed; further modifications and modelling by Francis Crick provided the answer to the "secret of life."

In these cases, discoveries emerged because of creativity, novelty from other perspectives, or abilities to see opportunities were none had existed for others. The discoveries that scientists arrive at are more often determined by the individual's own prior experience in other fields and by the accidents of the investigation. Static methods of observation can drastically restrict the range of admissible scientific belief. Kuhn suggests that certain characteristics summarize the way that discoveries are made: the previous awareness of anomaly, the gradual and simultaneous emergence of both observational and conceptual recognition, and the consequence change of paradigm categories and procedures.[13] That is,

> Discovery commences with the awareness of an anomaly, i.e.; with the recognition that nature has somehow violated the paradigm-induced expectations that govern positive science....Assimilating a new sort of facts demands a more than additive adjustment of theory, and until the adjustment is completed--until the scientist has learned to see nature in a different way--the new fact is not quite a scientific fact at all.[14]

Many scientific developments have evolved when scientists in other fields recognized something new or different. Scientific discoveries occurred when researchers found something new when they were researching something very different.

EXAMPLES OF PARADIGM SHIFTS
IN ORGANIZATIONAL THEORY

Creativity, prior experience, and the importance of the discovery processes are also extremely important in the developments of organizational theories. Two classic studies illustrate this. One study, carried out by researchers at the Tavistock Institute of Human Relations in London, provided the basis of sociotechnical theory.[15] Another study, was the Hawthorne studies. It drew attention to the fact that the need to be accepted and liked by one's fellow workers is possibly more important than the economic incentive offered by management.[16]

Development of Sociotechnical Theory

The notion of the sociotechnical system originated and was developed in Great Britain and arose in conjunction with the first of several field projects undertaken by the Tavistock Institute of Human Relations. These projects were undertaken in the British coal-mining industry where traditional coal mining technology was based on a pair of miners making up a single, small group organization structure. Work was done with hand tools, required great energy expenditure, and performance depended on an intimate knowledge of the mine and the working conditions. Members of the group were self-selected and multi-skilled all-round workers performed an entire cycle of extracting coal. The group performed without supervision in dispersed self-contained locations, was paid as a group, and developed high adaptability to local working conditions. These practices had disappeared as the pits became progressively more mechanized.

The successor to this traditional system became known as a conventional longwall system. In this system, mine output depended on the completion of the working cycle which consisted of preparing an area for coal extraction, getting and removing coal with the aid of conveyors, and advancing the machinery in roadways. These cycle activities were divided into seven specialized tasks, each carried out by different worker task groups. Each of the tasks had to be completed in the sequence and on schedule over three working shifts. The filling tasks, for coal removal, were the most onerous, and noncompletion frequency impeded the work cycle, reducing output. Having been assigned a specialized task and ostensibly equal work load, each worker was paid an incentive to perform his task with reference to the other tasks of workers.

The outgrowth of this organizational design was the development of isolated task groups, each with its own customs, agreements with management, and payment arrangements related to its own interests. This had enlarged the skill of operations and led to groups of men having their jobs broken down into one-man, one-task roles. Coordination and control had been externalized in supervision. Coordination between men in groups on different shifts, and control work, had to be provided entirely from the outside, by the management.

Management lacked the means to weld the individual task groups into an integrated team for performance of the cycle as a whole. Inability to develop work-team relationships resulted in hostility and conflict among workers. Each work group and worker viewed the assigned task in isolation, which is indeed how it existed. When mine conditions were bad, or prior work was not completed, the individual could not cope, and resorted to waiting for management to take corrective action. Thus, management spent most of its time in emergency action over technical breakdowns, system dysfunctioning, bargaining with workers over special payments to have resulting tasks completed.

The National Coal Board had asked the Institute to undertake a study of high-producing, high morale mine and a low-producing, low morale mine. However, the research team was not welcome at the coal base. At the time, there were six post-graduate fellows being trained for industrial field work in industry. After a year, the fellows were encouraged to revisit their former industries and make a report on any new perceptions they might have. One of the fellows, Ken Bamforth, returned with the news of an innovation which had occurred in a new seam in a colliery where he used to work in the South Yorkshire coalfield. In the new seam it had become possible to use a "shortwall" method because of improved roof control. The novel phenomena consisted of a set of relatively autonomous groups interchanging roles and shifts and regulating their affairs with a minimum amount of supervision. Cooperation between task groups and personal commitments seemed evident. Absenteeism was low, accidents infrequent, and productivity high. In order to adapt with the best advantage to the technical conditions in the new seam, the men had evolved a form of work organization based on practices common in unmechanized days when small groups, who took responsibility for the entire cycle, had worked autonomously.

The Tavistock group report to the National Coal Board was not, however, well received. Divisions on the Board resulted in the rejection of the report, and a refusal to let the Tavistock publish the findings. They feared the consequences of allowing groups to become more autonomous at a time when they themselves were intent on intensifying managerial controls in order to accelerate the full mechanization of the mine. They refused to allow the research to continue. It would lead, they said, to expectations that could not be fulfilled. While autonomous groups might be successful, they would not be feasible on longwall layouts which represented the prevailing method of mining. To a number of the people at the Tavistock, the self-regulating group held the clue to improvements in work organization. The interest in these developments pointed to a new form of work organization.

An alternative organization design, known as the composite longwall method, evolved to overcome the deficiencies in the conventional design. The composite design was aimed at providing an organization structure suitable for maintaining continuity of operations and for achieving early conclusion of a work cycle requiring more than one shift for completion. This was aided by setting goals for the performance of the entire cycle and making inclusive payments to the group as a whole for the completion of all tasks in one work cycle. The payments placed responsibility on the entire group for all operations, generating the need for individuals performing different tasks over interdependent phases of the cycle to interrelate. To maintain equal earnings, group members had to contribute equally, and interchange their tasks. The method of work employed was directed at maintaining task continuity. Each shift picked up where previous shifts had left off. When a group's main task was done, it deployed itself to carry on with the next task even if this meant starting a new cycle. All the required rules was internally allocated to members by the work group.

Sociotechnical theory is now an accepted part of organizational theory. In other industries, several important studies were carried out during the 1950s. In 1953 the late A. K. Rice carried out a study in the Calico Mills in Ahmedabad. Rice did no more than mention, through an interpreter, the idea of a group of workers becoming responsible for a group of looms. The employees in the loom shed took up the ideas themselves, coming back the next day with a scheme for which they asked management's permission to implement. Later, the change was diffused throughout the nonautocratic weaving sheds in this very large organization, which employed 9,000 people. The results surpassed expectation, and had long standing effects.[17]

Applications of sociotechnical systems theory in Norway began with studies of the role of workers' directors, a practice required by law in both state-owned and subsidized industries.[18] The Norwegian experiences produced a great deal of interest in Sweden towards the end of the decade, especially among employers and trade union associations. By 1973, between 500 and 1000 work-improvement projects of various kinds, small and large, were going on in many different industries.

The Hawthorne Studies

The Hawthorne Experiments, carried out from 1924 to 1932, undoubtedly crystallized a movement that was already forming. Under the sponsorship of the National Research Council, the experiment began in 1924 in the Hawthorne Works of the Western Electric Company in Cicero, Illinois, near Chicago. The subjects of the initial experiments were a group of women who assembled telephone equipment in Western Electric Company's Hawthorne, Illinois plant. The series of experiments were undertaken to determine the effects of such working condition as length of the work day, number and length of rest pauses, improved lighting, free lunches, and other aspects of the "nonhuman" environment.

The first set of experiments, sought to determine the effects of different levels of illumination on worker productivity. When illumination was raised in the test room, productivity increased; it also increased in the control room which received no additional light. With each major change, there were substantial increases in production. Output even increased when the workers were returned to their original poorly lighted work benches.

In the second group of experiments, a smaller group of six female telephone relay assemblers were put under closer observation and control. Changes were frequently made. Hot lunches, rest periods, Saturday morning work, and longer working days were added or eliminated. Whatever the changes, it seemed the productivity continued to increase. The production of the women continually increased whether the footcandles of light were raised, retained, or decreased. Obviously, some variables besides the level of illumination was causing a change in productivity.

After more than three years, the researchers at Hawthorne recognized that any of several changes introduced concurrently could have caused both the observed change in the individual's mental outlook and the increase in the output. It was quite evident that the workers developed a high morale perhaps, because: (1) the women felt special because they had been singled out for their research role, (2) the women developed good relations with one another and with their supervisor, and (3) the social contact and easy relations among the women made the work more pleasant. The research was conducted so that two female assemblers were initially selected and permitted to choose four others to join them in the test room, which was segregated from the rest of the plant. During the experiment, the women were often consulted and sometimes allowed to express themselves about changes that took place in the experiment.

A fourth phase of the Hawthorne studies consisted of several open-ended interviews conducted from 1928-1930 to provide information to improve supervisory training. Initially, the interviewers asked employees direct questions about their attitudes towards supervision, working conditions, and the job in general. The direct questioning technique resulted in standard, stereotyped responses and therefore in July 1929 a nondirective approach was taken.

In the final phase of the project, there was an attempt to investigate the problem more systematically. A new work group was selected, consisting of fourteen men, some of whom wired banks of equipment, which others then soldered, and which two inspectors examined.[19] The results in the bank wiring room were opposite those of the relay room. The workers had a different brand of emotional reasoning. They decided that there was a production quota and they should not exceed that. The men stopped at quitting time, they admitted that they could easily turn out more work. Tests of dexterity and intelligence indicated no relationship between the capacity to work and actual performance.

From a group dynamics standpoint, a number of sanctions, social ostracism, ridicule, and name-calling, were actually used by the group members to enforce the norms. In some cases, actual physical pressure in the form of a game called "Binging" was applied. In the game, a worker would be hit as hard as possible with the privilege of returning one bing or hit. Forcing rate busters to play the game became an effective sanction. In summary, the Bank Wiring room seemed to produce less productivity because members had the general fear of unemployment (don't work yourself out of a job). They had fear of raising the standard, and they protected slower workers by not overproducing beyond them. There was no sanction or repudiation.

A general interpretation of the preliminary findings is that workers involved in the experiment enjoyed being the center of attention; they reacted positively because the researchers and managers showed an interest in them. Informal work groups have a strong influence on the organization; they establish their own production norms (either high or low) despite attempts by management to increase productivity through task specialization and economic incentives.

SUMMARY

This chapter suggests that discoveries emerged from (1) unique preparations, (2) failures of traditional methods, and (3) persistence in understanding.

1. Preparation. Discoveries occurred when researchers or managers, educated with certain social science concepts, were prepared and interested in the process of problem-solving and discovery. This is a role of learning how to utilize existing concepts in identifying problems and potentialities. It is an "attitude" of science that prepares the researcher to adjust one's concepts based on new discoveries.

2. Failures of traditional methods. Discoveries emerged when researchers and managers were unsuccessful with traditional methods. As a result, some researchers began an inductive inquiry and sought to develop a process of problem-solving and discovery.

3. Persistence in understanding. Discoveries emerged when managers and researchers were persistent in a process of understanding and discovery, seeking to unravel and find explanations. Theory development occurred after creative leaps in relevant directions. The researchers did not just sit and wait for the theory to emerge in their minds nor did they become emersed in mountains of data. The creative leaps involved the search for new strands of thinking from the mass of possible interpretations. It involves "prospecting" the potential opportunities. It is analogous to the work of a miner prospecting for discoveries.

NOTES

1. G. I. Susman, and R. D. Evered, "An Assessment of the Scientific Merits of Action Research," *Administrative Science Quarterly,* vol. 23, 1978, pp. 583-603.

2. T. S. Kuhn, *The Structure of Scientific Revolutions,* 2nd ed. (Chicago: University of Chicago Press, 1970), p. 6.

3. T. S. Kuhn, *The Structure of Scientific Revolutions,* p. 111.

4. T. S. Kuhn, *The Structure of Scientific Revolutions,* p. 129.

5. T. S. Kuhn, *The Structure of Scientific Revolutions,* pp. 53-55.

6. I. B. Cohen, *Franklin and Newton: An Inquiry into Speculative Experimental Science* and Franklin's work in electricity as an example thereof (Philadephia, 1951).

7. F. G. Banting, *The Story of Insulin,* 1940.

8. F. G. Banting, *The Story of Insulin,* 1940.

9. See M. Bliss, *The Discovery of Insulin* (Toronto: McClelland and Steward Limited, 1982); *The Story of Insulin unpublished manuscript* (Banting Papers, University of Toronto).

10. F. G. Banting, *The Story of Insulin,* 1940.

11. J. D. Watson, *The Double Helix* (New York: Signet Books, 1968), p. 116.

12. J. D. Watson, ibid. p. 123.

13. T. S. Kuhn, *The Structure of Scientific Revolutions,* pp. 61-62.

14. T. S. Kuhn, *The Structure of Scientific Revolutions,* pp. 52-53.

15. E.L. Trist and K. W. Bamforth " Some Social and Psychological Consequences of the Longwall Method of Coal-getting," *Human Relations,* vol. 4, 1951; E. L. Trist, G. W. Higgin, H. Murray and S. B. Pollock, *Organizational Choice* (London: Tavistock Publications, 1963).

16. F. J. Roethlisberger and W. J. Dickson, *Management and the Worker* (Cambridge, Mass: Harvard University Press, 1939); C. G. Homans "Social Behavior as Exchange," *American Journal of Sociology,* vol. 63, 1958, pp. 597-606.

17. E. J. Miller and A. K. Rice, *Systems of Organization* (London: Tavistock, 1967); See D. Katz and R. L. Kahn, *The Social Psychology of Organizations* (New York: John Wiley and Sons, 1965, 1978).

18. F. E. Emery and E. Thorsrud, *Form and Content of Industrial Democracy,* (London: Tavistock 1969, Published in Norway in 1964).

19. The primary purpose was to make an observational analysis of the informal work group. An observer and an interviewer gathered objective data for study. The interviewer's main function was to obtain information about the worker's attitudes, thoughts, and feelings.

5

Adjusting Research Methods for Organizational Problem Solving

The scientific method of gaining knowledge is a logical process of gathering data and making predictions, interpretations, and explanations. It assists different observers to rigorously collaborate in building a body of evidence.

Scientific endeavors have, for more than half a century, provided the hope for a better, healthier, and safer world. The benefits of science are visible in medicine, chemistry, engineering, and biology. Human illnesses are more possible to cure than they were years ago. Comforts of life in the home and community and expectations for a healthier work life have drastically improved over the years. Traditional science has contributed to a world that would have been hard to imagine before the turn of the century.

In the last decade, scientific achievements have produced several social consequences. The more efficient freeway and transportation systems have created concrete jungles of noise and air pollution. The destruction of life through technological and biological warfare is a very real possibility. Efficient industrial system have increased the levels of air, water, and soil pollution. Most of us are growing to believe that we are living in a period of crisis which is potentially more devastating than before. We sit amidst our achievements and wonder about the effects of global warming, the holes in the ozone layer, and the pollution problems in developing countries.

Warfare and social ills are not a result of science. In every generation of mankind's existence, we have had to adjust our cultural values and goals to respond to our scientific achievements. Traditional science has simply been better at creating physical achievements than it has in providing the knowledge to help societies and organizations adjust to them. The methods of traditional science are not equipped for organizational problem-solving. They are useful for providing solutions to specific problems that are definable, observable, and technical. While traditional science has been very good in creating our "great society," it probably is not equipped to provide the knowledge for solving organizational problems.

This chapter outlines the traditional scientific method. It then summarizes a number of action principles which might be useful in assisting traditional science.

POSITIVE SCIENCE RESEARCH PRACTICES

When a question has been asked which could be handled reasonably within a single study, the scientist proceeds through several related steps from developing a theory or framework to providing a perspective for the problem and formulating hypotheses based on the concepts. Terms and concepts are specifically defined and evidence is gathered to test the hypotheses. The study's findings are most useful if they contribute to the general knowledge in this field and can be used to predict. A theory becomes more general if it can be repeated in different circumstances.

Certain principles are important to traditional and positive science: replication, specificity in definition, causal relationships, environmental control, a rigorous research design, and control of extraneous variables.

1. Replicability of the results. Replication is concerned with whether or not the results of an experiment can be repeated under the same conditions. Replication is much more than repetition or duplication. It means repeating a research study but usually with variations. Reliability is enhanced if a study is replicated and the same or similar results are found. Trust and confidence is greatly enhanced by a third replication because the probability of obtaining the same results by chance is lower than obtaining them just twice, and so on. Ideally, a change is introduced, the effects are observed, and the change is withdrawn and observed again to see if the pre-test conditions reoccur. Scientific theory and methodology is based on the belief that more general laws can be found to explain a broad range of circumstances.

2. Specificity in definition. A sound hypothesis is generally a simple one, in that it is specifically defined. One of the unifying ideas of the positive science was that everything consists of parts, and in order to deal with a "whole" it is necessary to take it apart until it is ultimately indivisible.[1] This is called scientific reductionism. If one wishes to explain something or solve a problem, one starts by taking the problem apart. The problems is broken into components to its ultimate or simplistic components. Then, by explaining the components or solving the mini-problems, it is possible to aggregate the explanations into a solution or explanation of a whole. So, analysis is a form of "up, down, up again" thinking and explaining things by the behavior of the parts. Managerial problem-solving is often described by such jargon as "cutting the problem down to size." Cutting the problem down to size is simply treating it analytically. It is reducing it to a set of solvable problems, solving the component problems, and then assembling them into a solution as a whole.

3. Causal relationships. The world is often explained by resorting to only one relationship, that of cause and effect. When one thing--call it an "X"--is the cause of another thing called "Y", we are really saying two things about it. One is that "X" is necessary for "Y." "Y" will not occur unless "X" occurs. The second is that "X" is sufficient for "Y"--if "X" occurs, then "Y" has to occur. Explaining the world in causal terms has very important consequences. When we try to explain something by its explicit cause, then, we do not need anything else to explain it, because the explanation is complete. If "X" is necessary and sufficient to cause "Y," then nothing else matters.

4. Environmental control in science is established by constructing a setting which is not affected by unplanned-for influences. The scientist's laboratory is an isolated setting independent of its environment. The laboratory is like a hermetically sealed clock--it keeps ticking away without change over time in accordance with the laws that derived from the structure of the clock. The only debatable issue is whether this is a self-winding clock or not.

5. A rigorous research design. Most researchers pride themselves on a research design that arranges conditions of observations and measurement to guard against sources of unreliability. This is especially difficult in field settings, where natural motivational forces are at work. In addition, field experiments are subject to real life constraints, as the managers and employees may have to make normal day-to-day changes in the organization and the composition of the membership. The research design may have to be altered because the membership changes, because other programs or initiatives are introduced, because expectations are high concerning the change, or because the subjects are aware that they are being observed. In this sense, the method of implementing the research design is as important as the care that is taken in its construction.

One of the research designs which seems to be popular for research in social situations is the pre-test post-test control group design and is illustrated as follows:

$$R \quad O(1) \quad X \quad O(2)$$
$$R \quad O(3) \quad \quad O(4)$$

The design indicates that one experimental group (top line) was tested before and after being exposed to X, while another control group (second line) was tested at the same two times, but was not exposed to X in the interim. The additional symbol R stands for randomization, and indicates that subjects in both groups were selected from a common pool of subjects and were assigned to one or the other group on a random basis. Random, here, does not mean haphazard. It is a method of assignment by which each member has an equal chance of being in either (experimental or control) group. Random assignment is a necessary condition for a true experiment.[2]

6. Control of extraneous variables. It should be possible, by observing certain rules, to guard against extraneous variables affecting the results. The research conditions should be arranged so that each set of observations and conditions will logically have only one interpretation. If a certain pattern of observations can be satisfied by two or three or more different interpretations, then it is not possible to tell which interpretations should be the guide to future work. The research has to guard against a number of contaminants or sources of invalidity.[3]

The Usefulness of the Positive Science Methods in Applied Settings

In understanding, explaining, and predicting behavior in applied settings, experimental research rules and practices have provided the dominant "guiding light." There is no individual who completely defines the rules of applied research in organizations, although the work of Campbell and his colleagues is a good illustration. In theory, laboratory research conventions provide the ideal model for advancing knowledge in applied settings, if one can control extraneous events before, during, and after the change.[4] Internal validity has grown to be the most used criterion in the organizational sciences, while much less attention is given to construct, statistical conclusion, and external validity.[5]

Questions have been raised about the usefulness of experimental research practices in applied settings[6] and about their link with ontological assumptions of what the world is like.[7] Many of these objections illustrate the many problems of using laboratory science technology, as well as those associated with different philosophies of science.[8] They imply that the biases introduced by a strict application of experimental research practices in a field setting may lead to conclusions which are not as scientific as one might hope.

An Example of Sound Experimentation

Milgram's experiments on authority is a classical example of sound experimentation useful to organizational practice.[9] Milgram's research was concerned with what he called the "Eichmann phenomenon." He attempted to illustrate the docility of people responding to directions, even when the source of the request has no established authority and when the requests themselves were in apparent conflict with one's own wishes and values. In fact, 62 percent of the subjects obeyed the voice of authority and administered (as they thought) shocks of 450 volts to supposedly moaning, protesting, and then ominously silent people hidden from view.

One distinguishing feature of these laboratory experiments is the frequent use of a series of discrete, independent trials, where the stimulus conditions are pre-programmed by the investigators. This procedure gives the laboratory experimenter greater control over the experiment and reduces confounding

TABLE 5.1
COMPARISON OF EXPERIMENTAL AND FIELD SETTING CHARACTERISTICS

	Experimental Research Requirements	**Field Setting Requirements**
Setting Reactions	Controlled	Varies between being controlled to dynamically changing
Measurement Reactions	Variables are: • specifically defined, • mutually exclusive, • unambiguous	Variables are: • generally defined, • interrelated, • ambiguous
	It should be possible to introduce and measure the exact degree of change (i.e., number of cubic centimeters).	It may not be possible to measure the level of changes especially in terms of degree of understanding, etc.
	It should be possible to introduce experimental condition, withdraw it, reintroduce it.	Once experimental condition is introduced, the field setting changes even if condition is withdrawn.
Investigation/ Respondent	Objective detachment of researcher.	Subjective involvement commitment and loyalty of researcher to organization.

variables. However, it does reduce the "felt realness" for the participants. Such research illustrates sound research practice in designing an experiment to guard against certain research biases.[10]

Janet Bavelas offered another type of comment on the difficulties of this type of research:

> Of all of the criticisms levelled against Milgram's "obedience" research, there is one I have not seen, the most important to me: We knew that. The world had just seen genocide on a very wide scale, in the Ukraine, in the Holocaust, and the dropping of two atomic bombs on civilian populations. We did not need a replica in the lab; we needed, and still need, to know why--to understand the process, not to repeat it. Milgram's experiment belittled and trivialized the phenomenon rather than leading us closer to its nature.[11]

Field settings present a number of systematic errors that may evolve if researchers attempt to apply the classical experimental model.[12] These biases emerge from the mismatch between the level of analysis of the experimental model and the dynamics in field settings. Table 5.1 summarizes some of these contradicting requirements.

Generally, the experimental model requires a controlled setting where independent and dependent variables can be specifically defined and observed empirically as concrete structures.[13] In such a positive science, it is possible to measure the exact level of a change--such as the number of cubic centimeters of penicillin or mercury--and observe its effect in controlled conditions.

All research paradigms must encounter the ecological structure in the setting studied. If there is truly a difference between the pursuit of the goals of experimental research with the ecology of a field setting, then there is reason to suggest that it may not be possible to use the experimental model appropriately. This is not to deny that scientific research can be done in field settings, but to emphasize the different needs which exist.

Searching for Criteria of an Action Science

In recent years, there has been a growing concern regarding the long standing debate on the adequacy of positive science research methods in field settings.[14] There appears to be a growing recognition of the difficulties of applying the traditional research paradigm for understanding organization events. There may be an inherent incompatibility between research and natural organizational change and development. Traditional scientific research is difficult to carry out when organizations are operating normally. Organizations cannot respond to rules such as randomization, scientific control, replication, specification of variables, causality, and applications of standardized instruments.[15] Whenever threats to validity might occur, the traditional scientist must respond with a more rigorous measures and controls. B. F. Skinner described the danger of doing this by admitting (through a fictitious character in *Walden Two*):[16]

> I remember the rage I used to feel when a prediction when awry. I could have shouted at the subjects of my experiments, "Behave, damn you, behave as you ought!" Eventually I realized that the subjects were always right. They always behave as they ought. It was I who was wrong. I had made a bad prediction."[17]

This scientific model has generally been associated with the term "positive science," which suggests that law-like causal-like relationships between events can be established and observed. Comte, generally associated with the emergence of positivism, used the term "positive" to refer to the actual in contrast to the imaginary, to certainty in contrast with the undecided, to the exact in contrast with the indefinite.[18] The positive science paradigm began to be associated with a science that placed a great deal of importance on a meticulous and detailed examination of the objects themselves, rather than the mind's mental faculties. Positive science eliminates the role of history in the generation of knowledge and assumes that a system can be defined by our existing language.[19]

Kant and later existential writers painted a picture of a nonmechanical, nonpredictable universe in which there is much human emotion and vulnerability. They offered the concept of the intentional mind where knowledge begins with experience, but other aspects of reality--the "a priori"--are not supplied immediately by our senses. For example, it is not possible to perceive time or space, nor can one see, smell, or taste either. The perception of time and space is intuitive and supplied by the mind. Otherwise, the world is unintelligible, like a jumble of colors, patterns, noises and smells without any meaning.[20] Husserl used the term "intentionality" to illustrate that individuals can perceive something only as intended to perceive it; that is, by fitting the stream of primary sensory data coming into some pattern recognizable as being associated with something seen or known previously. This explains why there are conflicting findings on the nature of the problem in an organization. Each observer had responded to the stimuli under observation in terms of his/her own intentionality. He/she has perceived the phenomenon as he/she intends to perceive it.

Emery suggests that Heider's work helped in explaining some of the characteristics of sensations on the basis of their relationships with physical events.[21] He pointed out that objects in the environment had an informational structure. The perceptual systems of living species have evolved to detect and extract this information from their environment despite a great deal of noise at the sensory level. Our conscious feeling of sensations is all but irrelevant to the role of the senses as discriminating perceptual systems.[22] This allows us to think about

perception and not just sensation. The striking features of this emerging paradigm
are:

1.   The environment is recognized as having an informational structure.
2.   This information structure of the environment is embodied in the invariances
     that exist in the relations between energy flows despite fluctuations in the
     individual flows and regardless of whether they impinge on the sensors of an
     organism.
3.   The perceptual systems of living species have evolved so as to detect and
     extract this information from their environments despite a great deal of "noise"
     at the sensory level.
4.   Our conscious feelings of sensations is all but irrelevant to the role of the
     senses as discriminating perceptions systems.[23]

This "environmental" paradigm suggests that the "universal" is not grasped
by a separate intellectual process of abstraction but is grasped from the
"particular." The kinds of concepts that represent perception are "structural
concepts," and are yielded by the perception of serial order in nested
spatio-temporal events. They are not the generic concepts yielded by a process
of abstraction and naming (e.g. of naming species and genes).

Positive science research has been labelled as a "machine age" model of
thinking,[24] because it seeks to understand problems and issues by defining them
by their smallest components and assuming that the solution of these smaller
aspects can be aggregated to explain the total problem. The environmental
paradigm can be partially explained by systems theory, in that problems and
issues are interrelated to other problems and aspects of the organization. Problems
evolve as the organization grows and maintains itself, seeks equilibrium in
reaction to stresses and strains, and carries out the tasks which are most essential
to its survival.[25] There is no absolute knowledge or universal laws in
organizations. Rather, knowledge is relative to what is being used or is useful in
a particular context.

There is a need for a scientific perspective which recognizes an
organization's natural need for change and development. This is more of an
"action" science which is concerned with improving decision-making and
problem-solving as well as contributing to the social sciences by providing ideas
for future experimentation.[26]

An action science would not rely solely on standards of internal and external
validity. It would recognize that each operationalization of a construct and
researcher perspective provides certain biases. Yet, each method, perspective, and
operation has a degree of truth associated with it.

PRINCIPLES FOR RESEARCHING ORGANIZATIONS

Any science has two jobs to do: explanation and discovery. Explanation is concerned with verifying and generalizing, while discovery is a job of stating and testing general relationships between properties.[27] For some organizational variables, especially those that describe less tangible human and environmental variables, there may be a need for principles which are concerned with decision-making, problem-solving, and discovery rather than explanation and generalization.[28] Thus, different research principles may be more appropriate for different research problems. There is generally an accepted format and procedure for explanation or verification. This generally means that a theory or framework provides a perspective for understanding a problem and formulating hypotheses. The concepts underlying the theory are specifically defined, evidence is gathered to test hypotheses, and the study's findings are interpreted in relation to the evidence in the literature. Certain principles which are used for ensuring valid explanation and generalizations include: replication, specificity in definition, causal relationships, environmental control, a rigorous research design, and control of extraneous variables.

The remainder of this chapter summarizes a number of research principles which may be more appropriate for purposes of decision-making, problem-solving, and discovery. They suggest the need for: being creative in defining the real research question; generating theoretical concepts from the field; integrating concepts with real-life assumptions; triangulating and using multiple perspectives; verifying interpretations with perspectives in the field, and treating the research setting as a case study.

1. Defining the real research question. There is sometimes a confusion in what is meant by a problem statement, depending on whether one is interested in basic or organizational research and change. A basic research problem statement indicates a need to test a theory with empirical data.[29] In the field of organizational development, a problem is a need for change, and both organizational members and change agents are jointly involved in discovering the causes of symptoms such as absenteeism, turnover, and so forth.[30]

As researchers, we are taught in graduate school that science requires rigor, control, planning, and the removal of uncertainty. However, the tolerance for uncertainty, failure, and accident may be an important part of a research process, especially for problems which are complex, changing, or messy.[31] How does one begin the process of innovative research? Some people review a list of articles on similar problems; others go about the task of talking to people who are experiencing the problems; others talk with colleagues and seek to creatively develop ideas.

Creative and significant discoveries are rarely possible to plan for, and rely on one's ability to describe a problem in unique and unexpected ways. For example, Charles Robert Richet received the Nobel Prize in Physiology and

Medicine for discoveries related to allergies and anaphylaxis. The discovery
resulted from the unexpected reaction of a dog to a tiny dose of poison from a sea
anemone. Richet recognized the extraordinary nature of this reaction and found
an explanation for it. His prize-winning work grew out of a totally unexpected
result, as he described at the Nobel Prize ceremony:

> Let me tell you under what circumstances I observed this phenomenon for the first
> time, I may be permitted to enter into some details on its origin. You will see, as
> a matter of fact, that it is not at all the result of deep thinking, but of simple
> observation, almost accidental; so that I have had no other merit than of not refusing
> to see the facts which presented themselves before me, completely evident.[32]

Living with opposition and tolerating uncertainty may be more valuable than
solving a problem by immediately reducing the opposition and uncertainty. A
study of the lives of Harvard graduates illustrates that some people employed
healthy, creative, and productive mechanisms while other less effective and
healthy people employed maladaptive mechanisms in dealing with opposition.[33]
In a review of the literature on complex thinking processes, Bartunek, Gordon,
and Weatherby, concluded that highly uncertain situations require cognitive
complexity.[34] Complex situations require an ability to perceive several different
dimensions in a stimulus array and an ability to develop complex connections
among differentiated characteristics--integration and differentiation.[35] This ability,
according to Bartunek, Gordon, and Weatherby, correlates with tolerance for
ambiguity, assumption of leadership, prediction accuracy, empathy, and conflict
resolution.

Cognitive complexity is very important in defining some research problems
and in the "reframing" experience which is part of a new comprehension of a
problem or issue. Quinn argues that the "ability to transcend or reframe
perceptual tensions is at the heart of change in all fields of endeavor."[36] The
creative persons who produce the breakthroughs--Mozart, Picasso, Einstein, and
many others--were able to do so because they were able to see the many
fragmented and differentiated parts and bring them together into an integrated
whole. The creative person was able to see the integrated functioning of
antithetical elements.[37] This person is able to "flirt with doubt and disorder,
enduring anxiety while intuiting the answer. . ."[38] In the reframing experience,
there is a synergistic integration "where the observer and the observed, the actor
and the action become one."[39] It is a more intense mental focus where the
individual and the research task exist in a spontaneous and harmonious
relationship.

The above comments are similar to those made by many others who write
about the creative, reframing experience. In the field of poetry, Stephen Spender
writes about two kinds of concentration, one is immediate and complete, the other
is plodding and only completed in stages.[40] He indicates that some artists scarcely
need to revise their works. For example, Mozart thought out symphonies,

quartets, and even scenes from operas in his head as he went about his day. Then, he transcribed them in their completeness on paper. A more plodding concentration is illustrated by those who write in stages, feeling their way from rough draft to rough draft. This type of concentration was illustrated by Beethoven who wrote fragments of themes in note books which he kept beside him, working on and developing them for years.[41] Although Mozart's form of concentration may seem more brilliant and dazzling, Beethoven's is equally impressive. The results, and not the process, are what are being judged.

Some research problems may be answered with a Mozartian type of concentration. Most research problems which are complex and involve a large number of different people and perspectives might be more naturally focused on with a more plodding "Beethovenian" model for those who are less gifted with the Mozartian talent. Spender's comments about his Beethovenian process might be appropriate for the field researcher.

> Myself, I am scarcely capable of immediate concentration in poetry. My mind is not clear, my will is weak, I suffer from an excess of ideas and a weak sense of form. For each poem that I begin to write, I think of at lest ten which I do not write down at all. For every poem which I do write down, there are seven or eight which I never complete.

> The method which I adopt therefore is to write down as many ideas as possible, in however, rough a form, in note books (I have at least twenty of these, on a shelf beside my desk, going back over fifteen years). I then make use of some of the sketches and discard others.[42]

2. Generating theoretical concepts from the field. Traditional research practices suggest that the test of the theory is best achieved by breaking it into identifiable parts which can be more easily investigated. If the problem is too general, it cannot be tested.[43] Investigators have to systematically think through how the independent variable affects the results.[44] An accepted convention is to use the theory to deduce testable assertions; this involves specifically defining the variables of the theory by breaking it into identifiable parts which can be more easily investigated.[45] This principle suggests that the analysis of each part will assist in understanding the whole.[46] In general, the more specific the problem, hypothesis, and variables, the clearer are the testing implications.[47]

Managerial problems are interlocked with a range of other events and happenings. For this reason, it is not possible to study one problem which is isolated from others. Field experiments simultaneously introduce a number of independent variables which are interrelated with each other.[48] It is not possible to test and introduce one isolated variable. For instance, assessing the impact of a compressed work week involves a number of independent variables, such as starting and quitting times, number of days of work, number of hours of work, and soforth. A sound laboratory experiment would attempt to test each one of these variables independently, introducing one variable and withdrawing others, and so on.

It may not be possible to specify the various components of a theory as if they were separate and unique parts of the whole. Many practical problems have interlocked and interrelated components, and any division of the whole into separate components is really only an assessment of these parts. In this sense, any component is not unique or constant but is related to others. The knowledge gained about each part or component may not be a statement of the interactions of these parts together.

When first involved with a research issue, there is a need to rely on field "prompts" rather than those found in some body of theory. In traditional science, a theory leads to a definition of the problem and then to the development of a design to clarify it. In field settings, a theory is developed for a better understanding of how the variables in the field are interrelated.

Eric Trist offered the following comment on how the field should provoke or prompt the field exploration.

> If you don't have something in the field to prompt you, you may find you have nothing at all useful for practice. The field must provoke you. I never think rigorously when I first look at a problem or research opportunity. But once I begin to understand the field, I can begin rigorously to arrange the new conditions--the constituent problems and issues -- into an overall configuration. New factors enter in from the most unsuspected places. Then, I look at the relations, and seek to investigate relations between system levels.[49]

The field may never provide a random sample or the ideal conditions for experimental research, nor will it provide the opportunity to observe the variables of an elegant organizational theory. Field problems force the researcher to devise new concepts and measures or adapt old ones. They force the development of relationships with managers who are involved in similar problems, and encourage researcher to develop mentor-protégé relationships in guiding the process. This implies that researchers must "earn the right" to be involved with problem-solving in real-life settings.

The researcher soon learns that organizations do not hold still while they negotiate entry, make the intervention, and wait for the appropriate time to collect the follow-up data. Any organization which could be controlled to the extent that we might hope would be rather static in nature, and unlike the vast majority of organizations which might be more normal.

Field concepts are uncategorized and unordered. In some cases, a sorting process can be used as a way to order and categorize field setting problems, issues, and other open ended indicators of data. It is a process of categorizing or developing a picture of how many parts of a universe fit together. It is based on the logic that, through the use of intuitive processes, it is possible to establish categories or factors of similar statements that are mutually exclusive. The statements within each category should be intuitively related. There are different versions or ways to carry out a sort. Sorting was used during World War II, by Eric Trist, as a method of selecting officers; candidates would be faced with a complex "field," and they would have to make choices in providing some meaning through a process of grouping and categorization. It has been used in several research methodologies which have sought to gather evidence inductively.[50]

3. *Integrating Concepts with Real Life Assumptions.* The goal in conventional science is to construct a research setting which is isolated from other influences. A research laboratory is an ideal model of an isolated setting where it is possible to isolate and control extraneous influences.[51] An experimental condition might be isolated so that it does not interact with phenomena it normally interacts with in its environment.[52]

Isolating and controlling any organizational system extracts it from its essential purpose and relationships. A real system under study is an indivisible whole, which relates to and is affected by other systems in its environment. The services and outputs of any set of activities are very useful to others. In one case, an organization uses raw materials and human labor to produce a useful service, and the benefit is used to obtain more raw materials and labor for production of services and so on. In another case, the organization can provide expressive satisfaction to its members so that the energy renewal comes directly from the organizational activity itself.[53]

Conventional research is based on a practice of vertical thinking where general problems are divided into more discrete and understandable parts. Vertical thinking is like taking a set of toy blocks and building them upward, each block resting firmly and squarely on the block below it. With lateral thinking, the blocks are scattered around and need to be connected to each other loosely or not at all. The pattern that emerges from lateral thinking is quite different, and answers are found by using ideas from other fields, variables from other theories, applications from other experiences, or new relationships between existing variables. In this sense, lateral thinking involves two aspects: the deliberate generation of alternative ways of looking at things, and the challenging of assumptions. Alternative ways of viewing problems might seem rather arbitrary. In research settings, this might involve defining the problem from a number of perspectives, using different theoretical frameworks to investigate a problem, and having different and opposing viewpoints to solving the problem.[54]

Assumptions are often agreed to by various people who are associated with a problem. These assumptions may be established and reaffirmed over history, rather than being challenged or assessed. Assumptions can be continually challenged by asking the question "why?" This technique has been well documented as part of a conflict resolution process of asking parties to define their interests.[55] The usual purpose of the "why" is to elicit information. One wants to be comforted with some explanation which one can accept and be satisfied with. The question evokes an understanding of the history behind the problem, and provides for a non-judgemental way of reasoning behind the facts.

In the same way, scientific knowledge is more than "detective work" where the patterns between events and "crimes" are discovered.[56] There may be a need for a "reality" perspective to recognize the discovery of conditions creating the crimes so that they do not happen again.[57] If one viewed knowledge solely as detective work, the views and observations of managerial work would not be appropriate. However, managers are endowed with causal powers which are concerned with efficiency, control, and cooperation. After the detective work is complete, more demanding questions still need to be asked.[58] The first stage is an explanation of the phenomena and resolving difficulties. This logic might be revealed by asking for participant's accounts of why the action has taken place. It then involves searching for the causes and the contingencies explaining this "why" in larger settings.[59]

4. *Triangulating and using multiple perspectives*. Concepts can sometimes be defined so that their dictionary-like definition is similar to their operational definition. Concepts such as weight, height, and size mean the same thing in operational terms. Many other measures may only represent a part of the total picture, and for that reason may limit the generalizability of the conclusion. For instance, the researcher may be forced to use measures of turnover, absenteeism, or productivity simply because they are available and easy to obtain. Questionnaire measures might articulate perceptions and feelings rather than actual behaviors. Thus, each type of measurement is biased by its partial description of reality.

Gaining data and information from a variety of perspectives and viewpoints is a developing tradition in the social sciences and has been described using terms such as convergent or multimethod/multitrait methods or "triangulation."[60] These concepts share the goal of trying to use qualitative and quantitative data together, and using multiple levels of information and perspectives to provide different viewpoints on a research issue.

The word triangulation has been defined as "a combination of methodologies in the study of the same phenomenon" measurement.[61] It has been defined as "a combination of methodologies in the study of the same phenomenon," and has been associated with practices in navigation and military strategy where multiple reference points are used to locate a ship's location.[62] In the social sciences, the word has been associated with the use of multiple methods to improve validation so that the variation reflected the trait rather than the method.[63]

There are different types of triangulation: (1) between methods, (2) within methods, (3) multiple frameworks or measures, and (4) multiple researchers. "Between methods" comparisons involve the use of different and distinct research methods.[64] Interviews would be combined with observations, psychological testing, or a review of records. If the multiple and independent methods reach the same conclusion, there is a higher level of confidence. "Within-methods" triangulation is the use of multiple techniques within a given method to collect and interpret data. This would involve multiple scales or indices focused on the same concepts. Different scales may not produce as wide a variety of perspectives as might be gained from combining others methods reflecting diverse observations or different levels of data (i.e., feelings, perceptions, behaviors).[65]

Triangulation can be something more than the use of different scales and indicators to improve reliability and validity. It can also involve "multiple frameworks or measures" and "multiple researchers." A multiple framework approach might be a combination of: quantitative and qualitative data, or scientific findings with common sense perceptions, or the analysis of economists with sociologists. A multiple research approach calls for different observers or groups who seek to analyze the same phenomena.[66] The various triangulation designs are based on one assumption. The weaknesses of one perspective, method, or design can be strengthened by the counterbalancing strength of another.

In seeking to carry out a discovery aspect of science, triangulation designs recognize that much can be gained from methods which seek to understand non-empirical data. It also requires information which can be obtained non-empirically. This led Tavistock researchers, in the early days, to work in teams and undergo psychoanalysis as a way of providing insight into problems.

5. *Verifying interpretations with perspectives in the field.* The scientific concepts of organizational theorists may or may not exhibit a close relation to reality, although it is often implied that theory should be practical and useful to applied settings.[67] A theory can operate like a paradigm, and can insulate the scientific community as many socially important problems are not reducible to the terms of the conceptual and instrumental tools the paradigm supplies.[68]

A systematic bias occurs when the perspective of theory is assumed to account for the perspective of the field setting. The theoretical concepts defined by the researcher are often very different from those operating in the organization. The scientist systematically builds theoretical structures, tests them for internal consistency, and subjects them to empirical tests. People in the organization have limited perceptions and operate with their own concepts. They often blandly accept fanciful explanations of natural and human phenomena.

Much of what is useful depends on whether it is valid within the eyes of those people in the setting. It must be acceptable to them. This is the act of developing acceptable and situationally valid measures of organizational problems. It involves developing research processes and resolutions that represent the culture, and are ultimately verified by the perspectives in that culture. There are, of course, dangers of such a verification process, as it can lead to tendencies to present only the positive information.

In organizational research and problem-solving, verification is necessary for the survival of an idea. Certain endeavors, are best left to individual artists, who have the instinct and intuition to provide a unique interpretation, even in the face of adversity. Most organizational and societal endeavors are usually social rather than individual experiences. They are expressions of what an assortment of individuals can accomplish by using their collective creativity.

Many ideas, measures, and hypotheses need to be verified with those who are going to use them. Organizational members are better able than anyone else to define their problems and propose solutions because they are more acquainted with their own situations. They are better able to define how concepts and measures can be understood. Many problems in organizations require creative solutions and are complexly intertwined with others; these problems are likely to be resolved through concerted effort rather than individual action.[69]

Many research studies, plans, decisions, questionnaires, and policies are poorly implemented because they are just not understood, because they are hopelessly out of context with the organization's needs, or because they produce resistance to change. An entirely different research process is implied when a researcher calls a group together to define concepts, develop knowledge, refine measurement tools, or make discoveries. The researcher's role is to state objectives and directions, act as coordinator, facilitator, and chairperson of the group. Problem-solving research processes seek to help develop the organization's employees--in developing their skills, abilities and shared interest in the problems.[70] In a pure form, a researcher should never specify the criteria or standards for development and discovery, because this would involve premature judgement and diagnosis.[71]

Using decision-making as a criterion, good research is determined by the degree to which the results are useful in solving practical problems and contributing to a general knowledge of organizations. The researcher's role is part of a cooperative activity of problem definition, consideration of hypotheses, translation of hypotheses into action, and interpretation of the evidence accumulated. His/her role is to aid decision-making as well as contributing to a field science.

6. *Treating the research setting as a case study.* Randomization and the assumptions of a normal distribution are difficult to achieve in field research. A large percentage (over 80 percent) of organizational researchers use convenience samples,[72] and reviews of many large sample achievement and psychological measures indicates that they are based on non-normal distributions (based on a reviews of 440 large samples). Thus, the underlying tenets of normality-assuming statistics can be questioned in some cases.[73]

There are known biases occurring when a sample is not representative of its population. Unimportant people may be most willing, while other appropriate people may resist involvement. This problem also exists for laboratory experiments, especially when it is easier to use students rather than chief executives.[74] The curious and the exhibitionist are likely to populate any sample of volunteers. How secure a base can volunteers be with such groups overrepresented, while the shy, suspicious, and inhibited are underrepresented?

There is strong evidence indicating that responders are a different breed of animal than non-responders.[75] Responders tend to be brighter, better workers, more motivated, more highly educated, and more educated about a topic.[76]

Many behavioral sciences are generally considered to be nomothetic sciences, where it is possible to establish natural laws of gravity, motion, and the like. At best, organizational sciences might be able to estimate the probability of an occurrence rather than establish law-like certainties. The science of organizational studies might be idiographic, like history and anthropology. In such a science, the goal is to provide an accurate description of singular events and establish their relations.[77] This suggests that many organizational studies are really case studies[78] which have low external validity because of the inability to generalize findings beyond the cases researched.

Information from science needs much more than can be gained from single case studies which summarize the natural similarities and differences between events. Case study research requires consolidating cases, studies, and explanations. Consolidating studies can provide insight for more generalizable social science knowledge if the same conclusions occur in a number of carefully selected cases.[79]

It is just as true that the research results of a case study are only one part of a scientific process. The scientific process is continuous and the case findings should lead to action, experimentation, theory construction, and further research. This episodic nature of field research distinguishes it from other aspects of problem-solving. Developing a continuous cycle of research involves getting legitimization, where the goal is to move from practice to theory and then to improved practice.

SUMMARY

In action research, good research is determined by the degree to which the results are useful in solving practical problems and contributing to a general knowledge of organizations. The researcher's role is part of a cooperative activity of problem definition, consideration of hypotheses, translation of hypotheses into action, and interpretation of the evidence accumulated. His/her role is to aid decision-making as well as contributing to a field science.

It is highly unlikely that the researcher can know definitely and in advance the exact theory that will be used or developed. The definition of the problem, the propositions to be tested, and the methods to be employed undergo modification as interim results are validated or invalidated in practice. The research generally seeks to answer questions such as: What are some of the consequences that resulted from a particular intervention? How can we develop a plan for training our employees? If the researcher is involved in the process of change or the act of discovery, he/she cannot be detached and neutral, as would be required by the criteria of scientific research.

All sciences are based on certain assumptions. These are the rules and philosophy under which the science tries to achieve its objectives. The objectives of action research are to assist an organization as much as to assist social science.

In assisting an organization, action research is concerned with aiding participants to solve problems, make decisions, and implement actions effectively. This involves assuring that: (1) the relevant information for problem-solving is available and understandable, (2) the information is useable and manipulable by the system, (3) the cost of obtaining understanding, and using the information is not beyond the system capacity, (4) the problem is solved and the decision implemented in such a way that it does not reoccur, and (5) the process of information use can be accomplished without damaging the implementing process.[80] The criteria of an action science are constructed in recognition that organizational initiatives usually follow an ill-defined cycle of diagnosing, planning, action taking, and evaluating, followed by recurring steps to perfect or adjust the implementation.

NOTES

1. R. L. Ackoff, "The Art and Science of Mess Management," *Interfaces*, vol. 11, 1981, pp. 20-26.

2. D. T. Campbell, and J. C. Stanley, *Experimental and Quasi-Experimental Designs for Research* (Chicago: Rand McNally, 1966).

3. D. T. Campbell, and J. C. Stanley, *Experimental and Quasi-experimental Designs for Research*; D. T. Campbell and D. W. Fiske, "Convergent and Discriminant Validation by the Multitrait-multimethod Matrix," *Psychological Bulletin,* vol. 56, 1959, pp. 81-105; T. D. Cook and D. T. Campbell, *Quasi-experimentation: Design an Analysis Issues for Field Settings* (Boston: Houghton Mifflin Company, 1979).

4. L. B. Barnes "Organizational Change and Field Experiment Methods," in M. Cooper, H. H. Leavitt, H. M. Shelly II (eds.), *New Perspective in Organizational Research*, vol. 79, 1964, pp. 57-111.

5. T. R. Mitchell, "The Evaluation of the Validity of Correlational Research Conducted in Organizations," *Academy of Management Review*, vol. 10, 1985, p. 194; D. P. Schwab, "Reviewing Empirically Based Manuscripts: Perspectives on Process," in *Publishing in Organizational Sciences* L. L. Cummings and P. J. Frost (eds.), (Homewood, Ill.: Richard D. Irwin, 1985), p. 173.

6. C. Argyris, *Intervention Theory and Method*, (Reading, Mass.: Addison-Wesley, 1970); C. Argyris, R. Putman, and D. M. Smith, *Action Science* (San Francisco, Calif.: Jossey Bass, 1985).

7. H. Tsoukas, "The Validity of Ideographic Research Explanations," *Academy of Management Review*, vol. 14, 1989, pp. 551-561.

8. T. S. Kuhn, *The Structure of Scientific Revolutions*, 2nd ed. (Chicago: University of Chicago Press, 1970); A. Kaplan, *Conduct of Inquiry* (Scranton, Penn.: Chandler,

1964).

9. S. Milgram, "Some Conditions of Obedience and Disobedience to Authority," *Human Relations*, vol. 18, no. 1, 1965; A. Bavelas, "A Method for Investigating Individual and Group Ideology," *Sociometry*, vol. 5, 1942, pp. 371-377.

10. D. T. Campbell, and J. C. Stanley, *Experimental and Quasi-Experimental Designs for Research*; T. D. Cook and D. T. Campbell, *Quasi-experimentation: Design an Analysis Issues for Field Settings*.

11. J. A. Bavelas, "Permitting Creativity in Science," in D. N. Jackson and J. P. Rushton, (eds.), *Scientific Excellence: Origins and Assessment* (Beverley Hills, Calif.: Sage Publications, 1989), p. 13.

12. In assessing the performance of human links of a communication system, Campbell defined systematic error as those constant errors that are part of the structure of the communication system, and can occur from the setting as well as the participants in the setting. See: D. T. Campbell, *"Systematic Errors on the Part of the Human Links in Communications Systems,* vol. 1, 1958, pp. 335-337.

13. G. Morgan and L. Smircich, "The Case for Qualitative Research," *Academy of Management Review*, vol. 5, 1980.

14. C. Argyris, *Intervention Theory and Method*; P. Shrivastava and I. I. Mitroff, "Enhancing Organizational Research Utilization: The Role of Decision Makers' Assumptions," *Academy of Management Review*, vol. 9, 1984; G. I. Susman, and R. D. Evered, "An Assessment of the Scientific Merits of Action Research," *Administrative Science Quarterly*, vol. 23, 1978, pp. 582-603.

15. T. D. Cook and D. T. Campbell, *Quasi-experimentation: Design an Analysis Issues for Field Settings*, pp. 51-74; M. L. Smith and G. V. Glass, *Research and Evaluation in Education and the Social Sciences* (Englewood Cliffs, N.J.: Prentice Hall, 1987), pp. 124-157.

16. B. F. Skinner, *Walden Two* (New York: Macmillan, 1948, 1959).

17. B. F. Skinner, *Walden Two* (New York: Macmillan, 1948, 1959).

18. F. Emery,"Educational Paradigms: An Epistemological Revolution", in E. L. Trist and H. Murray, *The Social Engagement of Social Science: Selected Writings* by Members of the Tavistock Institute. (Forthcoming and to be included in Volume II, 1989); W. A. Luijpen and H. J. Koren, *A First Introduction of Existential Phemenology* (Pittsburg, Pa.: Duquesne University Press, 1969).

19. G. I. Susman, and R. D. Evered, "An Assessment of the Scientific Merits of Action Research," pp. 583-586.

20. F. Emery, *Educational Paradigms: An Epistemological Revolution*; W. A. Luijpen and H. J.Koren, *A First Introduction of Existential Phemenology*.

21. F. Emery, *Educational Paradigms: An Epistemological Revolution*.

22. G. Johansson, "Visual Motion Perception," *Scientific American*, June, 1975.

23. G. Johansson, "Visual Motion Perception," *Scientific American*, June, 1975.

24. R. L. Ackoff, "The Art and Science of Mess Management," pp. 20-26.

25. R. L. Ackoff, "The Art and Science of Mess Management." pp. 20-26; D. Katz and R. L. Kahn, *The Social Psychology of Organizations* (New York: John Wiley and Sons, 1978).

26. C. Argyris, R. Putman and D. M. Smith, *Action Science*; C. Argyris, *Intervention Theory and Method*.

27. G. C. Homans, *The Nature of Social Science* (New York: Harcourt, Brace and

World, 1967).

28. C. Argyris, R. Putman and D. M. Smith, *Action Science*; C. Argyris, *Intervention Theory and Method*.

29. M. L. Smith and G. V. Glass, *Research and Evaluation in Education and the Social Sciences* (Englewood Cliffs, N.J.: Prentice Hall, 1987), pp. 7-9.

30. T. G. Cummings and E. Huse, *Organizational Development and Change* (St. Paul, Minn.: West Publications, 1989), pp. 64-65.

31. R. L. Daft, "Learning the Craft of Organizational Research," *Academy of Management Review*, vol. 8, 1983, pp. 539-546; R. L. Daft and J. Wiginton, "Language and Organization." *Academey of Management*, 1979, pp. 179-191; R.M. Roberts, *Serendipity: Accidental Discoveries in Science* (New York: John Wiley and Sons, 1989).

32. R. M. Roberts, Serendipity: Accidental Discoveries in Science, p. 125.

33. S. E. Smith, "Ego Development and the Problems of Power and Agreement in Organizations," Unpublished doctoral dissertation, the School of Government and Business Administration, the George Washington University, 1980; G. Vaillant, *Adaptation to Life* (Boston; Little Brown, 1977) .

34. J. M. Bartunek, J. R. Gordon, and R. P. Weatherby, "Developing 'Complicated' Understanding in Administrators," *Academy of Management Review,* vol. 8, 1983, pp. 273-284.

35. R. E. Quinn, *Beyond Rational Management: Mastering the Paradoxes and Competing Demands of High Performance* (San Francisco, Calif.: Jossey Bass, 1988).

36. R. E. Quinn, *Beyond Rational Management: Mastering the Paradoxes and Competing Demands of High Performance*.

37. A. Rothenberg, *The Emerging Goddess: The Creative Process in Art, Science, and Other Fields* (Chicago: University of Chicago Press, 1979).

38. C. Hampden-Turner, *Maps of the Mind* (New York: MacMillan, 1981), p. 112.

39. R. E. Quinn, *Beyond Rational Management: Mastering the Paradoxes and Competing Demands of High Performance*, p. 21.

40. S. Spender, "The Making of a Poem," in B. Ghiselin, *The Creative Process* (New York: Mentor, 1952), pp. 112-125.

41. S. Spender, "The Making of a Poem," pp. 112-125

42. S. Spender, "The Making of a Poem," p. 115.

43. F. N. Kerlinger, *Foundations of Behavioral Research* (New York: Holt, Rinehart and Winston, 1967), p. 26.

44. T. D. Cook and D. T. Campbell, *Quasi-experimentation: Design an Analysis Issues for Field Settings,* pp. 53-54.

45. D. A. Kenny and L. Albright " Accuracy in Interpersonal Relations: A Social Relations Analysis," *Psychological Bulletin*, vol. 102, 1987.

46. J. G. March and H. A. Simon, *Organizations* (New York: John Wiley and Sons, 1958).

47. F. N. Kerlinger, *Foundations of Behavioral Research*, p. 27.

48. N. Morse and R. Reimer, "The Case for Qualitative Research," *Academy of Management Review*, vol. 5, 1956; R. Likert, *New Patterns of Management* (New York: McGraw-Hill, 1961).

49. Quote from interview with Eric Trist, July 13, 1988.

50. A. Bavelas, "A Method for Investigating Individual and Group Ideology" *Sociometry*, vol. 5, 1942, pp. 371-377; F. Herzberg, *The Managerial Choice: To be*

Efficient and to Be Human (Homewood, Ill.: Dow Jones and Irwin, 1976); W. F. Whyte," Models for Building and Changing Organizations," *Human Organization*, vol. 26, no. 1 & 2, 1967, pp. 22-31; R. Dubin, *Theory Building* (New York: Free Press.1978); B. G. Glaser, and A. L. Straus, *The Discovery of Grounded Theory: Strategies for Qualitative Research* (New York: Aldine, 1967).

51. F. N. Kerlinger, *Behavioral Research: A Conceptual Approach* (New York: John Wiley and Sons, 1979), pp. 93-100; M.L. Smith and G. V. Glass, *Research and Evaluation in Education and the Social Sciences*, pp. 139.

52. D. P. Ashmos and G. P. Huber " The Systems Paradigm in Organizational Theory: Correcting the Record and Suggesting the Future," *Academy of Management Review*, 1987.

53. M. L. Smith and G. V. Glass, *Research and Evaluation in Education and the Social Sciences*, p. 147; G. Morgan, *Images of Organization* (Beverley Hills, Calif.: Sage Publications, 1986), pp. 66-69.

54. E. de Bono, *The Use of Lateral Thinking* (London: Jonathan Cape, 1967); E. de Bono, *Lateral Thinking: Creativity Step by Step* (New York: Harper and Row, 1970).

55. R. Fisher, and W. Ury, *Getting to Yes: Negotiating Agreement Without Giving In.* (New York: Penquin Books, 1981).

56. H. Mintzberg, "Managerial Work: Analysis from Observation," *Management Science*, vol. 2, 1971, pp. 97-110.

57. H. Tsoukas, "The Validity of Ideographic Research Explanations," *Academy of Management*, vol. 14, 1989, pp. 551-561.

58. H. Tsoukas, "The Validity of Ideographic Research Explanations," pp. 551-561.

59. H. Tsoukas, "The Validity of Ideographic Research Explanations." pp. 551-561.

60. F. N. Kerlinger, *Foundations of Behavioral Research* (New York: Holt, Rinehart, Rinehart and Winston, Inc, 1967), p. 33-38; F. N. Kerlinger, *Behavioral Research: A Conceptual Approach*, p. 41.

61. F. N. Kerlinger, *Foundations of Behavioral Research* (New York: Holt, Rinehart, Rinehart and Winston, Inc, 1967), p. 33-38; F. N. Kerlinger, *Behavioral Research: A Conceptual Approach*, p. 41.

62. T. D. Jick, "Mixing Qualitative and Quantitative Methods: Triangulation in Action." *Administrative Science Quarterly*, vol. 24, 1979, pp. 602-611.

63. D. T. Campbell and D. W. Fiske, "Convergent and Discriminant Validation by the Multitrait-multimethod Matrix," pp. 81-105.

64. N.K. Denzin, *The Research Act*, 2nd ed. (New York: McGraw Hill, 1971).

65. N.K. Denzin, *The Research Act*.

66. R. Reason, and J. Rowan, Issues of Validity in New Paradigm Research (Chichester: Wiley, 1981).

67. P. Shrivastava and I.I. Mitroff, "Enhancing Organizational Research Utilization: The Role of Decision Makers' Assumptions," *Academy of Management Review*, vol. 9, 1984, pp. 18-26.

68. T. S. Kuhn, *The Structure of Scientific Revolutions,* 2nd ed. (Chicago: University of Chicago Press,1970), pp. 35-37.

69. W. R. Torbert, "Why Educational Research has Been So Uneducational; The Case of a New Model of Social Science Based on Collaborative Inquiry," in P. Reason and J. Rowan (eds.), *Human Inquiry: A Sourcebook of New Paradigm Research* (Chichester: Wiley, 1981).

70. S. M. Corey, *Action Research to Improve School Practices* (New York: Teachers College, Columbia University, 1953), pp. 71-83.

71. See N. R. F. Maier, *The Appraisal Interview* (New York: Wiley, 1958).

72. T. R. Mitchell "The Evaluation of the Validity of Correlational Research Conducted in Organizations," *Academy of Management Review*, vol. 10, 1985, pp. 200-201.

73. T. Micceris, "The Unicorn, the Normal Curve, and Other Improbable Creatures," *Psychological Bulletin*, vol. 105, 1989, pp. 156-166.

74. M. E. Gordon, L. A. Slade, and N. Schmitt, "The 'Science of the Sophomore' Revisited: From Conjecture to Empiricism," *Academy of Management Review*, vol. 11, 1986, pp. 191-207.

75. R. Rosenthal and R. L. Rosnow, *The Volunteer Subject* (New York: John Wiley, 1975).

76. M. L. Smith and G. V. Glass, *Research and Evaluation in Education and the Social Sciences*.

77. H. Tsoukas, "The Validity of Ideographic Research Explanations," *Academy of Management*, vol. 14, 1989, pp. 551-561; D. P. Schwab, "Reviewing Empirically Based Manuscripts: Perspectives on Process," *Publishing in The Organizational Sciences*, in L. L. Cummings and P. J. Frost (eds.), (Homewood, Ill.: Richard D. Irwin, 1985).

78. D. P. Schwab, "Reviewing Empirically Based Manuscripts: Perspectives on Process," pp. 173.

79. H. Tsoukas, "The Validity of Ideographic Research Explanations," pp. 551-561.

80. C. Argyris, *Intervention Theory and Method.*

6

An Overview of the Action Research Process

A scientific solution, it would seem, should be easy to implement. That is, the smartest, most scientific people working together, should conceivably be able to develop the best solutions which users would logically accept. However, many logical and scientific solutions may not always gain acceptance. People may not like them because they prefer old ideas or ones they have grown used to.

The term "action-research" was introduced by Kurt Lewin in 1946 to denote an approach to research combining theory building with research on practical problems. In his definition of action research, Lewin emphasized the collaborative relationship between the social scientist and the "client." This relationship affects the "direction" of the research in that it implies that both the scientist and the client are jointly involved in change and research.[1]

Lewin's term "there is nothing so practical as a good theory" is used to guide action researchers. Action research aims to "contribute both to the practical concerns of people in an immediate problematic situation and to the goals of social science by joint collaboration within a mutually acceptable ethical framework."[2] As such, action research is a type of applied social research differing from other varieties in the immediacy of the researcher's involvement in the action process.

This chapter provides an overview of the ways to view the change process and then provides an overview of the action research process. This viewpoint on action research attempts to link it to other organizational development practices such as strategic planning. Subsequent chapters describe the action research process in more detail.

THE CHANGE PROCESS

Any change program usually involves sequences such as assessing, focusing, and implementing. These three sequences are highly interrelated. For instance, the conception of an idea may not be termed successful unless it is implemented. The successful introduction of some new method implies that it is communicated and understood.[3]

Table 6.1 illustrates two stereotypical definitions of a process of change: directive and planned change. The size of the circles is a rough indication of the time and energy a manager or action researcher might spend during each sequence of the process.

In a directive or "top-down" process of change, there is minimal involvement of participants and less time is spent in the assessment of the need for change and the conception and proposal of the idea. As a result, more time may be spent in the process of assuring that the implementation is carried out. This would involve communicating, dealing with resistances, and building support for the defined idea. In a "top-down" process, more time is spent in the actual implementation rather than the assessment stage.

An Organizational Development (O.D.) intervention or planned change process requires more time in the formative sequences of the process. Participants or organizational members are involved in the definition of the need, and have the opportunity to use their creativity in developing the idea and its proposal. As a result, less time may be needed during the implementation stage for making adaptations or dealing with resistances. The investment of time in assessing and focusing can significantly reduce the amount of time required to implement and institutionalize the change. It should also reduce the possibility of having to scrap an unworkable idea and start over again.

A planned process is highly inductive and loose, especially at the beginning steps. Overall, however, the approach should take no more time than one would take in a more "top-down" project. The participative approach does not argue for months of field work and voluminous case studies as practiced by some social anthropologists. It suggests that much of the energy in a change process might be used in developing an idea and getting commitment.

BEGINNING THE ACTION RESEARCH PROCESS

Action research is a process where employees become jointly responsible for managing the process of change through a steering committee or Action Research group (A.R.). Before action research can begin, there must be an acceptance of its goals and methods as well as a positive and cooperative attitude among those who are carrying it out. Five sequences are part of this initiation effort: entry;

TABLE 6.1
MODELS OF CHANGE

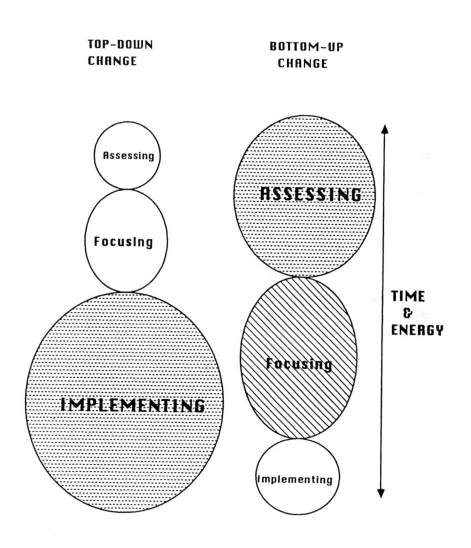

forming an action research (A.R.) group; developing goals for the group; training the action research group; and drawing up an agreement on the research that will be conducted.

1. *Entry.* Anyone in the organization can begin the A.R. process, but to be successful he/she must be personally interested in examining organizational processes and taking action. Commitment is motivated by problems, issues, and feelings that immediately concern organizational personnel. A.R. is suited for groups who are dissatisfied with or interested in some aspect of their organization. It is also very useful for testing the potential receptiveness of employees to new programs and issues.

Ideally, organizational participants, on their own, become aware of a problem and the need for change. They can either begin the action research themselves or have an A.R. consultant work with them. It is more likely, however, that awareness of the need for change in the organization may come from an A.R. consultant or an interested and motivated person lower in the organization. In all instances, however, commitment of top management and union executives should precede the research.

The action researcher must also gain the cooperation of other people who share his/her interest in the organizational problem. There must be, in addition, commitment to change and to take action upon the research findings. If an issue or problem does not receive this commitment, it may not be important. The action researcher must have access to individuals who support the research as well as those opposing it. While it may be difficult to engage the active support of those with opposing ideas, it is important that the researcher have access to them so that their arguments can be understood. Inclusion of opposing viewpoints may make the process more legitimate. Ideally, members of opposing groups will be included on the action research team.

There is a conventional wisdom that a researcher usually gains access to an organization through the person in charge. In addition, there are other important "gate-keepers" who need to grant permission to carry out the study. These are union executives, informal leaders, strong-willed individuals, and inflexible personalities. There are, therefore, multiple points of entry that require a continuous process of negotiation and coaxing.

The process of gaining access not only provides a commitment to action, but it also assists in refining the issues needing to be addressed in a study. It is an opportunity to gain an understanding of the criteria on which the success of the study will be judged. It is also an opportunity for the researcher to develop a research design to respond to the requirements of an action science.

The convergence of interest around the commitment to gather information and take action is an important first step. Commitment is motivated by problems, issues, and/or feelings of immediate concern to individuals. This commitment can be very fragmented, as individuals may be motivated to solve different problems. A researcher's initial task is to find the individuals who are committed to work on common problems.

2. *Forming an action research (A.R.) group.* Ideally, membership to the Action Research group would include all those in the focal organization or work group who are in a position to initiate action, those with the obligation to respond, and those committed to the problem's resolution. Since the A.R. group is voluntary, many people in the organization may not feel inclined to participate. It is therefore strategically desirable to hold preliminary recruiting interviews in which the purposes and interests of would-be participants can be identified. At the same time, it is important to explain the methodology and principles of A.R. to the participants who will be involved.

If certain individuals do not have the time or the desire to do research, this does not foreshadow the death of the research effort. What is essential, however, is that those who have the power to initiate action be kept informed of the group's progress. On the other hand, too many memoranda and progress meetings about the group's activities could become tiresome both for the A.R. groups and for the organizational hierarchy.

It is possible, although rare, for every member of a group or organization to be motivated to participate in a research effort. A group of unwieldy size could thwart the effectiveness of an action research group by inhibiting interaction and discussion. One answer to the problem of size is the division of responsibility among several teams, with a representative central steering group.

3. *Development of goals for the group.* For the A.R. group to function as a team, it must define common goals evolved from its need to solve a problem or plan an overall direction. The goals provide a helpful orientation for the research effort, effectively focusing and coordinating the many aspects of the research. Inappropriately stated goals, however, are worse than no goals at all. A.R. has its own particular criteria for stating goals:

- The goals must be very flexible. They cannot be long-term, but must be re-articulated in the step-by-step process of A.R.

- The goals must be important to the group and significant to the organizational functioning. Above all, the goals must capture and maintain the interest and commitment of all members of the group. As a test, a goal could be restated in the negative to see how the group reacts. If it has little effect, the goal may not be that important.

- The goals should be feasible to those concerned. Unrealistic, unapproachable goals evoke little commitment. Few of us desire to involve ourselves in effort designed to fall short of a purpose. Where goals can be attained, and where those involved can see the availability and accessibility of appropriate means, it is probable that commitment can be achieved.

- Pursuing a goal must be justifiable--there must be a definite need and the authority to do something about it. Justification is additionally important when the A.R. group approaches the organization-at-large seeking legitimization and sponsorship.

4. *Training of the Action Research group.* People cannot make intelligent choices about A.R. techniques unless they feel competent to deal with the problems of other people. "Group building" from the beginning is necessary to make the group's research genuinely cooperative and effective. Difficulties with group building--or with the skills of research--call for training and improvement.

The best way to train the research team is by demonstration or practical application. As Corey says, there is,

> a great difference between having mastered the vocabulary of group work and practicing the behaviour the vocabulary implies. Experience is almost certain to modify talk, but talk frequently has little effect on subsequent practice.[4]

Corey proceeds to specify the conditions that must occur if the group is to work cooperatively in an A.R. group.

- There must be freedom to change the established ways of working in groups. The status leader can play a decisive part in changing the methods of the group, for he is in the best position to create an atmosphere that encourages some freedom to change. An action as simple as arranging for someone else to chair staff meetings may initiate improvements. Another action that encourages freedom is self-criticism and a request for help by the status leader. Complete candor is probably not completely advisable at first. Most people test the limits rather gingerly when they feel some freedom to express themselves for the first time.

- Group members must evaluate group processes. It is a wise investment of time to take five or ten minutes at the end of the meeting to raise such questions as these: Have we gone about this in the best way? What might be done, and what should be done in the future to make our work more expeditious? This can be done either orally or by a simple written questionnaire. It might be said in passing that getting judgments from the members of a group about the success with which their work has been conducted is one of the most sensible and tangible ways of introducing action research procedures in group work. The post-meeting reaction data usually suggest some promising changes; these can be put into effect, and their consequences tested by subsequent post-meeting reactions.

- Group members must be willing to try out proposed improvements. Evaluation of group processes usually brings about proposals for improvement. The entire group can consider the desirability of implementing suggestions. If it has no other value, the decision serves to make the members of the group more keenly aware of the methods they are using to get the work done.

- Group members must be trained. Trying out new methods of group work under realistic circumstances and appraising its consequences are highly beneficial. Frequently, however, group members are reluctant to try out new procedures because they feel insecure and realize that they lack some of the skills required for giving these procedures a fair trial. Training sessions on group skills always have distinct advantages.

Learning how to do research by experimenting and working effectively in groups is not easy. A basic assumption of A.R. is that learning within the group through development of new attitudes is a basic resource for the research. Feelings of hostility and devaluation--whether directed at others or the self--must be confronted to avoid dysfunctional consequences to the research process.[5]

5. *The research agreement.* The Action Research group must obtain access to those who can authorize the research contract and facilitate research conditions. It is also important, although it may be difficult, to identify indifferent opposing organizational elements. Their arguments can then be inputted into the research process. Including opposing viewpoints tends to legitimize the A.R. effort.

The A.R. agreement can be secured in a variety of ways. It can be proposed directly by members of the Action Research group who hold formal positions in the organization. Or it can be secured indirectly through members of the A.R. group who are connected to other individuals and groups, which, in turn, have direct access to legitimizing agents. Top management commitment may be obtained more easily by a clearly defined contract. A well-defined agreement that includes a statement of needs, goals, justifications, and expectations leaves little question as to exactly what activities the organization is authorizing and supporting.

The A.R. group is never completely developed. At a certain point, the group will begin to feel anxious to start working on the research problems. This probably is the best time to commence the sequences of the action research and change process.

ACTION RESEARCH AND THE ORGANIZATIONAL DEVELOPMENT PROCESS

The remainder of this chapter provides an overview of how action research methods might be useful for carrying out the three sequences of a change process: defining the need for change; focusing a direction and developing a commitment to the changes; and implementing the plan. Subsequent chapters provide more detail on each of the steps.

Defining the Need for Change

Defining the need for change involves: (1) identifying the problems or needs, (2) using interviews to develop measures and ideas for the research, (3) sorting the interview information to develop questionnaires, and (4) collecting and reporting results.

```
┌─────────────────────────────────────────┐
│                                           │
│            Identifying problems           │
│                 and needs                 │
│                                           │
└─────────────────────────────────────────┘

┌─────────────────────────────────────────┐
│                                           │
│              Using interviews             │
│            to develop measures            │
│                                           │
└─────────────────────────────────────────┘

┌─────────────────────────────────────────┐
│                                           │
│             Sorting information           │
│               into categories             │
│                                           │
└─────────────────────────────────────────┘

┌─────────────────────────────────────────┐
│                                           │
│               Collecting and             │
│               reporting data              │
│                                           │
└─────────────────────────────────────────┘
```

Successful problem or need identification is the crux of an action research effort. Individual members of the A.R. group bring with them their own views of what is wrong with an organization or what should be researched.

The problem identification provides a starting point for beginning the research, as well as serving as an initial and important diagnosis of organizational members and their skills, perceptions, attitudes toward their work, and capacity to change. The temptation may be to proceed too casually, and to accept too quickly the initial views of a problem. Individual members bring with them their own personal motivations and views of what is wrong with the organization.

These personal agendas may not be an accurate testimony of the real problems.

One of the difficulties of the word "problem" is that it implies that there is something wrong. Rather, a problem is a definition of a need for change and describes how certain issues can be addressed. In the process of defining and identifying the problems to be studied, the A.R. group must determine how organizational members will articulate their views.

Successful problem identification must meet certain criteria:

1.   The problems must be important to the person naming them and also significant for organizational functions.
2.   The problems must be manageable.
3.   Problem statements must reveal some fundamental criteria for assessing a solution.

These criteria suggest that the identification of problems extends beyond the A.R. team and the manager's immediate concerns, and must recognize the needs of other perspectives.

The researcher can use two kinds of knowledge in identifying an organization's problems and structure. First, there are the concepts, variables, and propositions from the basic disciplines of the behavioral sciences. These could allow the researcher to search for key interdependencies of internal processes and functioning within the context of the external environment. It could allow the researcher to examine the behaviors of participants as they actually exist at the time of the change program and should be able to account for critical events and factors that brought about the existing situation. Such an understanding of organizational life is limited to the variables which are already defined by behavioral science. We should not discredit this type of data collection, as it is the basis of much of the writing in social sciences.

Valid knowledge can also include the particular data collected from the organization system, as it is exhibited within a participant's unique terminology, spatial organization, and response sets. This second type of data may only be partially linked to the concepts of behavioral science, but may have more presence in common sense interpretations, phrases, and modes of behaviour. This type of data is of most direct relevance to people in the particular organizational situation.

Action research is based on the idea that the interpretation of the problem depends on a combination of factors including the perspectives and histories of various participants. It is useful to think that most organizational problems can be defined from many different perspectives; the experimental researcher may be concerned with defining the problem from a theoretical perspective, and the manager is concerned with defining it to suit his managerial needs or objectives. The goal of the action researcher is to define the problem in a way that summarizes various perspectives and takes into account the organization's needs, managerial and union needs, and membership needs. In addition, it should build on how the action researcher has defined problems in similar situations.

This type of problem definition may not be scientifically rigorous within conventional science criteria. The major criterion for deciding on whether conventional science practices should be used depends on whether they are mutually relevant to the organizational practice and the needs of social science. Action research activities are often exploratory and discovery oriented. The activities can also be useful for providing information for social science when they recognize rules and canons of an action-oriented science.

One of the initial sequences in A.R. is to develop an understanding of how to assess or monitor the need for change. In doing this, *open-ended interviews* provide a way to understand the variables or criteria that might be important if a more extensive program of research were undertaken. The interviewee is asked to define: (1) some of the positive and negative feelings about an issue, (2) examples of issues, (3) ideas for how to carry out the research, and (4) ideas, criteria, or questions which might be used in a questionnaire. Interviews are a way of encouraging organizational members to brainstorm variables which might be used in a data gathering instruments. In this way, the initial interviews are a way to assist in defining a problem and the research measures and criteria. People who are interviewed are those who have a perspective on an issue. These perspectives might include union leaders, managers, and other groups as well as people who have different view of the problem.

There are a variety of ways of gathering data including unstructured or structured questionnaires, interviews, and focus groups. An action research consultant might be able to initiate a discussion with organizational members on how these methods can be used. One of the best data-gathering methods in A.R. is the open-ended, behaviour description interview. This technique focuses on the needs and problems of the organizational system, rather than on how the organizational system fits into some questionnaire. The behaviour description method enables people to articulate their needs or feelings better than when they are asked what they need or feel. Various research tools are described in the following chapters.

In A.R., organizational members should develop the skills for designing questionnaires, analyzing the data, and reporting. They are encouraged to use the interview information they have collected and develop a program for more comprehensive research on the issues which are important. Dealing with the interview data consists of two major steps: (1) summarizing the feelings and perceptions coming from the interviews and (2) content analyzing the interview data to provide a picture of the overall concepts and themes. These steps are necessary for developing a questionnaire to facilitate a more specific definition of the organization's problems. The questionnaire is constructed by structuring the interview data and open-ended responses into a questionnaire format.

The statements generated from the interviews--consisting of the individual's feelings and frustrations, examples of problems and incidents, and criteria for developing a survey-- can be transferred to file cards. The way that the statements are transcribed onto cards should reflect, as closely as possible, the manners and nuances of communication and thoughts of the individuals interviewed.[6] The statements are the basis for forming the concepts defining the issue or problem to be studied.

A sorting procedure can be used in ordering and categorizing interview statements (which can be written on cards) to represent a collective concept (or model) of the concerns and issues describing the problem. The sorting is based on the logic that, through the use of intuitive processes, it is possible to establish categories or factors of similar statements that are mutually exclusive.

Sorting procedures can be used for categorizing almost any type of organizational data, ranging from tidbits of gossip to hard scientific data and statistical information. In some cases, ideas from group members might be summarized through "brainstorming," and then arranged for sorting. In other cases, open-ended interviews might be used to derive information for a sorting procedure. The goal is to arrange the interview information into common categories and build a conceptual framework or grounded theory of the issues and problems being researched. As such, a questionnaire or interview format is a mechanism for operationalizing the framework.

When a questionnaire is developed from the interviews, it should meet the following criteria:

1. The measures should be derived from an open-end interview.
2. It should yield specific data.
3. It should provide data for client and organizational needs.
4. It should deal with particular, present issues.
5. It should be fairly easy to administer, analyze, and feed back to respondents.

Data collection is a process of selecting the people who can assist in providing information on an issue or problem being researched. The goal is to define the population of individuals who can provide a perspective on the issue. The A.R. group is then responsible for developing mechanisms to collect the data and present the findings.

Data gathering and analysis assignments are often left to those who are most interested and have a greater commitment to resolve a problem or issue. In any such effort, the A.R. consultant's or chairperson's responsibility is to assure that one perspective is not more represented than another, and that people do not offer their individual interpretations of the data.

The most significant characteristics of a data reporting are simplicity and objectivity of presentation. An efficient data presentation, which emphasizes simplicity and the minimal critical information, is worth hours of valuable group time. While it may be necessary to summarize all the data, only the most important should be presented in the main body of a report. Other summaries can be detailed in appendices or secondary reports.

Every study yields data showing many negative aspects of a given operation. It is useful to emphasize what can be done to improve the situation, since concentrating on weakness or failures produces a defensive reaction. Insisting on reporting negative data--no matter who it hurts--increases emotional resistance and creates a time lag for the acceptance and utilization of findings. Allowing the individuals opportunity to save face enables them to explore all of the different possible meanings which may surface from the findings. In situations where survey results are quite different from what has been expected, it is necessary to proceed cautiously--preferably letting the individuals who were surprised set the tempo.

There is a need to honor and protect the confidentiality of an individual's views. This may be particularly important where one is dealing with a client group with a small number of participants.

With a small number of people, it is inevitable that a certain amount of informal interaction takes place, where issues raised in interviews may be discussed, thus furthering an awareness of problems and hastening the individual's feeling that some action must follow. Rapoport recognised this point in discussing one of the dilemmas of the action researcher, the need to satisfy both the client and the scientific community.[7] The demands of the client for immediate action may conflict with the need to gather adequate research data to meet a more objective goal.

Focusing and Designing a Program for Change

The data gathering or assessment phase of any change project is a statement of the need for change. Even more, it is an opportunity for organizational members to indicate their positive and negative feelings about past events. The process provides a purging or cleansing; before the system can be renovated or redesigned, the old one has to be "buried." The reporting of results from an organizational assessment is an indication of the willingness to address the problems identified.

Focusing an organization in a new direction relies on understanding what is realistic and possible as well as what has occurred previously. The process encourages brainstorming and other idea generation activities for identifying issues and trends that the organization will have to respond to in the short and long term.

Focusing a change is much like an architect's task when beginning the process of renovating an old heritage building. The architect begins with ideas, sketches, and models, and works within the constraints of the existing construction to "focus" the renovation. An architect's concepts and visions are adapted to the present construction, needs of the tenant, and community norms.

The focusing step encourages the organization's membership to meet and discuss the most appropriate changes. This consists of a process where task groups meet and discuss various topics related to: (1) identifying opportunities and threats, (2) outlining strengths and weaknesses within the organization, (3) defining values and philosophies, (4) defining a mission statement, and (5) developing a vision for change.These discussions can be undertaken at short workshops or meetings designed to involve the organization's members.

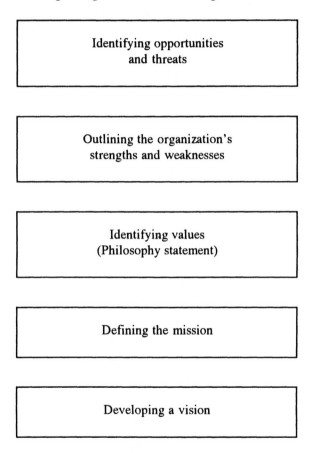

The *opportunities and threats* in the organization's larger environment can potentially affect the way the plan is developed and carried out. In "scanning" the environment, the action research group can become aware of the current and potential actions of competitors, economic trends, government policies and legislation, demographic changes, changes in market influences and tastes, and so forth. This is a definition of known opportunities and threats. These can be prioritized in terms of the probability of occurrence, their impact, and the ability of the organization to control or deal with.

Participants can gain another understanding of the need for change by analyzing the organization's *strengths and weaknesses*. This "organizational" scan provides participants with the opportunity to examine the way the organizational resources are presently committed. It is also an opportunity to identify the commitments deemed most valuable and those less useful to a "desirable" future.

Three other ingredients are important in focusing an organization's direction: a definition of the organization's mission, a statement of the organization's philosophy, and a vision of direction for the organization. An organization's *mission statement* describes its justification for existence. Organizations respond to social and political needs, and must justify their existence based on how well they meet these needs. It is "doubtful that any organization ever achieves greatness or excellence without a basic consensus among its key stake-holders on an inspiring mission."[8] A mission statement describes the organization's unique aim which sets it apart from other organizations. The statement refers to what the organization is in "business" for, or its purpose for existence. It is the "raison d'être."

After a general mission statement has been developed for the total organization, it is appropriate to become more focused and develop mission statements for each of the organization's units. These statements are more focused and more limited than that of the total organization, but they grow out of the general mission statement. Many organizations develop "credos" which are the public articulation of the mission statement or intent of existence. For example, the police credo is "To Protect and Serve," and Ford suggests that "Quality is Job One."

A *philosophy statement* can be useful for describing how the organization's members will work within this mission statement. It outlines the values for making decisions, principles for treating staff, and ways to relate to a client. It provides a listing of the values and assumptions that people feel are important and allows them to state what they would like to achieve. The statement of values and assumptions describe a attractive view of the organization, a condition that is rather ideal.

Mission and philosophy statements should be much more than just a statement of words and ideas. The process of articulating these statements is probably more important than the resulting words. The process should provide an opportunity to build a consensus of the most important values and beliefs. The discussions and debate clarify values of what staff feel are important and unimportant. They provide a signal to staff of what values are thought to be valuable, and a forum for people to debate issues. So, the resulting statements should, ideally, reflect the mission and values that people are committed to.

A *vision* or statement of the desirable future is like an architect's description or sketch before the plan is begun. It is the artist's description of the values, concepts, and ideas in designing a house. It provides enough detail so that people can understand the concept. In the same way, participants are asked to construct desirable futures for their own organization or work-groups. This is a statement of the desired directions--goals, focus on clients, and focus on people in the organization. It is also a statement of what currently exists within an organization.

A strategic issue or direction is like an architect's drawing of the design to be used in renovating an existing organizational system. Before an architect can devise the final scale drawing of the planned renovation, he/she begins with sketches or models. There is a "vision" of what might work. The architect must work within the constraints of the existing construction, using concepts and techniques of current construction for developing a plan or direction. It is a process of renovation using concepts of what might be, and adapting them to the present construction, needs of the tenant, and community norms.

"The only way to translate vision and alignment into people's day-to-day behaviour is by grounding these lofty concepts in the company's day-to-day environment."[9] This underscores the need to focus on a process of implementation.

Implementing and Developing an Action Plan

The planning activities of creating a philosophy statement, mission, and vision are creative exercises encouraging interaction with other people. The activities do not demand that people take on responsibility or use their time for carrying out tasks. That is, talking and interacting are fun and motivational in provoking changes in thought. They do not demand changes in the way people behave or carry out their activities.

The focusing process has provided an identification of many of the threats and opportunities within the organization's environment, as well as assisting the organization's participants articulate values and beliefs they want the organization to realize. The implementation sequence generally involves taking these philosophies, mission statements, and visions and developing plans and procedures for carrying them out. It involves a development of the strategic issues which are most important in responding to important threats and opportunities within agreed upon values.

The process also assists in identifying a number of operational strengths and weaknesses of the organization. Operational issues which are important, therefore, are those responding to these strengths and weaknesses within agreed upon values. The specific steps include:

```
┌────────────────────────────────────────┐
│                                          │
│         Developing the Strategic         │
│          Issue or Alternative            │
│                                          │
└────────────────────────────────────────┘


┌────────────────────────────────────────┐
│                                          │
│        Identifying strategic direction   │
│              for the issue               │
│                                          │
└────────────────────────────────────────┘


┌────────────────────────────────────────┐
│                                          │
│                Developing                │
│              an Action Plan              │
│                                          │
└────────────────────────────────────────┘


┌────────────────────────────────────────┐
│                                          │
│        Developing an ongoing process     │
│           of evaluating, updating        │
│                                          │
└────────────────────────────────────────┘


┌────────────────────────────────────────┐
│                                          │
│        Developing a commitment plan      │
│                                          │
└────────────────────────────────────────┘
```

There are three basic approaches to identifying *strategic issues* or directions, of where the organization might go: a direct approach; the goals approach; and visions of success.[10]

The direct approach involves the identification of strategic issues after reviewing mandates, missions, and SWOT's (strengths, weaknesses, opportunities, and threats). It is most appropriate in situations where the organization's internal and external environment are in high turbulence. These are situations where there is no agreement on goals, where the environment may be rapidly changing, where there may be a high degree of conflict between actors, and where interests are fragmented. In such situations, strategies may not be scientific or rational, but they satisfy the needs of the various actors.

The goals approach suggests that managers should establish goals and objectives and then develop strategies to achieve them. This approach is most appropriate when there is not a great deal of change and diversity and where there is a hierarchical structure where leaders at the top can coordinate or impose overriding goals and assist the organization's staff to achieve them. These are also situations where there is already a deep commitment or implicit understanding of the organization's goals and needs it has to respond to, such as police, fire, military, and many profit organizations. Such approaches are focused on the "best" strategies which optimize the organization's ability to achieve its goals.

Objective setting can be used to assist managers to set specific objectives for the future and encourage them to ask and keep asking what can be done to achieve results. Thus, objectives force managers to make explicit exactly what steps must be taken to fill the objectives. Also, they help subordinates learn what is required of them, thus coordinating an organization in a purposeful direction.

The visions of success approach relies on a manager's ability to develop a "best" or "ideal" picture of the organization and its future. The task is then to define strategies for moving from the way it is now to the way it will look and behave according to its "vision" or picture of the future. Such an approach is appropriate if the future is uncertain and if there is a fair degree of turbulence in the environment. These are cases of drastic change, where it is possible to mobilize people to work together. This approach replaces rational principles or mechanistic procedures.

The strategic issue or direction provides a specific sets of concepts and how they might be used within the specific organizational system. This is a statement of an idealized future, free of present-day constraints. It usually describes a five to ten year time horizon. It is not unusual to work within a short-term (i.e., one year) for some projects and a long-term (i.e., 5 years or more) future for others.

In the following example, a provincial ministry of education's royal commission on education defined a mandate and policy directions for the school system. Teachers, parents, and other groups were asked for their ideas and input. They described the mission as :

> The purpose of the British Columbia school system is to enable learners to develop their individual potential and to acquire the knowledge, skills, and attitudes needed to contribute to a healthy society and a prosperous and sustainable economy.

The strategic directions suggested that a healthy society and a prosperous and sustainable economy are achievable when "educated citizens," striving to be the best that can be are:

- thoughtful, able to learn and think critically and to communicate information from a broad knowledge base (in order to be able to solve problems efficiently and effectively);

- creative, flexible, self-motivated and possessing a positive self-image (in order to be able to make choices confidently and to take advantage of opportunities as they arise);

- capable of making independent decisions (in order to participate fully in society's democratic institutions);

- skilled and able to contribute to society generally, including the world of work (in order to help support the society and economy); productive, able to gain satisfaction through achievement and to strive for physical well being (in order to make a contribution to the well being of society while pursuing personal objectives);

- co-operative, principled and respectful of others regardless of differences (in order to foster the aims of a healthy society);

- aware of the rights and prepared to exercise the responsibilities of an individual within the family, the community, Canada, and the world (in order to ensure the improvement of society and the economy).[11]

However, this policy direction did not encourage teachers to "hook" in. In many of the School Boards throughout the province of British Columbia, teachers voiced their disagreement through strikes, many lasting as long as three weeks. The issue in these strikes revolved around teachers' concern about how the "vision" in "Year 2000" was being implemented. A strategy is a policy defining what the organization does or will do.[12] It consists of the following six steps:

1. identifying practical alternatives, and dreams or visions for resolving the issues,
2. identifying output requirements or standards to judge the usefulness of these options,
3. enumerating implementation requirements, and barriers to achieving these alternatives,
4. outlining the major actions,
5. identifying the resources needed,
6. identification of a working plan.[13]

Strategic alternatives are policy questions affecting an organization's mission, values, and vision. That is, if the organization wishes to work within its mission, values, and vision, how should it respond to the opportunities and threats in the environment while recognizing its strengths and weaknesses? The alternatives define the choices that organizational members are willing to make in better responding to their strategic issue or direction.

The future direction assumes that the data collected, the interest, experience, and expertise lead to the accumulation of observations which can be arranged within some uniting principle of the future. A statement of underlying principles is a useful first step. The goal is to summarize concepts and principles which relate to the problem rather than inventing new ideas which one is in love with.

The strategic alternatives provide specific sets of alternatives and how they might be used within the specific organizational system. The alternatives focus the organization to meet requirements of adaption, production, maintenance, and management coordination. Effectiveness is measured by criteria other than adaption and change; an organization also has to focus on internal structures such as production, maintenance and management coordination. Each of these requirements must be met.

Making Strategies More Specific

A strategy is operationalized by a list of more specific steps, projects, or working options assist in carrying it out. For example, a number of the strategic options that were developed to increase the number of female candidates in a university faculty included:

1. Seek out funding for a "Women in Management" position.
2. Develop a way to strategically communicate the new policy.
3. Develop mechanisms to satisfy faculty that the selection has resulted in the best person for the job.
4. Establish a recruitment process which is more proactive.
5. Carry out research to assist educational systems address this policy issue.
6. Hire female Master's candidates and support their work in obtaining Ph.D degree.
7. Remove sex, age distinctions on resumes, applications.
8. Develop mechanisms to make sure we are representative of society and that society can audit our selection procedure.
9. Develop a commitment to improve our gender balance over the next 10 years.
10. Define criteria of merit so that we can consistently evaluate candidates.[14]

These strategic options emerged from two problem-solving session. The initial brain-storming produced only a general listing of these and other points. These options were later refined into a policy statement for new hiring.

In this case, the faculty group identified objective criteria they felt should be used in judging whether or not these strategic options should be implemented. They were then asked to "flesh out" the strategic options they had defined. This required a more detailed listing of the above issues. The criteria for judging were just as useful for assisting faculty members think more specifically about "reasonable" policy options. This definitional process did not result in any major disagreements, even though the two year debate before this time might be characterized as vicious and divisive.

A *plan* is a list of actions to implement the strategic alternative. Plans can vary a great deal in form and content. The simplest form may be nothing more than a written agreement in the minds of key decision-makers about their organization's mission and what it should do, given the circumstances. In this sense, the process of planning is as important as the actual plan. The formal plan is most useful as a communication document. This is especially important if there is a need to coordinate with a range of people in a diversity of programs and for keeping people "on track" with the plan's intentions. As people forget and new people are added on, a formal plan can provide an important set of targets to focus activities. In addition, a plan can serve as an important public relations document for external and internal audiences.

A simple form of strategic plan might include the following heading.[15]

1. A statement of the mandate
2. A mission statement
3. A philosophy statement
4. A statement of opportunities and threats
5. A statement of strengths and weaknesses
6. A list of strategy issues (or a scenario, ideal future)
7. A list of strategies to realize these issues (these are practical alternatives, barriers, projects, and specific actions
8. A listing of responsibilities and roles
9. A program of implementation
10. A statement of visions of success

The plan is really a summary of the previous steps which have been undertaken. The major responsibility of the action researcher at this stage is to facilitate the transfer of information and decisions so that it evolves into a plan of action. Under normal circumstances, a program includes a list of projects which have identifiable tasks, target dates, and people responsible for undertaking. These targets can be defined so that they are likely to get commitments of time, effort, and logistical support.

1. Specific project tasks: General project tasks are less useful than specific ones; the specific ones define what will result when completed.
2. Realistic time constraints: The plan outlines when the tasks will be completed, guarding against over-committing and under-delivering.
3. Assigned responsibilities: People should be assigned responsibilities for the tasks.
4. Observable overviews: The plan is stated in a way that people know how the projects are linked together.

There are also several influences or "roadblocks" which detract from the organization's ability to attain its desirable future. Lack of training, low morale, poor management skills and other people-related deficiencies can be identified. The weaknesses can be seen as steps which need to be taken rather than as problems which are unresolvable.

There are several resources which may strengthen the organizations pursuit of its desirable future. The strengths of an organization can be tangible (plant, inventory, market share, salary levels, patents) or intangible (quality of management, employee loyalty, public support).

Common sense suggests that projects respond to the needs or fears of key interest groups--top managers, informal leaders, union executives, and the like. Or, if only one interest group feel strongly about an issue, it might be necessary to increase awareness. The design process involves re-articulating needs based on conversations with strong interest groups, involving interest groups in the definition of vision and objectives, and implementing projects which are most appropriate for the needs of the organization.

At some point in most change efforts, a number of questions are appropriate. These relate to assuring that the implementation is "on track" and that the change is having some of its expected impacts. These questions do not need to be asked in formal *evaluations*, but they can be posed at strategic times during the change effort.

Regardless of the specific action, the A.R. process remains the same. Every action is evaluated and the data fed back to the researchers to determine the validity of problem identification, general plan, action, and hypotheses. There are consecutive cycles of planning, execution, evaluation, or fact-finding, and replanning, action, and re-evaluation. Thus, A.R. has no terminus. The specific actions taken and the problems to which they are directed will, of course, change. But, organization improvement will always be an issue for the entire organization.

The times at which action plans are to be reviewed will differ. The plans will indicate when the checkpoints occur, and a schedule for review will be prepared for the organization as a whole as well as for individual departments. It will be necessary for the planning group to monitor this review to ensure that it is carried out and that a high level of involvement of staff is maintained. The phrase summative evaluation has been associated with many information gathering efforts using traditional scientific procedures and analyses. Such evaluations take place at the final stage of a change effort and are often used to satisfy outside funding agencies.

An important purpose of such evaluations is to solicit explanations for existing gaps, and ideas for reducing or eliminating them. The evaluation can also address the framework that was established in the research phase. It can consider whether the problems identified have been addressed, the level of commitment, and the effectiveness of certain actions. It can assess whether interventions are contributing positively to the change.

Getting commitment to a plan of action is possibly the most important aspect of the implementation process. The most effective implementation plan has a number of ingredients: they are incremental and recognize immediate needs; they illustrate a grand design and steps that need to be carried out; and they illustrate that the grand design or map will be modified at each stage of the change process.

Action research encourages a participative approach to planning with an emphasis on actions that are driven by the requirement adjusting organizational decisions to the overall strategies. The steps are driven less by a rational, grand design. It is akin to a sports strategy of winning one point at a time, or one game at a time. There may be a game plan and a strategy for "shadowing" certain players, but opportunities at certain moments are important to capitalize on. This idea of action planning is compatible with studies on technological innovation which indicate that small, rather than large, organizational changes play a key role in reducing production costs.[16] Daily accomplishments form the basis for a consistent pattern that allows people to see instant gains. The strategy includes:

- Dividing tasks into smaller units, or problems into identifiable chunks.
- Avoiding over-committing and under-delivering and practicing under-committing and over-delivering.
- Being patient and politely persistent.
- Accepting the principle that the more the researcher does, the less responsibility that people will take on.

The integral and most difficult element of getting commitment to projects is to allow individuals to articulate them in relation to their roles and responsibilities. In conventional "top-down" planning, goals or objectives are usually performed at the beginning of the process; it is the step on which all other steps are based, not the product of those steps. This is the crucial point of the whole process. Action research focuses on defining workable strategies and implementing them by creating opportunities and reducing restraints. It is a "bottom-up" process of developing goals and objectives based on participation and involvement.

Commitment does not only involve the sequence of events for carrying out a project. It also involves understanding who in the organization must be committed to the change and to carrying it out. This is an understanding of the politics of the change. As a result, most change agents have suggested such terms as: "getting the executive's approval," "getting key people on board," "making sure the union is committed," and "having the membership understand it."

Successful implementations require a systematic analysis of who is committed to the idea, who is able and willing to provide resources, and who is willing to carry out and persevere with the new process. In any change process, a critical mass of people are necessary to assure implementation. This may mean five of nine participants, but it may also mean two of nine participants who are the strongest informal leaders. In this sense, the critical mass includes "those individuals or groups whose active support will ensure that the change will take place. Their number may be small, but it is the critical number."[17]

An implementation plan describes a series of action steps devised to secure the support of people vital to the change effort.[18] It outlines who is involved and how their commitment is assured.

SUMMARY

The chapter provides an overview of the action research and change process. In writing this chapter, there was an attempt to link the action research process to some of the key steps which are normally part of organizational development and strategic planning process. This suggests that research and change is not simply an assessment activity. Rather, the action research process carries out the steps with attention to basic rules and procedures of action and decision-making.

NOTES

1. K. Lewin, "Action Research and Minority Problems," *Journal of Social Issues*, vol. 2, 1946, PP. 34-46.

2. R. N. Rapoport, "Three Dilemmas in Action Research," *Human Relations*, vol. 23, 1970, p. 499-513.

3. H. J. Leavitt, "Applied Organizational Change in Industry: Structural, Technological, and Humanistic Approaches," in J. G. March (ed.), *Handbook of Organizations* (Chicago: Rand McNally, 1965).

4. S. M. Corey, *Action Research to Improve School Practices* (New York: Teachers' College, Columbia University, 1953), p. 96.

5. A. H. Passow, M. B. Miles, S. M. Corey, and D. C. Draper, *Training Curriculum Leaders for Cooperative Research* (New York: Teachers' College, Columbia University, 1955), pp. 1-6.

6. J. B. Bavelas, A. Bavelas, and B. A. Shaefer, *A Method for Constructing Student-generated Faculty Questionnaires*, (Victoria,B.C.: University of Victoria, 1978).

7. R. N. Rapaport, "Three Dilemmas in Action Research. "

8. J. M. Bryson, *Strategic Planning for Public and Nonprofit Organizations* (San Francisco: Jossey-Bass, 1988), p. 48.

9. J. Naisbatt, and P. Aburdene, *Re-inventing the Corporation* (New York : Warner Books, 1985), p. 27.

10. J. M. Bryson, *Strategic Planning for Public and Nonprofit Organizations* (San Francisco: Jossey-Bass, 1988), p. 48.

11. B. M. Sullivan, *A Legacy for Learners- The report of the Royal Commission on Education*, Province of British Columbia, 1988.

12. J. M. Bryson, *Strategic Planning for Public and Nonprofit Organizations*.

13. For a similar listing of steps, see: J. M. Bryson, *Strategic Planning for Public and Nonprofit Organizations*.

14. *Internal Policy on Equity*, School of Public Administration, University of Victoria, October, 1991.

15. J. M. Bryson, *Strategic Planning for Public and Nonprofit Organizations*, pp. 174-175; See also: B. W. Barry, *Strategic Planning Workbook for Nonprofit Organizations* (St. Paul, Minn.: Amherst H. Wilder Foundation, 1986).

16. S. Hollander, *The Success of Increased Efficiency: A Study of Du Pont Rayon Plants* (Cambridge, Mass.: MIT Press, 1965).

17. R. Beckhard and R. T. Harris, *Organizational Transitions: Managing Complex Change* (Menlo Park, Calif.: Addison-Wesley, 1977), p. 53.

18. R. Beckhard and R. T. Harris, *Organizational Transitions: Managing Complex Change*, p. 54.

Part III

The Research

7

Types of Interviews

Interviews are an important part of any action researcher's project. They can be used for resolving disputes and problem-solving, brain-storming creative options, gathering data, or as a tool for developing a better understanding of the types of variables and criteria that can be used in a questionnaire.

The importance of different approaches to interviewing was underlined as early as the Hawthorne studies in the 1930s. These studies were primarily concerned with trying to understand how morale and productivity were affected by various aspects of the organization's design. However, in attempts to gain a better understanding of these factors, the researchers found that direct questioning often led to superficial, specific responses. The interviewers tried a radically new experiment where they sat back and decided to let the interviewee direct the interviews. The employees launched into long tirades to which the interviewer patiently listened. More importantly, the researchers gained surprising understandings about human relations.

Interviews, especially unstructured interviews, provide the opportunity for the researcher to investigate further, to solve problems, and to gather data which could not be obtained in other ways. This chapter provides an overview of how open-ended or unstructured interviews can be used for different purposes. It first outlines some general problems with interviews and then describes four types of interviews which can be used by the action researcher.

PROBLEMS WITH INTERVIEWS

There is a long and well-documented set of difficulties with open-ended or unstructured interviews. School teachers might assess the intelligence of the same five children and feel very confident about the accuracy of their assessments. However, they can disagree widely between themselves.[1] In selection evaluations, the same applicants can be interviewed by several classification officers and there may be little agreement among them. There are cases when one applicant may be ranked first by one selection officer and fifty-seventh by another. Thus, many early research studies rejected the value of unstructured processes for assessment and data gathering.

Open-ended interviews provide a rich assortment of information, but the information is often presented in ways which are difficult to interpret or generalize. The reliability and validity seems to be quite low.[2] The following conclusions are offered in reviewing the literature on interviewing:

1.   The interviewer forgets much of the interview's content within minutes after its conclusion. Interviewers have a relatively short and inaccurate memory. They can forget nearly half the information in a very short period of time.[3]
2.   Structured and well organized interviews are more reliable.[4]
3.   The interview is most valid in determining intelligence level, motivation, and interpersonal skills.

The open-ended or unstructured interview method provides an opportunity to get information first hand from the respondent in a face-to-face situation. It provides the presence of a sympathetic listener where people get problems off their chest. Interviewees experience what psychologists call catharsis (from the Greek work to make pure). Merely by talking things over, the interviewee can gain a better insight into the nature of his/her own problems. Speaking openly in a receptive environment is an opportunity to sort out one's own ideas.

The manager or research scientist who seeks to carry out scientific research faces two problems: he/she must increase the reliability in judging the problem under investigation, and he/she must provide some statistical proof that measurements are accurate and statistically valid. On the surface, the most sophisticated way to respond to these questions is to structure an interview or questionnaire process so that subject or applicant received the same set of questions in the same order. Structure increases accuracy, reliability, and validity.[5] There seems to be a dark cloud over those who wish to carry out open-ended, unstructured interviews. It would seem that improvements on the process would require that interviews be structured, so that the interviewer is trained and follows a procedure with a fixed set of questions. The following section outlines how unstructured interviews might assist the research process.

Those who argue strenuously for open-ended interviews are sometimes not the best defenders of the method. They spend a great deal of time gathering information that might be considered "low yield" information. They support their method by such statements as:

Open-end interviews give me a feeling for the organization. They allow me to better understand a number of quantitative measures.

I use direct quotes for some of the responses. It gives life to the data. It gives the
reader a feeling for the real statements and feelings of the interviewee.

This information is low yield because it is often volumous and unsynthesised, and
utilizes precious time of the interviewer and the interviewee.

Can unstructured, open-ended interviewing be improved?

The following section suggests that there are different types of unstructured
interviews, and each is unique to an interview problem. Thus, the key to
open-ended interviewing is to recognize how it has to be adjusted to different
interviewing needs.

TYPES OF OPEN-ENDED INTERVIEWS

Table 7.1 illustrates four types of open-ended interviews: the behavior
description interview, the sensing interview or discovery interview, the problem-
solving interview, and the helping interview. Each interview has specific purposes
and assumptions and is appropriate for certain situations.

The table suggests that there are two basic reasons for using interviews in
organizations: to gather data for understanding people issues or responding to
organizational interests. The vertical axis suggests that information can be used
for understanding the individual needs of interviewees or researchers (as a
therapist encourages a client to discover his/her own problems or as a researcher
gathers data that is only useful for testing the hypothesis). Or, interviewers might
seek to gather information which is of possible joint or mutual relevance, such as
the feelings and concerns about a change. The interviewer might gain information
for devising a questionnaire, while the interviewee has a opportunity to be heard,
and to offer suggestions for improving a situation affecting him/her.

The horizontal axis suggests that interview data can be used for the
organizational interests of the people in the setting (for the client solely), or it
might be used for more generalized purposes (solving mutual problems or
scientific pursuits). All the following interview methods are inductive,
open-ended, and unstructured. They seek to be useful for data collection, theory
building, problem-solving, or counselling. Each purpose requires a different
open-ended interview method.

Behavioral Description Interviewing

Behavioral description interviewing is based on the often quoted principle
of science that "the best predictor of future behavior is past behavior." That is,
reliable and valid evidence of past performance can assist in predicting the
future.[6] Being too rigorous in gathering data about past events and opinions may

TABLE 7.1
TYPES OF UNSTRUCTURED INTERVIEWS

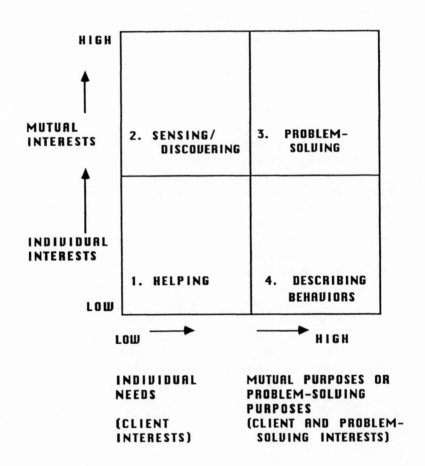

limit the research to the specific situations being studied. It will provide no insight into discovering new possibilities or solutions to problems.

Intuitive information about the future allows people to use their hunches, ideas, and feelings. Predictions of the future might be enhanced by combining various levels of information. That is, indicators of the past might be supplemented with intuitive information as well as actual past performance in similar circumstances. Circumstances in which the data will be used in the future are important. Although it is impossible to define totally similar and perfectly congruent circumstances, the goal is to draw data from a set of circumstances in the past which will give us an indication of those in the future.

Indeed, information about the past can provide a valuable reference point on predicting the future. However, three corollaries are appropriate.

Corollary One - Intuitive information and creativity is a powerful source of information on the future.

Corollary Two - Examples of past behavior provide the best example of what might happen in the future if they are based on similar circumstances and if they are consistent measures of behavior.

Corollary Three - Information collected in this manner is only one perspective on the future; other perspectives are also appropriate.[7]

Table 7.2 illustrates how behavior description questions relate to other types of questions which can be asked in interview situations. Various categories of information can be used in a questionnaire and interview.[8] Table 7.2 implies that a whole range of data may not provide very useful evidence about an organization's happenings. Some data may be of little use because it requires a large inferential leap in understanding behavior, or because it is judgemental, opinionated, and unsubstantiated. The goal of behavior description questions is to provide information about what actually happens; the questions assume that this is the best indication of future events.

The information requirements can be divided into three classes summarizing: characteristics, behaviors, and psychological states or attitudes. The more verifiable type of information to be gathered is concerned with biographical facts, technical knowledge, and descriptions of actual background and experience. The information may be reliable measures of a very limited and specific aspects of an issue or problem.

Behavior description interviews are a structured form of an open-ended interview. This interview method assumes that certain information gathered about past behavior can be a reliable prediction of behavior. It responds to the specific interests of the researcher and seeks to provide valid measurements based on specific criteria. The goal is to gather evidence for purposes of selecting personnel, hypothesis testing, and evaluating. The interview is guided by the general statement "We are looking for the answer to specific questions."

The goal, or so it would seem, is to derive data which describes, as closely as possible, the actual behavior that goes on in a given situation. These are the details of what people said, the unique interactions, and the specific character of the work setting.

The top part of information hierarchy in Table 7.2 presents questions relating to biographical facts, achievements, or technical information. Biographical data can describe age, marital status, and position. Achievement questions might refer to grade point average, publications, honors, and achievements. Technical knowledge questions refer to the person's technical capability to carry out a task and can include questions on the organization's overall general performance effectiveness. Experience-based questions refer to human capabilities such as the person's ability to type, write a memo, or fly an airplane. They also refer to technical information about the organization's capability or effectiveness in carrying out specific tasks. They can be questions related to experiences with the budgeting process, the manufacturing process, or other technical processes.

Much of the information in the top part of the hierarchy can usually be gathered through other methods than interviewing. In fact, such questions are usually difficult or cumbersome to ask in interviews. The information might be better collected elsewhere, like through formal organization records or through achievement tests that a person might carry out. Thus, these are not useful interview questions, unless the interviewer wishes to gain some rapport through such questions.

The middle part of the hierarchy suggests that questions about the past can be understood by what the individual will do in the future. The relevance of the past data and its appropriateness to understanding the future is the best reason for gathering data about the past. The following are types of questions that describe past behaviors.

1. Tell me about your best accomplishment in your last job, where did you get the idea, how did you plan it, how did you implement the plan, how did you deal with some of the major obstacles.
2. Tell me about your typical work day. For instance, what happened yesterday? I'm trying to find out some nitty gritty details of your day-to-day work period, that is, from the time you come into the office until the time you go home.

Some of these questions can focus on specific aspects such as motivational leadership, communication, conflict, etc.

3. Tell me about the last time you faced a situation where an employee was not performing. Describe the situation to me and how you dealt with it. What did you say to the individual? What did the individual say and what are some of the things that occured.
4. Tell me about the most emotional or most difficult situation that you've had.
5. Tell me about the hardest job you've ever had in the last couple of years.

TABLE 7.2
INTERVIEW INFORMATION HIERARCHY

TYPES OF INFORMATION   TYPES OF QUESTIONS

Measurable Characteristics

1. Biographical facts credentials and achievements	How old are you? What is your marital status? What is your G.P.A.? What publications do you have?
2. Technical Knowledge budgets, computers,	What skills do you have in dealing with: engineering principles, and the like?
3. Experience/Activity descriptions	What experiences have you had? What recognition have you received?

Observable Behaviors

4. Behaviour descriptions	Describe a recent experience which . . .

Psychological Characteristics

5. Self-evaluative information a. Likes and dislikes	What are the aspects you like most (least) about your job?
b. Strengths and weaknesses	What are some of the positive . . . What are some of the negative . . .
c. Statements of goal/attitudes, philosophy	What are your goals? What is your vision of the future? What are the formal plans? What are your personal plans?
d. Hypothetical/speculative Statements	What would you do if . . .
e. Opinions, attitudes, beliefs	What are your beliefs?
f. Solutions, recommendations	What suggestions do you have . . .

6.   Tell me about the co-workers you like least. Describe the co-workers you like most.

These types of questions, when they are followed with further behavior description probes, can provide approximations of what the person did. They ask the individual to describe the exact behavior that occurred in the particular work setting.

Behavior description questions set up a format so that individuals describe extreme cases. For instance, what is the most, least, last, toughest, worst? These are superlative attitudes. They assume that future action is best predicted from superlative attitudes, values, and behaviors which occurred in the past. These are the types of questions that seek to help to understand which is the most or least important aspect. In this sense, they are more realistic than questions which relate to "give me an example."

Questions about behaviors are very useful for an understanding of organizations, as they describe observable events and acts. They are not, usually, verifiable, because they are subject to differences in interpretation. In principle, these questions seem easy to get good information on, since they simply ask a person to summarize an event or experience. There are some difficulties with the reliability of the information because of memory loss, remembering less significant events, highlighting the most recent ones, threatening questions, confidential questions. Such statements, however, are valid to the respondent.

In the third level in the hierarchy are several types of self-evaluative questions to provide indications of feelings, frustrations, aspirations, and the like. They can be used to gather information on: likes and dislikes, strengths and weaknesses, goals, attitudes and philosophy, and hypothetical/speculative statements.

Questions on likes and dislikes seek to get at feelings of what the individual finds enjoyable/motivating or not enjoyable/punishing. Typical types of questions are: what do you like most about your job, what do you like least about your job, or what is your favourite job activity?

Questions on strength and weaknesses assume the interviewee's own interpretation is a relevant indicator of future behavior. These might be questions such as "What are your personal strengths (weaknesses)?

Goals provide an indication of what a person might be directed towards or what the organization might be directed towards. Questions might refer to: What do you plan to do? What are the goals of this organization?

These are types of questions which provide an indication of the future by providing the person with the hypothetical example. For instance: if you are asked to fire a person, how would you go carry it out?

Those who are more adept at answering, or those who are more intellectually alert, usually provide more coherent information. These questions are most likely to be intellectualized and can be answered better by people who are able to verbalize their responses. For this reason, their relevance for certain information gathering purpose might be questioned. We rarely perform in accordance with likes or dislikes, goals, or hypothetical futures. In fact, goals rarely provide an indication of what the organization would do in the future period. If anything, they may provide an indication of the person's or organization's visions but usually provide little indication of future behavior.

Questions about psychological states or attitudes are not verifiable, in principle. Attitudes and psychological traits exist only in one's mind and this is not directly accessible. Many psychological characteristics depend on the theory or concepts defining them. Even though one may have a clear idea about the criteria of these theories, differing ways of asking these questions can present different answers. Indeed, questions about some attitudes are more susceptible to question wording differences than others. Much of this information might be better gathered from personal interview, group problem-solving sessions, and observations.

The hierarchy of different types of questions provides a perspective on gathering information. In some cases it may be appropriate to ask technical types of questions. However, these types of questions do not provide an indication of behavior on the job. They provide technical details, emotions, or frustrations which may be quite different than actual behavior.

The Problem-solving Interview

The problem-solving interview responds to the mutual interests of the researcher and client and encourages individual problem-solving or goal setting. The researcher's purpose is to develop a climate where there are mutual interests in sharing ideas, exploring, and problem-solving. The interview encourages researchers and clients to develop joint responsibility. The interview is guided by the statement: "Let's resolve the problem."

The problem-solving interview format is based on the research of Norman Maier who carried out a series of classical studies illustrating the difference between problem-solving, tell and listen, and tell-and-sell interviews.[9] The latter methods assume that managers and supervisors take on the role of directing the solution.

Problem-solving involves decision-making where individuals are given the opportunity to make a choice among a number of alternatives. It assumes that individuals are responsible for selecting among the alternatives.

If personal growth and change are an objective of management, the problem-solving interview is a key component in this process. The objective of the problem-solving interview is to aid an individual, disturbed or otherwise, to identify ways to change and improve. It provides a context where the individual can work out a solution to a problem or issue and begin to take action to resolve it. Certain principles are important to the problem-solving process.[10]

1. Situations and incidents should be discussed while personalities and attitudes should not. The first statement describes a problem-solving situation while the second one illustrates a case where personality issues may be provoked.

As you know, we have a lot of deadlines to meet in this business. I wonder if there is a way of fixing this job so that these deadlines won't creep up on us?

You seem to be having difficulty meeting deadlines. I wonder if you have any ideas of how you can correct that?

2. Problem-solving is best served when people are jointly engaged in activities of interest. Both parties need not have the same interest or objective; however, both must feel that they can gain from the activity. The first set of objectives are examples with mutual interests; the second set illustrates objectives where it would be more difficult to locate mutual interests.

Set 1: (a) Ways to make people more safety minded. (b) Methods for improving quality. (c) Ways to make the job more interesting. (d) Areas where training is needed.

Set 2: (a) Being loyal for the good of the company. (b) Working hard so that the department will look good. (c) Responding to production goals. (d) Improving your efficiency.

3. Supervisors are often concerned that employees will be unaware of problems or will lack the ability to solve them. In order to stimulate interest in the problem-solving approach, the problem or issue needs to be stated so that the solution is not implied. Thus, the interviewer presentation should be limited to supplying needed information and describing the difficulty encountered. The goal is then to ask for opinions, refraining from offering suggestions. The first list of questions are stated so that the solution is already implied. The second set of questions are stated to take the issue closer to the origin of the problem.

Set 1: (a) Have you considered going to the teaching and learning center to get some of their material? (b) What effect does the failure to meet deadlines have on others? (c) What would you expect of a person in your job if you were in my place?

Set 2: (a) What is the reason for supposing that teaching performance may be lower in certain areas? (b) Why are deadlines so important? (c) How might we improve job interest?

The problem-solving process seeks to stimulate growth and development in the employee. It is based on certain assumptions: (1) employee initiated problems illustrate that their concerns are important, (2) determining employee interests and feelings may throw some light on others problems, (3) organizational problems should be stated from the perspective of the employees first, (4) initial discussions may be one-sided because of the general reluctance to discuss job problems with supervisors, and (5) possibilities for personality change are slight, although they increase when employees are given opportunities to increase their levels of responsibility, maturity, and self-confidence.

The process of getting ideas for solutions is different than the process of evaluating them. The skills include: remaining sensitive to feelings, reflecting ideas and feelings, using exploratory questions, and summarizing. These skills suggest that the problem-solving process is on-going and may not be completed in one interview.

The Discovery Interview

The discovery interview emphasizes the development of ideas, suggestions, information, or theories. The interviews encourage discovery and respond to the statement that: "We are looking for ideas."

Most managerial theories that appear in textbooks and academic articles are a product of critical, deductive theories. They usually draw on dominant theoretical traditions in specific scholarly disciplines. The theories are deductive and are most useful for future experimentation.

Many management theories are accused of having a low level of applicability, and have little use for solving organizational or social problems.[11] With few exceptions, they do little more than support the status quo. In fact, such formal theories may even play a negative role in the change process.[12] In one study, a team of American and Dutch social scientists studied 120 projects of applied social research in The Netherlands.[13] They found that the projects that used grounded concepts and qualitative methods had a higher level of utilization. They were theories developed to provide relevant information for feedback to the organization and for focusing an organization's direction. The road to implementation did not rest on elaborating catchy theory, devising ingenious models, seeking to emulate the advanced procedures of the physical sciences, adopting the newest mathematical and statistical schemes, coining new concepts, by developing more precise quantitative techniques, or insisting on adherence to the canons of research design.

Managers are recognizing the need for theories which are practically useful and relevant. Terms such as "grounded theory" have been introduced to suggest that researchers should be open to what the particular setting has to offer in developing a coherent framework.[14]

Grounded theorizing in research is concerned with the generation of theory, especially inductive theories in contrast to theories generated from logical deduction from *a priori* assumptions. Generating a theory from data means that hypotheses and concepts not only come from the data, but are systematically worked out in relation to the data during the course of the research. This concern is well marked in the literature on qualitative methods.[15]

The method entails continuous comparison of data with the concepts throughout the research. The data are not the sole instruments in the development of theory; human creativity and intuition are required.[16] The theory builder compares his/her ideas to empirical evidence, travelling back and forth between theory and data. Some ideas can be grounded, modified, or abandoned on the basis of the evidence.[17] The emerging theory may reflect commonalities and things shared rather than differentiation and things not shared,[18] but it might also lead to something completely new.

Many theories of behavior are based on empirical research applicable to a wide range of organizations. The theoretical assumptions are based on a body of research focused on motivation, leadership, and communication problems. Such social science theories evolve from a researcher's specific interests or hobbies. They demand certain controlled conditions where the theory is allowed to operate without the hindrance of other influences.

An organization's culture usually does not correspond to the behaviors underlying any theory of organizational behavior. An understanding of this culture and the features of the organization's technical system can emerge from a discovery sensing process of interviewing and brainstorming.

There are some compelling reasons for using such interviews: as a first step in the construction of measurement instruments, in developing a statement of goals, or in constructing a theory or concept. The style of interviewing illustrates how discovery occurs, through search, self-analysis, and creative insight. For this reason, the interview provides a model of one important aspect of the action research process.

The discovery interview can be valuable for understanding an organizational problem as perceived by the individual participants. It can be used for developing theories or research instruments which are valid for the situation. The purpose of this interview process is, ultimately, to create a manageable description of the numerous organizational interactions taking place.

The discovery interview is an open-ended interview process where the interviewee has the opportunity to explore ideas and thoughts in response to certain general questions. The interviewer encourages the interviewee to delve deeper into the exploration by reflecting comments, summarizing statements, and providing an atmosphere for the discussion.

The interviewer is only interested in information that the respondent feels is important, and provides minimal guidance by getting the respondent to explore his or her feelings and perceptions of areas that he or she chooses. The emphasis is on stimulating the interviewee to talk about ideas, information, or concerns. In conducting the interview, the interviewee is encouraged to talk about the problem, exposing feelings about the situation, and providing an environment where the interviewee can explore the problem and come up with his own interpretations.

Certain general questions may guide the interviewing. Good examples of open ended questions which cover most perspectives are:

1.   What are some of the difficulties with this system, organizational design? What are some of the problems you experience in working here?
2.   What are some of the positive aspects of this organizational design? What are some of the positive aspects of working here?
3.   What are some of the issues that we have to respond to in addressing these problems, responding to the future?
4.   What are your ideas you have for the future?
5.   What are some of the goals, behaviors, or outputs which might be important to guide us?

These questions are followed by specific probes which seek to encourage a greater exploration of issues.

The Helping Interview

The helping interview responds to the specific interests of the client and encourages the construction of concepts or theories for personal problem-solving. The researcher seeks to encourage a supportive, nondirective relationship so that individuals take responsibility for their own problem-solving. The interview is guided by the statement: "You are responsible for yourself."

The interview is closely associated with the writing of Carl Rogers and is based on the assumption that frustration, anger, and deep dissatisfaction need to be expressed before people can be changed.[19] It assumes that it is unnatural and unhealthy to submerge feelings in little pockets of the mind without expressing them. Failure to solve the problem brings about the replacement of the problem-solving attitude. Instead of creative feelings and constructiveness brought about through problem-solving, there are likely to be feelings of anger and frustration.

In the helping interview, a counsellor or mentoring supervisor creates an environment to allow an individual to express feelings and make his or her own decisions. Expressing feelings allows people to relieve tensions and act more naturally. When the frustration is reduced in this way, the person is able to get away from his own feelings and give a more honest look at the real source of the trouble. Of course, some feelings may be truly deep-seated and go back many years into childhood. These are obviously more difficult to locate.

In a helping interview, important questions might be: Did the interview help open the interviewee's perceptual field as much as possible? Did he/she discover his own self, or did he/she find the self he/she thought he should be finding? Did you help the interviewee move from an external to an internal frame of reference?[20] Did you help the individual get closer to himself/herself, to explore and express what he/she found there rather than deal with platitudes and evaluative labels? Did the interviewer explore what he/she wanted on his/her own or did the interview lead the person in a direction?

There is a difference of opinion, even among nondirective proponents, as to proper procedure. To some, any "structuring" or question asking is not helpful to the interviewee's needs.

Helping interviews can run through four stages: feelings, observations, reflections and actions or solutions.

Feelings: feelings expressed direct a motive rather than cognitive behavior.

Observations: Observations are descriptions of the here and now. Statements of fact are observations.

Reflections: these are examples or external reference points that could be used to verify or discount feelings and facts.

Action or solutions: This is the direction for action as a result.

These interview stages occur at different times. Sometimes individuals seek to work at solutions first and external reference afterwards. In addition, the interview may move between these stages rather rapidly. The goal of the interviewer is to encourage the interviewee to deal with feelings and facts as much as possible with occasional thinking to external reference points. Solutions or actions are those decisions which the interviewee develops.

There are several "don'ts" connected with the development of the helping interview: don't give advice; don't give sympathy; don't try to persuade; don't give reassurance; don't tell the person that things will come out okay; don't tell the others about your troubles; don't make fun of them, and so on. These rules of thumb are intended to encourage interviewers to be active listeners rather than parents, directors, or advocates.

SUMMARY

One important component of all research, but particularly important in interviewing is the experimental effect. This phenomenon is well recognised by sociologists and psychologists.[21] In Schein's terms:

> Every decision to observe something, or to ask a question, or to meet with someone constitutes an intervention into the ongoing organisational process. . . . If I interview someone about his organisation, the very questions I ask give the respondent ideas he never had before. The very process of formulating his own answers gives him points of view which he may never have thought of before.[22]

The term "experimental effect," first coined in psychology, implies that the experimenter or researcher, in the very act of research, is introducing a variable that changes the nature of the situation.

The process of inquiry itself may therefore act as a change agent, particularly the interview situation. In his studies on students, Sanford notes that students would report changes in themselves "as a result of being interviewed. "

> Many interviewees reported great benefit from the self-analysis that was set in motion (one made a life-changing decision in the middle of the interview)... Most important, it seemed, was the fact the inquiry started a process of change in the whole institution.[23]

The process of inquiry can act as a change agent. During the formal programme of interviewing, coupled with informal conversations, respondents begin to formulate their own solutions to problems. Problems were not only raised during the interviews, but a process of problem-solving can be set in motion. This process might be called "haphazard interviewing" to distinguish it from formal interviewing. Decisions and actions are based upon self-analysis rather than a conceptual analysis. This informal, haphazard process occurs too fast to be superseded by the slow and pedantic formal action theorizing process, where researchers have to take time to compile the gathered data and feed it back to the client group. The interviews are a catalyst and crystallizer of ideas and events. This highlights the importance of recognizing the purpose of the interview.

NOTES

1. D. J. Wagner, *The Growth of Sociological Theories* (Beverly Hills: Sage Publications, 1949, 1984); See T. Jantz, L. Hellervik, and D. C. Gilmour, *Behaviour Description Interviewing: New, Accurate, Cost Effective* (Toronto: Allyn and Bacon, Inc., 1986).

2. L. Ulrich and D. Trumpo, "The Selection Interviews since 1949," *Psychological Bulletin*, February, 1965, pp. 100-116.

3. R. E. Carlson, P. W. Thayer, E. C. Mayfield, and D. A. Peterson, "Improvements in the Selection Interview," *Personnel Journal*, April, 1971, p. 272.

4. There seems to be strong support that structured and organized interviews are more valuable than unstructured interviews. Unstructured interviews make very low inter-rater reliability. R. E. Carlson, P. W. Thayer, E. C. Mayfield, and D. A. Peterson. "Improvements in the Selection Interview," p. 270.

5. E. E. Mayfield, S. H. Brown, and B. W. Hamstra, "Selection Interviewing in the Life Insurance Industry: An Update of Research and Practice, *Personnel Psychology*, vol. 33, 1980, pp. 725-740; See T. Jantz, L. Hellervik, and D. C. Gilmour, *Behaviour Description Interviewing: New, Accurate, Cost Effective*.

6. T. Jantz, L. Hellervik, and D. C. Gilmour, *Behaviour Description Interviewing: New, Accurate, Cost Effective*.

7. T. Jantz, L. Hellervik, and D. C. Gilmour, *Behaviour Description Interviewing: New, Accurate, Cost Effective*, p. 14; Table 7.2 is adapted from this book.

8. Dillman suggests that this information can be sorted into four categories: attitudes

(how people feel about an attitude object such as a person, idea, or institution), beliefs (what people believe to be true), behavior (what people actually do or have done), and attributes (characteristics such as sex, age, and income). D. A. Dillman, *Mail and Telephone Surveys; The Total Design Method* (New York: John Wiley, 1978).

9. N. R. F. Maier, *Principles of Human Relations* (New York: John Wiley, 1952).

10. These principles have been adapted from N. R. F. Maier, A. R. Solem and A. A. Maier, *Supervisory and Executive Development. A Manual For Role Playing* (New York: John Wiley, 1957), pp. 112-113.

11. C. Argyris, *The Applicability of Organizational Sociology* (London: Cambridge University Press, 1972), pp. 70-74

12. E. Van de Vall, M. Bolas, C. Bolas, and T. S. Kang, "Applied Social Research in Industrial Organizations: An evaluation of Functions, Theory and Methods,"*Journal of Applied Behavioral Science*, vol. 12, 1976, pp. 158-177.

13. These included projects in industrial and labor relations (40), regional and urban planning (40), and social welfare and public health (40). Most of the conclusions were drawn from interviews because the researchers felt that they could not reliably judge the range of projects.

14. B. G. Glaser and A. L. Strauss, *The Discovery of Grounded Theory: Strategies for Qualitative Research* (Chicago: Aldine, 1967); H. Mintzberg, *The Stucture of Organizations* (Englewood Cliffs, N. J. : Prentice-Hall, 1979); R. I. Sutton "The Process of Organizational Death: Disbanding and Reconnecting," *Administrative Science Quarterly*, vol. 23, 1987, pp. 542-569.

15. B. G. Glaser and A. L. Strauss, *The Discovery of Grounded Theory: Strategies for Qualitative Research*; N. K. Denzin, *Sociological Methods* (New York: McGraw-Hill, 1978); J. Lofland,"Styles of Reporting Qualitative Field Research," *American Sociologist*, vol. 9, 1974; H. Blumer, *Symbolic Interactionism: Perspective and Method* (Prentice-Hall, Englewood Cliffs, N.J.: 1969); and E. J. Webb, D. T. Campbell, R. D. Schwartz,and L. Sechrest, *Unobtusive Measures: Nonreactive Research in the Social Sciences.*

16. H. Mintzberg, *The Stucture of Organizations* (Chicago: Rand McNally, 1966).

17. R. I. Sutton and A. L. Callahan "The Stigma of Bankruptcy: Spoiled Organizational Image and Its Management," *Academy of Management Journal*, vol. 30, 1987, p. 411.

18. J. Van Maanen "Epilogue: Qualitative Methods Reclaimed," in J. Van Maanen (ed.), *Qualitative Methodology and Social Psychology*, vol. 51, 1983, p. 257.

19. C. R. Rogers, *Client-centered Therapy* (New York: Houghton Mifflin, 1951).

20. C. R. Rogers, *Client-centered Therapy* .

21. N. Sanford "Whatever Happened to Action Research," *Journal of Social Issues*, vol. 26, 1970, pp. 3-23; E. Schein, *Process Consultation*, (Menlo Park: Addison Wesley, 1969).

22. E. Schein, *Process Consultation*, p. 97.

23. N. Sanford "Whatever Happened to Action Research," p. 12.

8

Developing Data
Gathering Instruments

A great variety of diagnostic instruments are available for studying organizations. Questionnaires and other data gathering instruments make it possible to study a whole range of topics from productivity and efficiency considerations to behavioral factors such as morale, organizational flexibility, and job satisfaction.

It may always seem easier to take a standardized questionnaire or instrument "from the shelf" and implement it according to the specific steps outlined. Such instruments provide information on many questions as well as providing a basis for comparison with other settings.

Organizational researchers use self-report instruments far more than any other form of data gathering. The measures persist because respondents can easily tally the results for large samples using the growing power of computers. The following comment may illustrate the consequences of this form of evaluation.

> Heavy reliance on self-report information has excluded crucial populations from organizational inquiry, postponed cross-checking of propositions, inflated the apparent consequentiality of minor irritations in the workplace, and imposed a homogeneity of method which raises the prospect that the findings of the field are method-specific.[1]

As a rule, standardized instruments are not used in action research, as they reflect the indicators of a large number of organizations. An action science suggests that data gathering tools--questionnaires, observations, and unobtrusive measures--should be designed as closely as possible to respond to each unique organizational setting. They should reflect the timely organizational issues, ideas, and manners of communication. Individuals in an organization have attached a certain importance and meaning to their statements and communications, and data gathering tools should respond to this.

This chapter suggests that we should gain an understanding of the complex issues in the organization being studied, and then develop our questionnaires or measurement tools to reflect this. If standardized instruments are used, they should reflect the variables and nuances identified from the organization's participants. The following chapter provides a perspective on how interviews can be used for developing research instruments.

DEVELOPING QUESTIONS FOR DATA GATHERING

How does one generate questions for interviews or questionnaires? Does a researcher derive questions because he or she feels they are useful? Does he or she search the textbooks on what other people have asked? Does he or she borrow questions from other questionnaires?

The formulation of the questions to guide an action research project can be relevant for scholarly and practical purposes. This is a dual relevance of being theoretically interesting to a scholarly audience who would appreciate hearing more about it, and being practically interesting to a practitioner audience.[2] Action research is based on the assumption that research questions should respond to both areas of relevance.

Starting a study does not involve a comprehensive review of the literature, but relies on inductive processes, especially at the very beginning stages. When I first begin a research project, I go immediately to my field. I immerse myself in the organization and talk to various people. I try to meet the informal leaders and to understand their perspective. It is only then that I feel comfortable with beginning to define the research objectives and my plan of attack. I try to get agreement and respond to suggestions and ideas. Then I begin the process of developing research instruments.

Developing an action research questionnaire is a "bottom up" process. This emerges from consultations with people in the field, from people who are involved with the issue, and from those who have an interest in learning more about it. The process involves open-ended interviews, on-site observations, and other explorations. The process may seem long and unnecessary to some people, as it requires patient and careful editing of items so they "echo" the phrases and words used by the people being researched. However, time spent at this stage should decrease the time one spends later on, as well as improving the relevance of the questions.

The complete process is ongoing and involves developing an understanding of the issues, criteria, and variables related to the problem, as defined in the field; sorting and arranging the interview statements into common categories; developing questions or statements to measure the main categories of the theory; designing the recording format; and finalizing and pilot testing the questionnaire instrument or interview schedule.

The bottom-up exploratory process is useful even if the plan is to develop a set of structured questions in an interview guide. The exploratory process is not normally part of the final data collected. The exploratory/sensing process should, even when the researcher is an expert in the subject area, ground the concepts of the questionnaire within the setting under investigation. It is also an opportunity to gain commitment and collaboration from the people being researched.

Developing an Understanding of the Issues

Concerns for internal and external validity represent two major counter trends in the use of open-ended questionnaires and interviews. The researcher might seek to standardize interviews schedules so that less trained interviewers can carry out the task of interviewing. Or, we might seek to develop highly trained researchers, who can follow a more flexible and discovery oriented research approach, probing for further detail and understanding for different respondents. Both trends have their place.

Standardized instruments appear to offer the same form and same set of questions to each respondent. This is possibly not true, since the same question may be interpreted differently by various groups and individuals. There is, as a result, an unknown level of reliability in the results.

The second method does not offer the same structure or set of questions to each respondent. However, the skilled researcher can make sure, by using probes and further questions, that the same questions are understood by the same respondents. This flexibility of choice introduces a lack of control over the questions being asked, and might make the traditional researcher question whether science has actually been carried out. Indeed, skilled researchers are also prone to error.

Interviews provide many possible distortions. These are introduced in the way the interviews add to or subtract from the real data which is being gathered. People of different values have their own personalized descriptions of events.[3] The use of probes and secondary questions might also be viewed as distorting the real data and encouraging unheld opinions.[4] Extremely deviant opinions and memory bias have long been suspect when obtained by personal interviews. These and other distortions are often accused of being present in gathering interview data.

Often, the most preferred solution is to structure the questionnaire and interview process and gain the "scientific" rightness in data collection but sacrifice the relevance of the data to the organizational setting. The alternative is to develop a process relying on the skills of the interviewer.

How does one develop instruments specifically relevant to the organizational problems being studied? Ideally, we would become totally immersed in the organization's reality to develop an intimate understanding of it. Then, one must rise above these day-to-day happenings and construct a picture of how these many events are working together.

There are probably many ways to do this, and this may depend on the situation needing analysis and the type of information being gathered. A first step, for several situations, is to begin a process of open-ended interviewing with the goal of immersing the researcher in the underlying problems defining the organization. The goal of using open-ended interviews is to improve the external validity or relevance of the data gathered. There will also be questions about the internal validity of the measurement.

In the action research process, interviews are a valuable way to gather indicators for a questionnaire or interview schedule. Such interviews rely on the use of probes and specific questions to evoke more thought; interviews ask for critical incidents ti illustrate the issue being studied.

Probing for Depth in an Interview

Probing is an attempt to continue the same line of questioning but to probe for more information. Responses can be expanded by soliciting examples and further explanation from the person being surveyed.

"Could you give me an example?"

Interviews can support and supplement data from other sources such as observation and survey techniques. They provide more in-depth information and personal experiences that could not be obtained from other data gathering instruments.

"Let me check out some data I have collected."

The language of the interview is the respondent's language expressed with the jargon he/she has become familiar with. It is not predefined by the structured questions or phrases common to the researcher.

"I'd like to understand the terms you use to describe this."

Using Questions Which Evoke More Thought

Persons who participate in interviews are more likely to believe that their contributions are useful if they are allowed to structure their own responses. The style of interviewing encourages others to recognize that the world does not fit into neat, well-defined boxes. It encourages people to recognize ambiguity, uncertainty, insecurities, and the like.

It is often suggested that questions evoking open-ended responses provide more information and detail than questions encouraging closed-ended responses such as "yes," "no," "don't know."

Certain questions enhance conversation. For instance, questions beginning with "what," "why," "where," and "how," facilitate the thought process. Questions beginning with "are you," "when are," and "where is," lead to very simple answers, elicit yes/no responses, and limit discussion.

Being too open-ended is likely to get no response. For example, "What are some of your concerns?" "How do you feel about working in this organization?" Such questions are likely to be as unprovocative in getting participation as closed-ended questions. They may yield responses, but there may be a higher degree of variation from different interviews. The interviewee could appropriately respond by saying "Concerns about what" and "Feelings about what."[5]

In improving participation in question asking, certain types of questions are more appropriate: (1) High level (thinking) vs. low level (rote) questions; (2) Divergent (many answers) vs. convergent (few answers) questions; (3) Structured vs. unstructured questions; (4) Single direction vs. multiple direction questions.

(1) The *level of questions* refers to how the question evokes thinking. *High level questions* require individuals to think rather than simply recall, paraphrase, or summarize.[6]

"What are some of the important contributions you might . . . ?"

Low level questions are those asking the individual to merely recall, repeat, summarize or paraphrase what has already been stated or written down.

"What is the exact purpose of the machines . . . ?"

(2) The *number of possible right answers* indicates a question's divergence. *Divergent questions* are those for which there can be a number of "correct" or discussible answers.

"What are some of the conclusions you might draw from the high level of absenteeism?"

Convergent questions imply that there is one right answer.

"What is the exact number of absenteeism for the secretaries during the month of August?"

(3) Certain questions are more *structured* that others. *Structured questions* provide background information, specify or narrow the focus, and otherwise orient the respondent to the question and its aims.

"One way to approach the problem is to examine the differences and similarities between organizations. Let's do this for the southern and northern divisions. What are some similarities or differences between the divisions?"

Unstructured questions are wide open and amorphous.

"What about the various divisions in the company? How do you see them."

(4) The number of answers to a question is another variable which affects the likelihood of responses. *Single questions* contain one main direction for exploration. They may also contain structured information to facilitate answers. Note that a single question does not necessarily require convergence or a single answer.

"After the reform, corruption wasn't eliminated. It took new forms. What were some of the underlying dynamics or forces that reinstitutionalized corruption?"

Multiple questions contain more than one direction in which people can respond. They may also contain asides, elaborate explanations and elaborations.

"After the reform, was corruption eliminated? I mean, to the extent that it wasn't, can you explain why? What institutional factors led to a new kind of corruption? I don't mean that the original form of corruption was still intact-I mean the new forms. What were they and why were they? Do you see what I'm getting at?"

The most promising questions are obviously high level, divergent, unstructured and single direction. However, other variations may be necessary for certain subject areas and interviews.

Using the Critical Incidents Technique

The critical incidents technique, introduced toward the end of World War II, might be important for developing questions. The process emerged as psychologists interviewed field commanders, officers, and soldiers in attempting to improve the performance of bomber and tank crews. They observed that when an officer or crew member was asked to describe the behaviour of an effective tank crew, he responded with a list of traits or vague descriptions such as courage, leadership, know-how, and the like. If the interviewer asked for an example of what he was getting at, the officer or soldier described a specific incident that was an example of effective or ineffective tank crew performance. These stories about specific tank crew behavior helped the interviewers identify performance problems and improve tank crew effectiveness. The term critical incidents was used for such stories because they illustrated real events describing specific effective or ineffective performance.

Critical incidents provide data or incidents reflecting behavior. They usually are not opinions. Opinions as such, are limited by a person's insight, intelligence, or attitudes and beliefs. In describing an incident, however, a person usually does not rely on opinion or intelligence. A person relies on memory and observational skills. The interview situation seeks to gather all the information that the person observed, rather than asking the person to make inferences about it.

The goal in developing questions for data gathering and exploration is to initially become aware of critical incidents representing the general concepts to be investigated. This provides a pool of information for developing a battery of questions for interviews or questionnaires. Such a pooling of incidents gives a wider perspective on the variables underlying an event, at least more inclusive than those in a researcher's repertoire or one individual's perspective. A pooling of incidents from different people is also less subjective than the biases of one perspective.

A researcher, in beginning the process of exploration, can develop a battery of questions to evoke critical incidents. The incidents may cover topics such as motivation, communication, leadership, or other general areas which need study.

The following is an example of questions seeking to gather information about motivation. In seeking to better understand the characteristics which maintained and sustained motivation for entrepreneurs, the following two questions were asked.

1.   Think about a time when you felt especially satisfied or motivated. Describe the situation. What motivated you (What turned you on?)
2.   Think about a time when you felt especially dissatisfied or unmotivated. Describe the situation. What was it about this situation that you found demotivating or dissatisfying?

The critical incidents can provide an indication of the criteria for measuring or directing an interview, but only if they are asked within an appropriate sequence, and with the appropriate probes.

Basic Skills in Interviewing

A major element in action research process of data gathering is the possibility of discovery. It is a commitment to learning about people in their own terms rather than through preconceived or outsider's measures and constructs. The research task is to find out or "discover" what is fundamental or central to the people being researched.

Listening does not involve absorbing and understanding so intensely that one's internal frame of reference has difficulty being separated from the interviewee.[7] It involves keeping one's own frame of reference separate from the interviewee. One of the tests of listening is being able to restate in one's own words what the interviewee has said. If the person accepts this, there's an excellent chance that the interviewer has listened and understood the messages. A reflective summary is a way of summing up the feelings another person has expressed, disregarding the factual details and incidentals. It involves: making summary statements of what the interviewee has said; pointing out important phrases of the discussion as voiced by the interviewee; and rephrasing what the interviewee has expressed, using such terms as "you feel that" or "you think that."

The interviewing process relies on the proper use of pauses. The interviewer should not be afraid to allow a pause to persist. One case is cited of a high school girl coming for counselling who sat through several counselling sessions uttering no more than three or four words a session. At the end of that time, she had apparently resolved her difficulty, faced up to the fact and learned to attack the problem in a problem-solving manner. She no longer had an adjustment difficulty in her school work or with her fellow classmates. This probably is an extreme case. Nevertheless, pauses can be constructive, a time when the interviewee is collecting thoughts, struggling to find adequate expression for them and to clarify true feelings.

The respect for silence is a key skill to enhance the process of interviewing. Silence may occur for various reasons. The interviewee may require time for thinking. Confusion can create silence either because of the issues dealt with or because of the interviewer's probes. Silence may also occur due to the interviewees' uncertainty of the interviewer's expectations. The interviewee may be silent because he or she is resisting what he/she considers to be probing. There are short pauses when one is simply looking for thoughts.

In developing questions, the procedure is to interview those people who are aware of the problem and have some feelings (positive or negative) about it. For assessing satisfaction of employees, the goal would be to obtain a sample of most of the employees in the organization, recognizing people who were highly dissatisfied and satisfied. If the concern was absenteeism, it might be sensible to sample those employees with some record of absenteeism, as well as those who do not. If the problem was turnover, it would be sensible to sample some of those who were contemplating leaving the organization, those who had left, or are considering leaving.

Sorting the Interview Statements into Common Categories

If the researcher has a good perception of the issues in the organization and understands the organizational language, an essential first step to instrument construction is already accomplished. The questions, statements, or observation criteria should parallel, as closely as possible, the manner in which the individuals in the organization articulate the issues. They should summarize main phrases and ways of working in the   same words and manners of the organization's participants. This is the terminology and logic that individuals in organizations find most relevant, and if accurately summarized, will be a useful reflection of the individual's impressions of the organization or problem situation--an expression of manifest and latent feelings.

The interview is very useful for gaining an understanding of the concepts to be used in a more general sense. These steps are also useful in developing a questionnaire, goal statements, and skill requirements, and are especially relevant when individual input and ideas are needed. The goal is to summarize each person's statements to reflect, as closely as possible, the manners and nuances of communication and thought of the individuals interviewed.[8] The individuals in an organization have attached a certain importance and meaning to their statements. For this reason, general instruments will not be especially significant, as many of the measures will not be relevant for a specific situation.

Interviews might be recorded and transcribed in studies which are more systematically carried out. Copies of the interviews can be made, and sorters can then read them and mark each unique concept (with a colored marker). The concepts can then be cut up so that they can be sorted. An interviewer's notes can be recorded on note cards so that each card represents a concept.

The sorting is an intuitive process of ordering the concepts in common categories. It can be carried out by one individual, although groups add extra energy and ideas, as well as guarding against preconceived biases. In addition, groups are a way of involving individuals who are working in an organization.

Dealing with the interview data consists of transcribing or summarizing it and developing some system to reference and store it as raw interview data. Then, it is ready for sorting into common categories. The responses can be collapsed into categories based on common or similar intent of meaning. Questions can then be developed.

Developing Questions or Statements for Measuring

Questionnaires can provide a range of data about people and organizations. They are used to measure anything from customer and worker satisfaction to underlying beliefs and values. On the surface, questionnaires are convenient to use and can economically provide more information on questions from a larger number of people.

Action research questionnaires, by definition, are not standardized instruments developed from theoretical concepts. Rather, they are developed and validated for the specific perspective in the organization. For this reason, standardized instruments are usually less appropriate.

Action research questionnaires, because they are aimed at the process of discovery and development, include a range of question types. Some of the questions are rather open-ended in nature and are generally oriented to a process of discovery. In this sense, questionnaires are essentially self-administered structured interviews. Questions which focus on specific areas of the study are presented to the respondent in printed form. The respondent reads the questions and provides an answer, either by writing statements or by choosing from alternative predetermined responses.

Questions are developed for each category. A set of questions can be used to derive data about different aspects of a concept. The importance of the concept may be reflected in the number of statements emerging in the discovery interviews. The wording of the questions should reflect, as closely as possible, the actual words used in the interviews. However, normal rules of editing are appropriate to guard against vagueness, multiple indicators within one question, and so forth.

Open-ended responses can provide a picture of what the respondent has in mind, the intensity of feelings, the meaning, and the frame of reference for answering. They provide a format for spontaneous responses rather than a definite choice among alternatives. This type of response is particularly valuable in preliminary and exploratory stages of research. Follow-up questions can add more in-depth information to open-end questions, in order to clarify or amplify the initial response.

Researchers often attach open-ended questions at the end of a survey and ask respondents to provide comments. The answers to these questions are often little more than frustrations and feelings that the respondent may have. Questioning should guide the respondent into recalling behaviors or ideas relevant to the study.[9] There are two ways to do this: question guides and probes.

Question guides encourage the respondent to recall a range of relevant activities. The following is an unguided question:

"What do you do to encourage employee motivation and development?"

Examples are other ways to guide the response. For instance,

"What managerial activities do you use to motivate people (involvement, incentives, interesting work, and the like)?"

A guided question might list fifteen activities or possible answers asking a manager if he/she uses them for motivating employees. See Table 8.1. In this list of activities, the researcher might list the total range of variables from the interviews. Of course, there is a danger of creating too long a list of examples, and respondents might feel more inclined to fill in the first items on the list.[10] Although such lists may improve reporting, very few items not on the list are likely to be reported.

Specific lists of questions are easier to answer, because they allow a "hook" to a specific behavior, time period, location, who was involved, and why it

TABLE 8.1
RANKING QUESTIONS

Please rate the degree to which you use the following tools to motivate your employees, on a scale of 1 to 5. (1 = low use and 5 = high use).

(A.R. Cohen, "Erring Around the Collar: Whitening the Blue-Collar Blues Exercise," *Exchange: The Organizational Teaching Journal*, N.D.)

_____ Chance for promotion

_____ Person in charge who is concerned about you

_____ Not being caught up in a big, impersonal organization

_____ Job that doesn't involve hard physical work

_____ Freedom to decide how to do his/her work

_____ Good job security

_____ Good pay

_____ Chance to use your mind

_____ Interesting work

_____ No one standing over him/her, being own boss

_____ Not being expected to do things not paid for

_____ Clearly defined responsibilities

_____ Friendly co-workers

_____ Time for outside interests

_____ Participation in decisions regarding job

TABLE 8.2
POSSIBLE PROBLEM QUESTIONS

1. How often do you drink beer?
   1. Daily
   2. Several times a week
   3. Weekly
   4. Monthly

2. How often do you watch T.V.?
   1. Daily
   2. Several times a week
   3. Weekly
   4. Monthly

occurred. Otherwise, respondents may interpret the same question or event differently. For instance, the general question "What is your general impression of your manager?" is an example of a question which can be answered differently for each individual. One's impressions may be based on friendship, while another's might reflect on an argument which just occurred.[11]

Probing open-ended questions should not only provide a statement of the world in the eyes of the respondent, they should also probe for further depth. Probes can be used to provide further details or other aspects of a question. Newspaper reporters often use probes to follow their questions. They are like the five W's: who, what, where, when, and why. They seek to encourage a person's own interpretation rather than attitudes and feelings of others. That is, "What do you do during the crisis?" or "What do you think happened during the crisis?"[12]

Questions can provide an indication of when the events occurred. This is the time period, for example, during the day, week, month, or year. Questions also provide information on what occurred and why it occurred. They should not ask "What do you feel that others felt during a crisis?" However, it would be appropriate to ask a question like "What did you see them doing during the crisis?"

Designing the Recording Formats

As a general rule, survey researchers prefer closed questions because they are easier to process and they reduce coder variability. They usually ask the respondent to rate the level, intensity, or frequency of an issue or concept. However, highly specific questions are prone to respondent biases.

The questions in Table 8.2 seem to be quite logical for a questionnaire. However, they could evoke untrue responses, since some heavy drinkers would probably avoid extremes; others might have a tendency to exaggerate. In such cases, it may be more appropriate to use open-ended questions, since they will allow people to provide their own numbers. When researchers set the range of a scale, there is a tendency to see the high or low values as extremes.

Types of Recording Formats

Recording formats for designing a questionnaire are of four types--open-ended, closed ended with ordered choices, closed-ended with unordered choices, and partially closed-ended.[13] Other classifications of the types of scales include: agreement-disagreement, rank order, and forced choice.[14] Open-ended items allow respondents to use their own words. See Table 8.3.

Closed-end items with ordered choices provide a statement followed by more than one response option. See Table 8.4. The respondent picks the items or place

TABLE 8.3
OPEN ENDED ITEMS

    A. (attitude) What was the most important reason you had for disagreeing with the new management plan?

         _____

         _____

    B. (behavior) Think of your typical work day. Describe it and the tasks and activities that are part of it.

         _____

         _____

TABLE 8.4
CLOSED-ENDED WITH ORDERED CHOICES

    A. (behavior) In your job, how would you rate your ability to complete your tasks?

        1. Very Low
        2. Low
        3. Moderate
        4. High
        5. Very High

    B. (attitude) How would you rate your satisfaction in pay?

        1. Very low
        2. Low
        3. Moderate
        4. High
        5. Very High

TABLE 8.5
CLOSED-ENDED WITH UNORDERED CHOICES

    A. (behavior) What sources of information do you find most useful to your decision-making?

        1. Newspaper
        2. Internal memos
        3. Other managers
        4. Employees

    B. (attitude) Which one of the following do you prefer in your job ?
        1. Friendly co-workers
        2. Job security
        3. Adequate pay
        4. Interesting work
        5. Helpful supervisor
        6. Other (explain) _____

---

on a scale which best summarized his/her attitude, belief, or attribute. The responses can be arranged on a continuum such as degree of satisfaction or level of agreement, and allowing individuals to choose among alternatives. Closed-ended items with unordered response choices do not form a continuum or scale. See Table 8.5.

Open-ended responses can provide a picture of what the respondent has in mind, the intensity of feelings, the meaning, and the frame of reference for answering. They provide a format for spontaneous responses rather than a definite choice among alternatives. This type of response is particularly valuable in preliminary and exploratory stages of research. Follow-up questions can add more in depth information to open-end questions, in order to clarify or amplify the initial response.

Open-ended questions can be linked to other types of questions. Ideally, they can be linked to the central concepts addressed in the survey. For instance, one might be trying to measure concepts of job design, satisfaction, and motivation. This might mean that 3-5 closed ended questions might be used for assessing each concept. One might also include open-ended questions on behaviors and feelings for each of these general concept areas.

A.R. questionnaires seek to obtain a measurement on concepts derived from

TABLE 8.6
QUESTIONS THAT SEEK TO USE VARIOUS SCALES

SECTION A

A.   (to measure an attitude) How would you rate your satisfaction with pay?
1. Very low
2. Low
3. Moderate
4. High
5. Very high

B. (to measure an attitude) How would you rate your satisfaction with your supervisor?
1. Very low
2. Low
3. Moderate
4. High
5. Very high

C. (to measure an attitude) How would you rate your interest in your work?
1. Very low
2. Low
3. Moderate
4. High
5. Very high

SECTION B

A. (attitude) Which one of the following do you prefer most in your job?
1. Friendly co-workers
2. Job security
3. Interesting work
4. Helpful supervisor
5. Other (explain)_____

SECTION C

A. (behavior) Think of a time when you were exceptionally motivated in your job. Describe this feeling and the reasons you felt motivated?

_____

_____

B. (behavior) Think of a time when you were exceptionally dissatisfied in your job. Describe this feeling and the reasons you felt dissatisfied.

_____

the open-ended interviews or observations. They seek to gather more detailed information on particular statements uncovered in the interviews.[15]

Action research questionnaires, because they are aimed at the process of discovery and development, include a range of question types (closed and open ended). Some of the questions are rather open-ended in nature and are generally oriented to a process of discovery. See Table 8.6.

Finalizing the Questionnaire or Interview Schedule

No respondent will answer questions appropriately after gaining a bad impression at the beginning of the questionnaire. Thus, there are certain "rules thumb"of finalizing the questionnaire or interview to enhance its presentation.

The spontaneity and spacing of the questions can indeed enhance interest. There are several issues to be answered when arranging questions.

1. Should emotionally neutral and easy-to-answer questions be answered in the first section or should the most central and important questions appear first? Should easy questions or those of different orders of magnitude precede the more important ones?
2. Should open ended questions be used to supplement each set of questions?
3. Should questions be arranged in sections or jump from different types of questions?
4. How long should the questionnaire be?

Many researchers usually begin a questionnaire with biographical questions. Biographical questions such as age, income, employment status may be considered threatening to some. Thus, they might just as well be placed at the end of the questionnaire.[16]

Once the respondent is thinking about a topic, it may be sensible to ask other questions related to it. Some researchers argue that it is appropriate to switch back and forth between topics to reduce the monotony, or to check on reliability. In general, respondents resent answering this ordering, and their impatience is tested by encouraging respondents to change their thought processes back and forth. While these procedures have been devised to check on reliability, they may actually reduce reliability because of reduced motivation. Logical groups of questions may encourage the respondent to continue thinking within the specific content area. If the content was to be changed, it may be appropriate to warn the respondent with introductory phrases. Instead of asking the same questions in different sections, it may be useful to ask the same question in a different way (varying from closed to open-ended, for example).[17] Many questionnaire schedules are constructed to make sure that a response set is not constructed, and this may be important for certain types of questionnaires (indexes or scales). That is, positive and negative questions might be interspersed so that the interview does not develop a response set.

A questionnaire can be constructed by developing measurement scales to suit the people surveyed and concepts measured. This selection might be made with the assistance of the sorters who develop the categories. It may also be useful to encourage the sorters to arrange the questions on the questionnaire, while emphasizing the importance of reliability checks and so forth. To eliminate some problems of negativity, it may be more advisable to word all questions or statements in the affirmative, for example, satisfaction with the job as opposed to dissatisfaction with the job. Additional comment space might be avaliable for "non applicable" and "don't know" options.

The funnel principle is most used in interviews. It suggests that more general questions might be followed by more specific probing ones.[18]

One might ask questions which are really a series of more in-depth probes.

"Describe what it means to be challenged in your career. "
"Describe how it might feel to be challenged. "
"Are there periods in your career when you felt especially challenged?"
"Are you challenged in what you do now?"
"What do you find challenging now?"
"What do you find not challenging?"

The inverted funnel principle is often found in questionnaires. The goal is to ask specific questions and then ask for more general summarizing questions, or even open-ended questions.

The length of a questionnaire is difficult to judge. Many researchers have conducted three-hour interviews and asked respondents to complete one-hour surveys. The length seems to be determined more by the salience of the topic to the respondent than anything else. However, rather than justifying a longer questionnaire, one important factor is to seek only information that is crucially important. So often, when there is doubt about the salience of an issue, researchers choose to include it rather than eliminate it. The rule might be stated as "when in doubt, leave it out."

The best guide to salience is to use issues and questions important to the respondents, forgetting about future analytical possibilities. On highly salient topics, it is possible to construct questionnaires of as many as twelve to sixteen pages, without a loss in cooperation. Beyond that point, noticeable drops in cooperation occur.[19] The final sections of the questionnaire might ask for comments about what the respondent found important and not important in the questionnaire. It might even be asked how the questionnaire might be improved. A note of thanks is always an appropriate ending to a questionnaire; details on how and when respondents can expect feedback can also be provided.

The format of the questionnaire should, in   principle, recognize the respondents' needs as more important than that the researcher's style or coding requirements. Poor formats lead to erroneous responses, lower cooperation, and reliability.

The Pilot Test

No amount of thinking, editing, and brilliance will take the place of a pilot test. The pilot test provides a means of catching and solving unforeseen problems on: the phrasing and sequence of questions, and the length of the questionnaire. It is useful for gaining insights on the appropriateness of certain questions and the ways which statements are worded. It can provide data for pre-analysis and a way to observe how individuals react to procedures used in data collection.

A qualitative pilot study is a way to field test the instrument as if it were an interview schedule. The researcher directly asks respondents to answer questions normally to be answered in written form. During this stage, the interviewer will try to make note of questions that are interpreted differently than intended. The interviewer can always be alert to reactions of these respondents and can keep a record of observations of these reactions.

The research pilot test is the actual "dress rehearsal" of the study. The procedure is laid out exactly as it would be in the actual study. This would include specific instructions, form letters, and the like. The researcher will ask respondents to complete the questionnaire in the same type of setting as they would normally be expected to complete it. This can provide information on the time the questionnaire takes and whether respondents actually follow the instructions they are asked to. The tabulation and initial analysis of the data can present interesting problems of coding, as well as identify important areas where questions are needed or not needed.

The process of designing action research questionnaires based on open-ended interviews usually reduces the need for substantial changes as a result of the pilot test. However, if the pilot produces a need for major changes, something might have gone awry in the instrument development process. A careful and sensitive interviewing process is the most appropriate way to improve wording. Usually, the pilot test is a way of "roughing out" the edges in the instrument.

The Mechanics of Administering Questionnaires

Anonymity depends on the research setting and some organizational members may be very reluctant to identify themselves. Identification may be important for assuring that the appropriate members are sampled, although other devices--checkoff lists--might be more appropriate.

Good questionnaires may still get poor response rates if they are not administered properly. Research administration is more than picking up the questionnaires and making sure all questions are answered. It means the development of a system for assuring that the questions are answered appropriately. This involves developing mechanisms for (1) distributing the interview or questionnaire to the respondent, (2) assuring the questionnaires are received and that the respondent does not need assistance, (3) receiving and picking up questionnaires, (4) assuring that late people are reminded, (5) checking the form, (6) filing and numbering questionnaires, (7) coding, (8) checking the coding, (9) creating mechanisms for computation or analysis, and (10) displaying the results so that they can be communicated, and so on.[20]

In most cases, the action research steering committee can offer valuable assistance when members have the commitment and interest in the project.

SUMMARY

In an "ideal" survey or interview study, the criteria to gather information and the phrasing of the questions have been carefully worked out in pilot studies. Each item or question provides information about a theory the researcher has developed. The important questions to be asked are those related to a sound theory or conceptual framework.

No research setting is ideal and it is rarely possible to know in advance the problems, theory, and criteria relevant to study. An action research questionnaire or interview schedule recognizes that the theoretical framework for the questionnaire must emerge from the setting being researched and include the perspectives of the researcher as well as those of the participants.

However, there are hundreds, perhaps thousands of tests and scales which are commercially available. Scales are composite measures of attitudes and values and usually combine responses to several items measuring the same variable. Psychological tests are often considered in measurement of a wide range of characteristics including: values, feelings, ability, aptitude, intelligence and achievement tests.

Most such scales and tests, it would seem, would not be used in an ideal definition of an action science because they are based on predefined constructs or theories and do not gather data inductively. However, a qualitative science need not reject the standardized instruments and methods just because they are based on a different paradigm of science. It should seek to use them when they are evoked in the process of discovery, and offer another perspective on a problem.

There are various concepts--such as self-esteem, confidence, intelligence, personality, attitude, and creativity--to be measured through quantitative scales. In most of these cases, these instruments are subject to many biases and are limited by specific time periods, populations, cultures, and the like. For many such cases, standardized tests lose their relevance and validity for particular local programs. Thus, it may be useful to use qualitative measures to document behaviors which coincide with quantitative instruments.

There are several types of standardized instruments which can be used to supplement qualitative measurement.[21] Most tests and scales can be divided into the following classes: intelligence and aptitude tests, achievement tests, personality measures, attitude and value scales.[22] Lists of such instruments can be found in the *Psychological Bulletin,* the *Journal of Educational and Psychological Measurement,* and the *Encyclopedia of Education.* However, they represent only one perspective on the issues addressed.

NOTES

1. E. Webb and K. E. Weick, "Unobtrusive Measures in Organizational Theory: A Reminder, " *Administrative Science Quarterly*, vol. 24, 1979, pp. 659. See also R. L. Daft and J. Wiginton "Language and Organization," *Academy of Management Review*, vol. 4, 1979, pp. 179-191.

2. R. E. Walton, "Strategies with Dual Relevance" in E. E. Lawler III, A. M. Mohrman, Jr., S. A. Mohrman, G. E. Ledford, Jr., T. G. Cummings and Associates, (eds.), *Doing Research That Is Useful for Theory and Practice*, (San Francisco, Calif.: Jossey-Bass, 1985), pp. 192-193.

3. L. Schatzman and A. Strauss, "Social Class and Modes of Communication, *American Journal of Sociology*, vol. 60, January, 1955, pp. 329-338, as summarized in A. Lindesmith and A. Strauss, *Social Psychology* (rev. ed.) (New York: Holt, Rinehart and Winston, 1956), p. 237. See also A. Strauss and L. Schatzman, "Cross-class Interviewing: An Analysis of Interaction and Communication Styles," *Human Organization*, vol. 14, Summer, 1955, pp. 28-31, in which the actors claim interviews should control the lower class respondent by directing his answers through probes and guiding remarks.

4. See H. Garfinkel, "Common-sense Knowledge of Social Structures: The Documentary Method of Interpretation," in J. M. Scher (ed.), *Theories of the Mind* (New York: The Free Press, 1962), pp. 689-712; See also, M. Kuhn, "The Interview and the Professional Relationship," in A. Rose (ed.), *Human Behavior and Social Process* (Boston: Houghton Mifflin, 1962), pp. 193-206 and Irwin Deutscher, "Words and Deeds: Social Action and Social Policy," *Social Problems*, vol. 13, Winter, 1966, pp. 235-54.

5. The four categories are found in J. D. W. Andrews, "The Verbal Structure of Teacher Questions: Its Impact on Discussion," *POD Quarterly*, 1980, vol. 3(4), pp. 129-163.

6. They are characterized by Bloom's intellectual operations of application, analysis, synthesis, evaluation. See: B. S. Bloom et al. (eds.), *Taxonomy of Educational Objectives: Cognitive Domain* (New York: David McKay, 1956).

7. A. Benjamin, *The Helping Interview* (Boston: Houghton Mifflin, 1969); I. E. P. Menzies, "A Case Study in the Functioning of Social Systems as a Defence Against Anxiety: A Report of a Study of the Nursing Services of a General Hospital," *Human Relations*, vol. 13, 1960, pp. 95-121.

8. J. B. Bavelas, A. Bavelas and B. A. Shaefer, *A Method for Constructing Student-generated Faculty-evaluation Questionnaires* (University of Victoria, 1978).

9. Respondents interpret broad questions more specifically than the researcher

intended. W. A. Belson, *The Design and Understanding of Survey Questions* (Aldershot, England: Gower, 1981).

10. S. Sudman and S. S. Bradburn, *Asking Questions* (San Francisco, Calif. : Jossey Bass, 1982), pp. 36-39; A. R. Cohen, "Erring Around the Collar: Whitening the Blue Collar Blues Exercise," *Exchange: The Organizational Behavior Teaching Journal*, N. D.

11. Bounded recall is a device where researchers interview the same respondents. The initial interview is unbounded, and the data are not used for subsequent interviews. However, the subject is reminded of the behaviors reported previously, and the interviewer checks new behaviors reported. Bounding, unlike a list of questions for recall improve the details gathered rather than providing a broad list. See J. Neter and J. Waksberg, J. "A Study of Response Errors in Expenditure Data from Household Interviews," *Journal of American Statistical Association*, vol. 59, 1964, pp. 18-55.

12. S. L. Payne, *The Art of Asking Questions* (Princeton, N. J. : Princeton University Press, 1951).

13. D. A. Dillman, *Mail and Telephone Surveys: The Total Design Method* (New York: John Wiley, 1978).

14. F. N. Kerlinger, *Foundations of Behavioral Research* (New York: Holt, Rinehart and Winston, 1967).

15. There is still the opportunity to provide extra questions for reliability checks or to measure the influence of changes in wording. The latter may be done by administering two parallel forms of the questionnaire to equivalent samples of the population where the two forms have some questions in common but other questions are worded differently with the content still remaining the same.

16. It may also be appropriate to indicate why these questions are being asked: "So that we can see how your opinions compare with those of other people, we'd like a few facts about you. " See S. Sudman and S. S. Bradburn, *Asking Questions*, p. 219.

17. S. Sudman and S. S. Bradburn, *Asking Questions*, pp. 222-223.

18. The term "funnel" refers to a procedure of asking the most general and unrestricted question in the area first, and following it with successively more restricted questions. In this way, the content is gradually narrowed to the precise objectives. One of the main purposes of the funnel sequence is to prevent early questions from conditioning and biasing the responses to those which come later. The funnel sequence is especially useful when one wants to ascertain from the first open questions something about the respondent's frame of reference. R. L. Kahn, and C. F. Cannell, *The Dynamics of Interviewing: Theory, Technique, and Cases* (New York: Wiley, 1957), pp. 159-160.

19. S. Sudman and S. S. Bradburn, *Asking Questions*, pp. 227.

20. S. Sudman and S. S. Bradburn, *Asking Questions*, pp. 252-258: S. L. Payne, *The Art of Asking Questions* (Princeton, N. J.: Princeton University Press, 1951); William J. Goode and Paul K. Hatt, "The Collection of Data by Questionnaire," *Methods in Social Research* (New York: McGraw-Hill, 1951), pp. 132-161.

21. There are several decisions that have to be made about the content, wording, form of response and placement of questions, and a detailed list of these is available in Appendix C in C. Selltiz, M. Jahoda, M. Deutsch, and S. W. Cook, "The Collection of Data by Observation." *Research Methods in Social Relations* (New York: Holt, Rinehart and Winston, 1959), pp. 200-234.

22. A. Anastasi, *Psychological Testing* (New York: Macmillan, 1982). Many practical instruments and tests have appeared in publications like the *Annual Handbook of Group Facilitators*.

9

Other Data Gathering Methods: Using Observations and Unobtrusive Measures

It may seem appropriate to use interviews and questionnaires for measuring many aspects of an organization, including values, degrees of satisfaction, or levels of interest. Scaling experts can point to a vast array of highly sophisticated instruments that have been statistically validated and can be used for almost any purpose.

Several facets of organizational life do not lend themselves to questionnaires and interviews. Organizational data are often qualitative, rich in detail, and full of subtle and unique events. These details are hard to obtain by asking a person to assess experience on a five-point scale ranging from extremely unsatisfied to extremely satisfied. Such data includes specific experiences, histories, details, and holistic descriptions.

Observations or unobtrusive measures are often suggested as ways to supplement questionnaires and interviews. This chapter describes the use of participant observation and unobtrusive measures and summarizes some of the difficulties in using them. It then offers a perspective for how they can be used in action research studies.

OBSERVATIONS AND UNOBTRUSIVE MEASURES

Observational and unobtrusive measures are ways of developing information on a setting, its history, processes, personalities, and events.[1] The methods assume that meanings, perceptions, emotions, and beliefs can only partially be recorded with questionnaires and interviews.

Observational Methods

Direct contact in a setting for an extended period of time provides an opportunity to gain other data presented in the form of personal histories, stories, feelings, and experience.[2] The descriptions are the eyes, ears, and feelings for those who read them.

Observations are much more than one-to three-hour interviews where both subject and researcher act in unnatural ways. Participant observation allows the observer to take on, to some extent, the role of a member of the group and participate in its functioning. The observer is asked to experience the problem practically and personally. This is an opportunity to see the conflicts and miscommunications which might never have been recognized by asking questions in an interview. In one study of a nuclear power plant, we had the opportunity to observe the "shut-down" of a unit of the plant as the operators worked to deal with many of the activities for assuring safety. We observed operators, responding in a crisis-like manner brainstorming reasons for gas leakage and possible ways to resolve them. We gained an important perspective on the problems they faced and how they relied on others when decisions were nonroutine. "Being there" certainly offered details enhancing our ability to understand the way they made decisions.

In some cases, it may be difficult to observe such exceptional events. For example, decision-making effectiveness during a disaster sometimes cannot be observed because it is difficult to know when and where that disaster will occur. Or, decision-makers may be unwilling to allow observers to see their behaviors in action. In such cases, interviews may provide a more total picture of the problems experienced.

There are a range of roles an observer can take on. At one extreme, the observer might be an onlooker seeking to implement an explicit scientific structure. At the other extreme is the observer who enters the setting as a participant observer with a genuine openness and unstructured approach. Various combinations of these facets are used for different types of observation. See Table 9.1. Observational questions can be posed in an exploratory/sensing fashion to gain insights for theory or further testing. They can be used to supplement other data sources such as interviews, questionnaires, and unobtrusive measures. Or, they might be used as the primary data collection device for testing hypotheses in action. In general, the purpose depends on whether one is testing a research hypothesis, or providing direct insight for action.[3]

The observation can be structured with explicit guidelines and instruments. Or, unwritten guides or frameworks can be used as a guide. In this sense, the observer is the data collection instrument. There may be some questions about the specifics of the job such as: where does the employee get his or her raw materials from, what types of interactions did the employee have with others, and so on. Usually, very little structure is given to the evaluation other than watching the

TABLE 9.1
THREE DIMENSIONS OF VARIATION
IN OBSERVATIONAL STUDIES

Exploratory with
no explicit definition
  of purpose
	Scientific with
	a very specific statement
	  of purpose

Unstructured	Structured
Covert relationships (Full participant)	Overt relationships (Onlooker)

employee perform the job. The recording process, however, can be highly structured. After the observation is over, the researcher creates a picture of the dimensions of the job.[4]

Structured observations rely on instruments and procedures for observing, and include questions like: who talks to whom, how many interactions were initiated by the person, how many times did the individual leave his or her desk, and so on. Researchers can develop a set of reliable measures for systematic observation and recording. There is less freedom of choice and encouragement to understand other interesting happenings, and observers may be asked to rate the behavior they observe.

One can learn a great deal about a setting by being involved as a full participant and attending all the normal functions and duties and not letting people know about the research being carried out. What kind of relationship is constructed when the investigator deceives the other party, and how might it hurt future research and attitudes? Will participation in a setting affect or harm the long term product of what is being produced? Will participation put others in danger? Will full "participant" roles involve the researcher so much that they no longer gather data or record the observations possible.

An "onlooker" observer usually makes no secret of the investigation, often making it explicit that the research is the overriding interest. The purpose is to observe and to move "where the action is." However, there are certain dominant biases from being present and visible as an observer. In such brief encounters, it may be difficult to gain access to the meanings that participants have in the setting.

Most observational designs will be of the "onlooker" variety and suffer for biases associated with "being there." Not interrupting the natural setting is a key requirement in understanding the persons involved, their behaviors and perceptions, and the dynamics of the physical and social environment. The problem, then, is to become accepted and respected as a researcher in a way which encourages people to be as natural as possible. The term naturalistic suggests that a researcher does not interrupt the natural setting while trying to understand the persons involved, their behaviors and perceptions, and the dynamics of the physical and social environment.[5]

UNOBTRUSIVE MEASURES

Many aspects of an organization's operation can be measured with the use of actual numbers. It makes sense to count the number of people who enter a program, the number who leave the program, and the number of people who are absent from work.

There are mountains of materials produced by organizations and individuals as part of their everyday functioning. Most organizations do an immense amount of data collection during the normal course of activities, and they contain huge, but often hidden, data banks. The various organizational documents, records, and written materials are usually abundant. They appear like a "mountain of information" that seem rather "incoherent."

Organizational information is undoubtedly useful in providing some insight into the nature of the setting and the subjects. It is also useful for suggesting hypotheses, propositions, or ideas needing further studies. This occurs when the measures provide an indication that something is uniquely different for a certain part of the population, or when some data do not fit with normal expectations.

People who use such unobtrusive measures in organizational analysis presume that one of the best indicator of a possible hypothesis may be the variance from the norm.[6] For example, many processes of change are initiated by those who are in disagreement with the status quo, a fact which is probably hidden when researchers are most concerned with the average agreement.

Unobtrusive data can also be used for testing hypotheses or propositions. Certain classical organizational studies illustrate this. For instance, Lewin compared the Hitler Youth and the Boy Scouts of America to test the hypothesis that similarly organized but ideologically different groups would stress different themes in their literature. He analyzed and compared member and leader literature published by the Boy Scouts and by the Hitler Youth.[7] Trist and Bamforth compared the production records of differently organized coal mining operations to suggest that production is affected by the way that people are organized to carry out their tasks.[8] These studies illustrate how unobtrusive measures were used to illustrate the hypotheses and propositions to be tested.

Generally, the more natural the measure, the lower the possibility of bias from the act of measuring. Such information is specific and personal. There are mountains of such information in accounting reports, such as telephone calls made, costs of lighting and heating, number of customers served, and so forth. The problem is in determining how these measures represent the concept or idea being researched.

Types of Unobtrusive Information

Using various internal documents is one of the most unobtrusive ways to collect data. Most organizational materials have already been produced and the basic problem is to use them in a logical way. Some data are secondary, and are collected from secondary sources rather than directly from the respondent. This data is produced because of organizational requirements or practical needs.

There are various types of unobtrusive measures that are of importance for organizational analysis. These include: available records, legal and taxation information, operational and budgeting information, and personal documents, and personal diaries.[9]

Available Records

Most countries have a large national storehouse of records that are generated from census and registration data; these are available in almost every university library. In addition, newspaper and periodicals can be systematically summarized to indicate the influence of events and policies. Finally, voluntary organizations and special interest groups often collect specialized records to further their cause.

Legal and Tax Information

Organizations are required to summarize a host of details for tax purposes including the number of people, their salaries, the number of hours worked, and the financial status of the company. They are required to produce information illustrating they are obeying legal requirements for safety, hiring, compensation, and the like. They will be required to assure governmental bodies that the building codes are being upheld, that the vehicles and equipment have been maintained and inspected, and that the standards of safety and health are being observed. Many organizations, for example, keep detailed records of turnover, accidents, and grievances.

Operational and Budgeting Information

Organizations also produce information as part of the day-to-day functioning. *Budgetary* information is used to pay people, to purchase materials, to keep stock, and to be aware of profits. *Operational* information is used to summarize the details of production and sales, and to handle key questions of scheduling and inventory control. *Performance* data summarize productivity, reject rates, repairs cost, complaints, breakdowns, and other accounting information such as electricity bills and sign-out sheets for after-hours work. In school systems, there are various measures of grades, age, achievement tests, parent meetings, class size, and test scores. In hospital systems, there is a wide array of accounts of illness, drug used, types of operations, and the like. Criminal justice statistics summarize a great deal of detail about criminal and legal records. *Records* are "any written statement prepared for an individual or an agency for the purpose of attesting to an event or providing an accounting." Examples of records include: airline manifests, city directories, expense accounts vouchers, police records.

Personal Documents

Individuals have their own records used for daily schedules, identifying priorities, personal budgeting, and note keeping. These include letters, diaries, autobiographies, essays, memos, and notes. A document is "any written (or filmed) material other than a record and which was not prepared specifically in response to some request from or some task set by the investigator."

In using records, certain questions must be asked: Can they be verified from other sources? Do other documents exist which might assist in providing additional light on the picture? Is the document complete? Does the document represent a personal perspective, an official perspective? What was the intention of the author? What were the assumptions of the author?

Diaries

The respondent or diary keeper is asked to record events immediately after they occur, or at least on the same day. Diaries have been used to summarize how people have used their time or to catalogue their eating habits, consumer expenditure, and television viewing. They are appropriate when trying to record frequent, non-salient events that are difficult to recall and easy to exaggerate. Ledger diaries, where events are entered in a category, yield slightly more accurate information in that they are easier for the diary keeper to respond to.

Observations and unobtrusive measures are extremely valuable for substantiating people's perceptions and ideas. Often, in groups, people make judgments and assume their interpretations of the facts are correct. Thus, the actual observations or records are valuable in checking out assumptions which may mistakingly guide decision-making.

PROBLEMS WITH OBSERVATIONS AND UNOBTRUSIVE MEASURES

Observations and unobtrusive measures are common in the course of our daily lives. Most people have filled in a tax form, a diary, or application for employment. The terms observation and unobtrusive measures have become something of a ceremonial citation use to indicate researchers have measures other than questionnaires. They are initially viewed with enthusiasm as priceless gems of information, but are often left aside because they are unmanageable and full of errors. This section summarizes some of the errors present when using these methods.

Problems with Observations

It is not always easy to record events simultaneously with their occurrence. There may be too many things happening at one time or it may not be possible to predict when the important events will occur. Problems develop when two or more activities occur simultaneously. Activities may be used to accomplish several purposes as, for example, a manager spending time with a certain employee to communicate something as well as improving the level of motivation.[10]

Observations offer an opportunity to participate in the daily life of the group or organization in question. Ideally, one does not interrupt the natural sequence of events. However, observer effects are probably inevitable in any study. The problems of observation are vividly obvious as one tries to observe the problems and issues faced by drug addicts or prostitutes. There is an obvious problem of entry or in being accepted as a "true participant observer." Members of these cultures, as most cultural groups, are very leery of those who would dare put on their façade. There are obvious questions of risk for the researcher. "Going native" might be extremely dangerous.[11]

Better information comes from the amount of time and the quality of the relationship with people in the setting. The observer relationship demands certain skills and personal attributes, such as the ability to listen and gain a rapport. The stronger the personal relationship, the greater chance researchers will be able to observe people as they really are. Suspicion is something that is overcome by time and familiarity, and the task of the researcher is to establish such a relationship. It is, at this stage, that the observer begins to become a participant by taking part in the organization's activities and getting beyond the mere observations. The goal is to become known as a "regular" and start to know people on a social footing. It is an opportunity to fade into the background simply by virtue of being in the same place for a longer period of time and gaining the trust and confidence of those observed.

The limitations of observations, either because of sample size, inaccuracies or omissions are well known.[12] Participant observation studies are subject to at least two classes of error--control effect and biased-viewpoint effect. *Control effects* occur when the measurement process becomes an agent working for change. In the act of observing, the participant may influence the setting. A *biased viewpoint* effect occurs when the observational instrument may selectively expose the observer to the data. The observation may summarize selectively aspects of the situation or shift the calibration of the observation measures.[13] There may be a tendency for the observer to be disposed toward exotic data, and be more likely to report on those things which are different from his or her own of viewpoint.[14] The only way to control such errors is to look for confirmation from different perspectives.[15]

Problems with Unobtrusive Measures

Most organizational records "were produced for someone else and by someone else."[16] Thus, there must be a careful evaluation of why they were produced, for the risk is high that they are full of errors. One is uncertain of the data when only a limited body exists, or uncertain of the sample when so much exists that selection is necessary.[17]

Unobtrusive measures have been the basis for much of the research of historiographers.[18] The measures have the same sort of biases as do other documents, as the records themselves may not describe the organizational events of interest. In addition, a recorder might make an error in completing the record, such as a misspelling, typing, or errors of omission or memory. There are administrative errors of misfiling and using the wrong forms. Other errors occur when the recording system is changed and the old records are not presented in the same format.

Besides the low cost of acquiring a massive amount of relevant data, one common advantage of archival material is "nonreactivity." There may be substantial errors in the material, just as there are biases in filling out a questionnaire. However, the reaction to being tested are minimized because the producers of the data are not aware that they will sometimes be studied by social scientists. The running record may be spotty, and the missing parts may be the most interesting and potentially controversial.[19]

There are two major sources of biases in archival records--selective deposit and selective survival. *Selective deposit* exists in the storage of the data. What data should be recorded and what not? Are the director's letters the only ones filed because a secretary does the filing? Letters to the editor and suicide notes have the same sort of problem. Do people who do not write suicide notes have the same thoughts as those that write them? Less than one quarter of all suicide victims write notes. Sometimes selective editing creeps in through administrative practice. Various archival materials such as roll-call votes, crime reports, reports of congressional speeches, letters to the editor, and other records are subject to content restrictions in their initial recording.

The risk to *selective survival* is also a real possibility. Some records survive because they are not consumed in use, are indifferent to decay, and are not distinguishable. The most interesting evidence may have ended up on somebody's desk and was never returned because a person was never quite finished with it, spilled coffee on it, or wanted it for a personal file. Certainly, in statistics, we recognize that missing data is a problem, and most survey evidence is based on an average of fifty percent of the sample.[20] The selective survival of records is also an important methodological question. Why were certain records kept while other disposed? Possibly, the most valuable records disappear first because they are the most in demand and of political interest.

Some of these errors can be resolved through data transformation and indexing methods--if they can be known. Some of this information loss can be captured from other sources, and indeed this might be a real requirement. Columbus kept two logs--one for himself and one for the crew. Record keepers may keep two logs. Police may compile records for the criminal justice system and another set of logs for their own personal decision-making. Accountants have to conform to standard format, while keeping a personal set of accounts for specific purposes. The archival materials on birth, marriage, and death often can be checked with other information from the census. The political bias of a newspaper's letters to the editor might be compensated by an analysis of the congressional or legislative records.

Unobtrusive measures are usually one-sided, although no more one-sided than self-report information. Unobtrusive information is usually collected to respond to such purposes as taxation, regulation, or record keeping. Researchers usually have different purposes such as analysis, problem-solving, prediction, or evaluation.

If organizational measures do not capture the data needed for responding to the research objectives, it may be necessary to develop surrogate measures of performance or behaviour. These usually include records of some form of output or behavior. These are cases where participants or subjects do not see the forms as part of the research process, but as a more natural part of what is needed for working normally.

It may take a variety of data to provide insight on organizational events and interactions. If organizations are complex, then many different types of methods should be involved to collect data simultaneously.[21]

A PERSPECTIVE ON OBSERVATIONS AND UNOBTRUSIVE MEASURES

How does one begin a process of observing an organization's interactions and finding out about the most useful unobtrusive organizational records? This is similar to a fire inspector who is trying to unravel the details of how a fire destroyed a building. Much of the evidence has been destroyed or concealed. The fire inspector is presented with a mass of information and much of it has been partially destroyed. The immediate goal it to gather the information with the most potential before the building is torn down and reconstructed.

It is rarely possible to gather all the details at the scene of the fire. Such a comprehensive observational study would require a large number of fire inspectors who would look into each separate detail of the disaster. The costs of such efforts are in most cases prohibitive. Thus, most data collection efforts have to respond to choices of what to observe and collect information on.[22]

Studies using observational and unobtrusive measures might have much in common with the work of a fire inspector.[23] They proceed through steps including: exploratory observations and record collecting within generalized categories of data which might yield possible solutions; developing more comprehensive ways to observe and analyze; performing the more detailed observations; observing the frequency; recording the observation; and verifying the accuracy.

Initial Observations, Recording, and Interviews

The researcher, like the fire inspector, may be inclined to seek to observe "everything," at least initially. However, there is usually a purpose underlying any observation, whether implicit or explicit. In preparing for observations and record collecting, researchers have, and should have, some broad questions in mind. Experience with previous disasters, provides an understanding of what to look for in the rather chaotic remnants of a building. The inspector is likely to have developed a grounded understanding to focus the probe in certain directions over others.

During the initial observations and record gathering, the observer looks for problems and concepts that promise or lead to the most understanding. These observations are supplemented with open-ended questions probing for what is happening. In organizations, these questions may be asked to organizational participants. In a disaster, a fire inspector has a series of open-ended questions to focus his/her observations and record collecting. Most observers will want to answer some general questions about the participants, their tasks, the setting, the behavior and outputs, timing, and unique causes and consequences.

1. *The Participants.* Who are the participants? How many are there? How can they be characterized (age, sex, roles, occupations)? Where are they situated in relationship to each other? Is there any key groupings or relationships?

2. *The Tasks.* What are the functions of the various groups of people? How are they relating in this setting? What are they doing during the key events or observations? Are these functions formally defined? Do individuals and groups have a variety of purposes for being there? Are there conflicting goals of various groups or individuals? What are these conflicting goals?

3. *The Setting.* Each setting has unique features which are described by the technology--the equipment, facilities, and resources. As a result, a nursery school may be very different than a clothing factory. An airplane disaster is different than a burned building. How can I preserve the data or information which describe the equipment, facilities, resources by sampling the records, taking pictures, or reconstructing the facilities elsewhere?

4. *The Behavior and the outputs.* How do people actually behave during the event? Describe this behavior in descriptive terms. What are the specific movements made and activities that they carried out.

5. *Timing.* The timing of the behavior is described by the time it occurred, the time it takes, and the frequency. What time did the behavior, output, or event occur? How long did it occur? How often did it occur?

6. *Unique causes and consequences.* What unique occurrences affected the people, tasks, setting, behaviors and outputs, and timing. What unique consequences affected the people, tasks, setting, behaviors and outputs, and timing.

This list of general topic areas cannot be approached as a cookbook list of things to observe in an organization. However, they might be used as an overview of some of the events and interactions taking place. During the initial observations and recordings, the above categories might be used as a guide where observers summarize the behavior and interactions occurring. The content of the observation may change as the observer continues to probe in different directions.

The initial observations become the basis for the formation of a set of guided concepts to form subsequent evaluations and might be used, in certain cases, to conduct a second site visit. These concepts are formed in much the same way that a researcher forms the grounded concepts in a questionnaire, by sorting the various items of information into categories that evolve from the data and other appropriate concepts. Many conventional observational procedures borrow strongly from ethnography, a field work method long associated with anthropology.[24] Ethnography does not encourage researchers to become emersed in a setting with a completely open mind, nor does it encourage explicit hypotheses testing. An ethnologist seeks to understand what organizations are like by seeing how the events and activities are interwoven around some purpose or meaning. These events and activities are not some logical theory of motivation or leadership, but they are the situational theory of that specific setting.

Understanding of an organization evolves from choices one makes in observing or interviewing people or events. These are choices of whom to interview, what questions to ask, and what to codify. Choices are also involved in identifying the activities to observe.

One can always fall back on some accepted theory or set of constructs in understanding organizations. Ethnographers have traditionally drawn their research practices from anthropology and related research on culture. Thus, the constructs, variables, and activities describing a culture have been the "choice" variables for observation and analysis. These are concepts which describe values, norms, beliefs, symbols, and other cultural terms. In organizations, one might assess goal achievement, management functioning, group dynamics, functional theory, efficiency, or others.

To enter the observation without a theory is theoretically possible, until choices are made about the variables and relationships to study. These choices provide a set of constructs or set of criteria with some logical, political, systematic, and situational coherence.

Developing More Comprehensive Ways for Recording or Analysis

Conclusions and interpretations from these initial observations and recordings provide the groundwork for the development of the indicators to be used in the data gathering. Observers are continually making choices about what data they will pick. However, the more questions we ask to ourselves or others and the more we "listen" to different interpretations, the more chance that we have at abandoning preset theories or beliefs.

Lack of structure presents the possibility of observer bias. Observer bias may be substituted for a bias of too quickly imposing one's own definitions on the respondents. When the goal is exploration and discovery, such observer bias may be justified. In such cases, the observer is creatively developing a clearer understanding of problems and issues. Interviews and focus groups may be an important guide to focus the observation and to provide it with a direction.[25]

At some point, the researcher will have to ask: what constitutes data? In trying to answer this question, Spradley suggests three kinds of data:[26]

---

1. Descriptive questions	Setting, people, events
2. Focused questions	What occurs
3. Selective questions	How, why

Descriptive questions summarize the setting, the people, and the events. They are the basic units of field data which can be described in terms of dress, age, gender. They include what is seen and what is heard, and generally this data provides an indication or overview of the setting. Much of the data can be gathered during the initial observations might be more organized.

One can ask and answer more *focused questions* after describing the systems characteristics. The key descriptive data in the command and control center of a nuclear power plant might be the operators and their tasks. In observing he communications among these operators, we asked a number of questions to focus on communications during certain key events (incidents) or times of the shift. For example, in trying to understand the communications that occurs during a "shift-turnover" in a control room of a nuclear power plant, the following questions might be asked:

1. What occurs in the time period before the shift change?
2. What are the major communication linkages which you have with others at the end of the shift (last hour or so)?
3. What would be the mode of communication usually used (i.e. phone, radio, face to face, etc.)?
4. Approximately how long and how often does this communication occur and how?
5. Could you give some reasons why you would communicate with this person or group? Could you give some examples?

On the basis of these observations, more *selective questions* might be asked. Considering the above questions on communications linkages during different parts of the shift, we asked operators to identify the nature of their working relationships with each individual or group.

1. For each individual or groups:
   a. Could you give some specific examples of things that this individual or group does which are helpful to you in your job.
   b. Could you give some examples of things that this individual or group does that are not so helpful to you in your job?
2. In your working relationships, there are times when miscommunications occur, which may or may not lead to problems. For each of the individuals and groups identified earlier.
   a. Could you give some examples of miscommunications that have occurred, in which, for instance, something you said was misinterpreted by the other person, or you misinterpreted something they said?
   b. Is there a time in the shift when these types of miscommunications tended to occur more frequently . . .
   • Beginning of shift
   • Middle of shift
   • End of shift

These questions allow one to move from a more general definition of the key interactions to specific questions which unfolded in the process. The importance of questions going beyond mere description is underlined in criticisms of managerial studies indicating how managers spend their time.[27] The emphasis on the description of an activity without recognizing its purpose had led to some accusations that some researchers missed out key aspects of a manager's behavior. Observing an operator carrying out an activity may not indicate what they felt they were doing and why it was important, or how it relates to other overall activities. Thus, observations are only one perspective on what is occurring. The self-questioning and interviewing is an opportunity to provide a perspective on why these events occur.[28]

Carrying out the Observations and Recordings

While observing and recordings, several choices have to be made involving the credibility of those observed and the statements people make. Many statements may be forced by the act of observing and recording. Individuals may be overly willing to pass on statements reflecting groups norms. On the other hand, an informant may not want to say things until alone and assured of confidentiality. Such statements are not to be ignored, but recognized as interpretations.

Certain questions, used by history researchers, might be used to assist in judging the information received. Is there a reason for the informant to conceal the truth? Does a person's ego or vanity play a part in what was stated? Did the person actually witness what was described or is this hearsay evidence? Can the person describe the actual behaviors which occurred? Did a person's feelings about a particular person affect the way that the event was perceived?[29]

Interviews may assist in an initial understanding of the organization's activities and interactions. They can suggest where and when to observe and identify the issues and dynamics attending the observations. In the early stages of an observation, interviews can help the observer locate key interactions, people, or expected events. They can indicate where and when to observe, as well as a perception of the key events that might be occurring.

Interviews also provide data on the dynamics occurring during an observation. They continually verify what is happening and, more importantly, why it is happening. One good strategy is to ask what people are doing as they are doing it. The goal, then, is to capture interpretations and intents while they are fresh in the participant's mind. More importantly, interviews help the observer to see the actions in context, where participants do not have to recall or interpret why they are doing something. In this way, informants can assist the participant observer in collecting data about the core features of a program. Participant observers are very involved in the daily lives of their subjects.

However, in order to give some precision to their data, they need to continually ask questions of what is happening and why.

Observations and recordings, when combined with interviews, provide a two-facet approach to understanding. Thus, we might spend less time devising provocative and fool-proof questions on what we think important. We might spend more time in observing the content and nonverbal cues of what people normally talk about. That is, people's values, beliefs, ideas, and interpretations are displayed regularly in what they do. The researcher's task is to describe what they are doing and why.

These observations and recordings may not describe certain aspects such as formal outputs or activities, but they will describe the dynamics in the setting. They illustrate the social meanings, the individuals interacting, and the decisions and the rules avoided and not used. They reveal the meanings, beliefs, and practices that organizational participants use to organize their activities.

The mere co-presence of a particular set of phenomena may not be enough to establish co-occurrence. Rather, both phenomena had to be co-present and function relevant to some other phenomena of interest. Certain things follow when a given set of phenomena are present in a particular context. For example, when people attended a meeting, they discussed certain issues. Something else may routinely occur when one or two people or phenomena are absent. Certain people may be routinely late; certain people may be routinely unprepared. In such cases, when a participant offers an account of why something did not happen, this might be a inference on the behavior. Unprovoked explanations or nonnormal events are indications of something going against the norm. Many of these sanctions illustrate the importance of established and accepted rules and behaviors. Participants who routinely sanction particular types of behavior are telling others the rules for appropriate action.

Observing the Frequency

One of the analyst's major choices involves a definition of what are the organization's key activities and what represents significant data. The goal is to center the inquiry on whole events which have a beginning and an end. These are events that routinely occur and compose the central threads of the organizational activities. While other non-whole events may be undertaken, these are usually less relevant and personal. The key events are the whole events or activities central in the eyes of the participants. There is a need to search for patterns, themes, or categories to describe the activities observed. There is also a need to describe frequencies, key activities and interactions, and standards for perceiving, believing, and acting which group members are using to organize their affairs.[30]

Patterns of co-occurrence are the main base of ethnographic assessments. These patterns recognize those facets which routinely go together at particular kinds and moments and those that routinely follow one another in sequence. What happens next when the behavior is present is systematically different from what happens when the action is absent. From this perspective, deviant or discrepant cases, those that do not fit the norm, are not treated as unexplained variance as they are when statistical methods are employed.[31]

Methods for Recording

Many observational studies have been presented as case histories without any attempt to quantify. Pioneering work using observational techniques was done by anthropologists who were studying small, isolated cultures. They presented data which were rich in detail, but which provided few concepts to guide others. The typical notetaking or recording provides a sketch of the interaction, why it occurred, and who else was involved.

When and how should notes be made? The best method to follow, unless one is adept enough to record detailed observations on the spot in shorthand, is to jot down a few key words or phrases bringing to mind certain events. These can be summarized in detail soon after the observation .

The greatest asset of direct observation is the recording of behavior as it occurs without influences produced by a research setting. It is independent of the participant's ability to report or the ability to translate actions into words. People may try to create a particular impression, knowing that they are being observed. However, it is probably more difficult for them to alter what they do or say in a life-situation than it is to distort an oral or written report of what they have done or said.

The best time for recording is undoubtedly the time the observation is made. This is a process of describing the various characteristics of the situation in a form representing how it occurs. The goal is to provide a series of notes which act as a "sketch" for the later "pictorial" description of the setting.

The process of recording seeks to develop the initial sketch of notes into an actual picture of the system. This is a "back-and-forth" process of developing an initial description, comparing it again with a second observation or the observations of others, and then finalizing the description. The observation becomes more focused and the categories for description can be revised in later stages of the observation.

The act of recording is often lost in too sketchy a picture or too detailed a sketch. As the observer gains experience in observation, the "recording" skill can be fine-tuned. The best recording principle, it would seem, suggests that we should be detailed enough to communicate the system to another person while not so sketchy as it would require constant verbal editorializing by the observer.

The Accuracy

Experience and self-insight is often the best guide to accurate recording, but this too can be rightly questioned by skeptics who are concerned about reliability and validity. The most useful way to increase the accuracy of the data collection method is by using multiple observers of the same event. They can then compare their records with each other and address anomalies. It is desirable to make independent records first, so that written records can be compared. Differences should be identified and, ideally, the observers should go back to the setting to "observe again." When multiple observers are used, it may be desirable to have observers with different backgrounds.

When an observer is forced to work alone, objectivity can be increased by indicating which observations represent actual behaviors and events, and which represent interpretations. Researcher interpretations are important in cataloguing the gestures, discrete hesitant movement, and other subtleties of the setting. However, any overdose of one type of interpretation or set of data cannot respond to questions of reliability and validity. Being involved with participants will always be judged as affecting the judgment or the sharpness of the observations.

There will always be a tendency to become absorbed by the values and feelings of the culture being observed. The researcher can seek to respond to this in the following ways:

1. *Recognizing feelings.* Researchers at the Tavistock Institute were continually involved with psychoanalysis, as an attempt to assist their exploration, and so that they did not become the destination of others' problems. They also worked in research teams, and constantly questioned their observations. Diary writing is another way of capturing feelings and events during the intervention; progress reports to "disinterested others" or managers can also be helpful.

2. *Changing the focus.* One tactic is to shift the focus to see events and happenings from other points of view. This might involve changing the focus of observation from person to person, or event to event. In some settings, certain people or groups may be the center of the research. The tactic is to shift the focus to see the events and happenings from others' perspectives.

3. *Shifting perspectives.* Another tactic is shift the perspective from being a full interviewer, to being an observer, surveyer, or "detective" gathering unobtrusive data. This is valuable because many understandings are not always communicated and have significance because they are not mentioned.[32]

4. *Insider verifying.* Findings can be verified by re-checking with the people observed.

5. *Outsider verifying.* The checks provided by significant disinterested colleagues is another way of verifying, the accuracy of findings.

The above procedures on observing and gathering unobtrusive data is open-ended and unstructured. It offers suggestions on the researcher's role, what should be observed, the data, and methods for recording. As in the development of an action research questionnaire, the categories and questions for observation emerge from the initial exploratory interviews and observations.

Instead of arguing that a conclusion is true or false, we might ask how likely the frequency or distribution is an accurate reflection of the interactions. Obviously, one of the best ways to assure that the data are accurate is with several kinds of evidence. Thus, a norm or behavior said to exist might be verified if it can be actually observed.

The data recorded are rather loose at this stage and need organization through content analysis and model building. This is a process of building models and maps to summarize the information so that it is easily visualized and understood.

SUMMARY

Using observations and unobtrusive data can be more time consuming than questionnaires and interviews dominated. These methods might be used in providing another perspective, and used alongside other data collection efforts. For example, it might be appropriate to carry out more extensive observations to compliment surveys or self-reports.[33]

NOTES

1. J. P. Spradley, *Participant Observation* (New York: Holt, Rinehart and Winston, 1980); J. P. Spradley, *The Ethnographic Interview* (New York: Holt, Rinehart and Winston, 1979).

2. There are several terms which might illustrate an observational method of data collection and include: participant observation, naturalistic inquiry, case study, field study, ethnography, and so on. See L. Schatzman, and A. L. Strauss, *Field Research: Strategies for a Natural Sociology* (Englewood Cliffs, N. J. : Prentice Hall, 1973); J. Van Maanen, "Making Things Visible," in J. Van Maanen, J. M. Dabbs, and R. R. Faulker (eds.), *Varieties of Qualitative Research* (Beverly Hills, Calif: Sage Publications, 1982).

3. M. Q. Patton, *Qualitative Evaluation Methods* (Beverly Hills, Calif: Sage Publications, 1980).

4. C. Selltiz, M. Jahoda, M. Deutsch, and S. W. Cook, "The Collection of Data by Observation. " *Research Methods in Social Relations* (New York: Holt, Rinehart and Winston, 1959) pp. 200-234.

5. M. L. Smith and G. V. Glass, *Research and Evaluation in Education and the Social Sciences* (Englewood Cliffs, N. J. : Prentice Hall, 1987), pp. 252-280.

6. E. Webb, and K. E. Weick, "Unobtrusive Measures in Organizational Theory: A Reminder," *Administrative Science Quarterly,* vol. 24, 1979, p. 653.

7. K. Lewin, "Hitler Youth and the Boy Scouts of America," *Human Relations*, vol. I, 1947, pp. 201-227.

8. E. L. Trist and K. W. Bamforth, "Some Social and Psychological Consequences of the Longwall Method of Coal-Getting," *Human Relations*, vol. 4, 1951, pp. 3-38.

9. E. J. Webb, D. T. Campbell, R. D. Schwartz, and L. Sechrest, *Unobtrusive Measures: Non-reactive Research in Social Sciences* (Chicago: Rand & McNally, 1966).

10. M. J. Martinko, and W. I. Gardner, "Beyond Structured Observation: Methodological Issues and New Directions," *Academy of Management Review*, vol. 10, 1985, pp. 676-695.

11. C. Marshall and G. B. Rossman, *Designing Qualitative Research* (Newbury Park, Calif. : Sage Publications, 1989), pp. 92-93.

12. In the observational studies of management, several limitations are apparent such as: small sample sizes, lack of reliability checks, activities which occur at the same time, and the inability to differentiate between groups. See: M. J. Martinko and W. I. Gardner, "Beyond Structured Observation: Methodological Issues and New Directions," pp. 676-695.

13. N. W. Riley, *Sociological Research: I. A Case Approach.* (New York: Harcourt, Brace and World, 1963).

14. Control effects may be reduced by the observer assuming an incognito role, where the observer can become completely emersed in the system being studied. One might also take care in choosing informants, and recognize or sample those who might be classified as good informants (knowledgability, physical exposure, effective exposure, perceptual abilities, availability of information, motivation. See: K. W. Back," The well-informed informant," in R. N. Adams and J. J. Preiss (Eds.), *Human Organization Research* (Homewood Ill.: Dorsey Press, 1960), pp. 179-187.

15. M. L. Smith and G. V. Glass, *Research and Evaluation in Education and the Social Sciences*, p. 256.

16. E. J. Webb, D. T. Campbell, R. D. Schwartz and L. Sechrest, *Unobtrusive Measures: Non-reactive Research in Social Sciences*.

17. This dilemma is often called "Croce's problem. " One part of this suggests that it is difficult to establish the merit of a limited body of data. The second part of this dilemma, the degree of confidence of the sample, is easier to assess.

18. See G. W. Allport, *The Use of Personal Records in Psychological Science* (New York: Social Science Research Council, 1942); J. Dollard, and O. H. Mowrer, "A Method for Measuring Tension in Written Documents," *Journal of Abnormal and Social Psychology*, vol. 42, 1947, pp. 3-32.

19. E. J. Webb, D. T. Campbell, R. D. Schwartz and L. Sechrest, *Unobtrusive Measures: Non-reactive Research in Social Sciences*.

20. T. D. Cook and D. T. Campbell, *Quasi-experimentation: Design and Analysis Issues for Field Settings* (Boston: Houghton Mifflin, 1979).

21. D. K. Weick, *The Social Psychology of Organizing* (Reading, Mass: Addison Wesley, 1979), pp. 188-193.

22. There are, or course, cases of more comprehensive data collection efforts, as after the bomb explosion aboard Pam Am Airlines over Lockerbie, Scotland. These inspectors did not only sample the data after the disaster; they reconstructed it for further analysis.

23. It shares many goals with a pure description of a naturalistic qualitative assessment which derives its philosophical orientation from phenomenology. Phenomenology suggests that groups of people have different views of the reality and

different ways of interpreting it. Thus, people take action based on ideas and beliefs about the world, regardless of what the world is objectively. In this sense, it would be important to "get inside" the organization and try to explain its consequences in terms of participants realities and meanings. E. G. Guba, "Criteria for Assessing the Trustworthiness of Naturalistic Inquiries, " *Educational Communication and Technology Journal*, vol. 29, 1981, pp. 75-92.

24. M. Q. Patton, *Qualitative Evaluation Methods* (Beverly Hills, Calif: Sage Publications, 1980), pp. 44-45.

25. The goal in any such observation is to search inductively for the "patterns, themes, and categories" in the data. M. Q. Patton, *Qualitative Evaluation Methods*, p. 306.

26. J. P. Spradley, *Participant Observation* (New York: Holt, Rinehart and Winston, 1980).

27. H. Mintzberg, *The Nature of Managerial Work* (New York: Harper and Row, 1973).

28. N. Snyder, and W. F. Glueck, "How Managers Plan-the Analysis of Managers' Activities," *Long Range Planning*, vol 13, 1980, pp. 70-76. See also M. J. Martinko and W. L. Gardner, "Beyond Structured Observation: Methodological Issues and New Directions," pp. 676-695.

29. See: L. Gottschalk, C. Kluckhohn, and R. Angell, *The Use of Personal Documents in History, Anthropology, and Sociology* (New York: Social Science Research Council, 1945).

30. The choices of an event to observe can be described in two ways. Vertical co-occurrence is when phenomena occur at a particular moment in time and function conjointly. Horizontal co-occurrence is when they recur consistently together in sequence and function in relation to one another. See S. Ervin-Tripp, "On Sociolinguistic Rules: Alteration and Co-occurrence," in D. Hymens and J. Gumperz (eds.), *Directions in Sociolinguistic: The Ethnography of Communication* (New York: Holt, Rinehart and Winston, 1972), pp. 213-250.

31. F. Erickson, "Talking Down: Some Cultural Sources of Miscommunication in Interracial Interviews," in A. Wolfgang (ed.), *Research in non-verbal communication* (New York: Academic Press, 1979); F. Erickson and J. Shultz, *The Counselor as Gatekeeper: Social Interaction in Interviews* (New York: Academic Press, 1982); E. G. Guba, and Y. S. Lincoln, *Effective Evaluation: Improving the Usefulness of Evaluation Results Through Responsive and Naturalistic Approaches* (San Francisco: Jossey-Bass, 1981); D. W. Dorr-Bremme, "Ethnographic Evaluation: A Theory and Method," Educational Evaluation and Policy Analysis, vol. 7, no. 1, 1985, pp. 65-83; Y. Lincoln, and E. Guba, *Naturalistic Inquiry* (Beverly Hills, Calif.: Sage Publications, 1985).

32. P. K. Manning, "Problems in Interpreting Interview Data," *Sociology and Social Research*, vol. 51, 1967, pp. 302-316.

33. In one study, for example, self-report measures were compared with records of single-day absences for the same employees during the same period of time. The results indicated that the number of reported single-day absences recorded did not match very closely with official records. Self-reports, in this case, may have been invalid because of inabilities to recall, unwillingness to provide accurate data, and so forth. See C. W. Mueller, D. S. Wakefield, J. L. Price, J. P. Curry, and J. C. McCloskey, "A Note on the Validity of Self-Reports of Absenteeism," *Human Relations,* vol. 40, 1987, pp. 117-123.

10

Analyzing Messy Data

There are several text books and articles with suggestions for analyzing data generated from questionnaires and other sources of codifiable data. They offer sophisticated statistical techniques and procedures for illustrating relationships of large data sets and large numbers of variables. Analysis has been described as a process of "cutting the problem down to size" or reducing it into smaller more comprehensible parts. This is a process of solving the component parts of the problem and assembling them into a solution for the larger problem.[1]

William James, a nineteenth century psychologist, made the observation that people do not start a day's work with problems to be solved. The start of a day resembles a "great big buzzing confusion" or what his student John Dewey called "an indeterminate situation." Russell Ackoff called this situation a "mess," and indicated that what we usually confront are messes and not problems.[2]

If information and organizational data is so conceptless and messy, how do we take steps to analyze it? This chapter first provides a perspective on the systematic errors that are likely to occur in field research. It then outlines methods for improving the value of the information collected and analyzed.

SYSTEMATIC ERRORS IN QUALITATIVE ANALYSIS

Researchers can expect to find three types of systematic errors when they attempt to use qualitative data collection and analysis procedures in field settings. These errors occur during a study's composition and conceptualization, implementation and data collection and recording. These biases emerge from the mismatch between research requirements and field setting dynamics.

The *composition and conceptualization* of the research can produce systematic errors which may "add," "distort," or "delete" unique information.[3] For example, certain relevant variables might not be included and irrelevant ones included. It may not be possible to appropriately define all the components of a theory, their interactions, and their relationships to events in an organization. This error can be exemplified in a symphony orchestra when a composer attempts to define the way the composition is to unfold and the many instruments needed to produce the sounds. The requirements of the conductor might dictate practices not truly consistent with the nature of the instruments in the orchestra or the capabilities of certain players. Certain instruments are suited to certain types of music; horns may be more common for military marches; violins may be more common for classical compositions; and guitars might be more suitable for country and western selections. The use of some instruments might add or delete elements to the composition. These errors represent imperfect "attempts to define a composition."

Implementation errors illustrate the lack of uniform relationships between the intervention and field setting. The experimental interventions may be well defined, but there are certain distortions--personalities, relationships, personal histories--affecting their application in field settings. This type of systematic error grows out of the inconsistencies and differences in relationships, and are usually "environment generated." Implementation errors in an "orchestra," for example, exist when the sound of one instrument cannot be heard because of the strength of another. Or, certain important instruments may be indistinguishable because of the mass of instruments working together. The conductor and orchestra might be working well but the many instruments may not be interrelated because of the seating arrangements, acoustics, intensity of the notes, number of instruments, size of the orchestra, and so forth. These errors occur because of the dynamics of organizational life. Many events do not remain stable for a long period of time and might not be expected to, given the many activities in an organization. Implementation errors result from reactions produced by the intervention. They are like a "culture shock" as if the culture of one system of rules interferes with another.

A third type of systematic error evolves from the mechanisms for *measuring and recording*. These may "delete" certain sounds. Recording methods--questionnaires and observations, for instance--may force the definition of variables which may not be sensitive to certain information. Deletions might be exemplified by the methods of recording the movements of the orchestra or from biases from the microphones or filters.

Compositional Errors

When we, as action researchers, set out on the task of gathering data in organizations, there are certain "compositional" errors which add or distort the information collected. These errors occur because: our concepts and theories may or may not capture the most important interactions we are trying to understand

and measure; the variables to be measured often interact with each other; and the setting may be difficult to control.

Theory is important in research for its systematic explanation of observed phenomena. A theory is a set of interrelated constructs (concepts), definitions, and propositions that specify relationships among variables. Its purpose is to explain, predict, and provide a systematic explanation. However, action researchers enter organizations knowing that a wide range of their *theories and concepts may or may not exhibit a close relation to reality.*[4]

Thomas S. Kuhn's book, *The Structure of Scientific Revolutions*, describes a paradigm as a set of assumptions within which a group of researchers and practitioners function. Every paradigm tends to define the world in a limited way and to deal with it efficiently--with its own sort of criteria. "Normal science" research is directed to the articulation of those phenomena and theories that a paradigm already finds relevant.[5] A crisis of normal science occurs when the original paradigm is incapable of disposing of the problems encountered. At this time, a new candidate for paradigm status emerges.

Scientific research generally, but also that which is applied in field settings, has much in common with Kuhn's description of the growth of paradigms in the natural sciences.[6] There are those who are very accepting of one viewpoint or paradigm, and they may become protagonists who too easily reject other paradigms or processes of intervention.[7] They may become so familiar with their methods that they take them for granted and overlook assumptions of their application.

Are action researchers and qualitative researchers calling for a new paradigm of research based on grounded theories, qualitative data, and inductive principles? Most action researchers have grown up within certain disciplines or schools, and have come to believe that certain theories and methods are more appropriate in the analysis of certain problems. If action research and the qualitative sciences are an emerging paradigm, will its procedures and tools describe the real dynamics of organizational life? It would seem that an organization cannot operate within a unique paradigm of science.

Ideally, one chooses theories and methods of data collection to objectively analyze a problem. A systematic error occurs when the perspectives, theories, and methods of action research are not appropriate for the operational issues or scientific efforts it is responding to. There are dangers that the concepts are too remote and different from those used by people in the organizations studied. As such, the objectivity of action research needs to be acceptable to lay people.

The culture of an organization develops in response to its own needs which are molded by the technology and people. In many cases, these needs manifest themselves with respect to the needs to produce outputs within a limited amount of time. The organization's procedures and methods of working are dictated by this culture rather than by the paradigm of science.

The initial problem definition is often motivated by beliefs about oneself and goals about what should be achieved. These beliefs play an important part in the way that the initial problem is presented, especially since it can encourage the researcher to go into specific directions over others. These beliefs may merely be symptoms of the problem, they might be one person's solution, and may not reflect the real problem. Often, the real problems are concealed and need to be unravelled and untangled from beliefs and emotions.

The variables in field settings are highly *interactive*, and cannot be explicitly defined as a hypothesis. Hypotheses in field settings are not micro-sets of larger problems.[8] They are interactive; they are propositions to be tested where a combination of independent variables X1, X2, X3 . . . Xn will dynamically affect conditions Y1, Y2, Y3 . . . Yn. These hypotheses are more interactive than static.

A field situation *cannot be controlled* to the same extent as a laboratory experiment. A model of a social system's operation is not always definable within cause and effect terms; some events may be catalytic, some buffering, circular, reciprocal, positive, and negative.[9]

If research objectives are strictly adhered to, there may be threats to organizational survival. The pressures that an executive must face stem from the requests of others in and out of the organization. Specific organizational pressures and personality considerations are often responsible for decisions being reached without an adequate analysis of the problem or the consequences. It would be unrealistic to insist that the executive fulfil the strict requirements of the research design, as this would diminish the ability to respond to new ventures. This may be like limiting the natural course of the organization's development for the sake of the experiment, or invalidating the organization's validity for the sake of an experiment's internal validity. As a result, researchers have had difficulty in collecting data on individual characteristics from a range of situations and comparing people with one another.[10]

Most field settings have *response sets* emerging from the way they are designed. For instance, schools of engineering and architecture use efficiency concepts in designing the spacial arrangements in building. Response biases can also occur from the design of office equipment, street and parking, and the physical shape of building. These biases are similar to response biases on a questionnaire and can encourage individuals to respond in certain ways and move in given directions at specified times.

The most salient threat to the internal validity may be the likelihood of a "third" variable correlating with X and Y, or both. These are cases where it may not be possible to define specific variables important in the change. For example, one might argue that age was associated with compliance; the younger the subordinate, the more compliant he or she might be. One might also argue that a third variable called experience was also related.[11]

Implementation Dynamics

Marshall MacLuhan introduced the phrase "the medium is the message" to indicate the process and method of communication may be more than its content.[12] Similarly, when introducing organizational changes, the medium may be as important as the variables describing the change. All interventions or changes are intermixed with a process of intervention. The content describes the change, while the medium is the implementation process. Like the phonograph or orchestra playing off tune, the changes introduced in a field setting may be incompatible with the process which is used to introduce them. The process of implementation is affected by a range of issues concerned with the communication of the change, threats to validity, and field setting interactions.

In traditional science, one methodological goal is to carry out the research so that subjects are not alerted to the purposes of the research or intervention.[13] The research should be designed to reduce the feedback, and extraneous interactions and communication between subjects and researchers.[14] However, *organizational communications and interactions* are vital to the functioning of an organization. There is an on-going management responsibility to increase the level of communication and interaction to respond to new objectives and needs to change. The inputs of a system consist not only of energy, which becomes transformed in the work done, but also of communication and feedback signalling the way the work is carried out. If there is no purposeful direction and corrective device to deal with negative feedback, the system's internal structure will lose its effectiveness.

Most field research face a number of threats to invalidity from the implementation of the research. A very prominent bias, the Hawthorne effect, describes how the awareness of being tested affects the results.[15] Other threats include novelty and disruption effects resulting from the enthusiasm or unfamiliarity of being involved in a new program.[16]

The process of introducing a change is subject to interactions including resistance, difficulties in understanding, and tendencies to adapt, rearrange, and discard less useful ideas and suggestions. In introducing any change, there will be a period of adjustment, such as in the physiological functioning of the body.[17] In addition, people react to influences because of their cognitive structure or their selective perception of the world.

In field settings, the initial introduction of independent variable(s) can reinforce or hinder continued interactions.[18] A social change cannot be introduced in the same way as one would install a part in a machine; a social change involves acceptance and learning, with various degrees of understanding and resistance by different individuals. The effects may have a regenerative capacity; the momentum for the continual use or non-use of these changes may depend on the perceived usefulness to participants. For example, the acceptance of computers increases with the understanding of their use. The momentum from this use increases as a person finds new applications.

Implementation is subject to difficulties in understanding and communicating. Rapoport first coined the term "rejection phenomena," when referring to a defensive reaction on the part of the client, particularly to the presentation of data by a researcher in a "brusque or unskilled" manner, and whose perception of problems might not accord with that of the client.[19] Other writers make reference to this phenomenon in describing a defensive, hostile attitude to information which may prove threatening.[20]

The momentum in many changes may be the positive reinforcement of working toward a goal, or the motivation derived from accomplishing a sub-goal. Thus, after the first transmission of a change or the initial accomplishment of an objective, the subject may be more motivated to do the second task. This will affect the second task. The individual may have learned something after the second use, and this will affect the third. The motivational and learning function will be different after each output but there may not be much more learned after, say, the tenth or eleventh transmission. In the same way, withdrawing the change may not be completely possible, as individuals cannot de-program themselves in machine-like fashion. Long-range effects are greater than immediate effects for general attitudes, although weaker for specific attitudes. Immediate post-tests or measures at any single points in time may not be conclusive, suggesting that measurements have to occur at various stages of the process.[21]

In organizational settings, there are a range of field setting effects from attitudes, the political environment, and the way the problem was initially defined. Individuals' attitudes and values toward being researched are conditioned by years of history with the organization, and experiences while being researched. Some people may be quite be quite neutral, some opposed or positive, fearful or fearless, and so on. Some people may be tired of being researched while others are overly keen to be involved. Some of these historical associations may have formed deep rooted subconscious and conscious reactions.

The political environment in any organization can influence the definition and importance of the problem to various people. The politics surrounding certain facts and issues can influence the definition and importance of the problem and the methods used for gathering data. A detached researcher may gain little commitment for a hypothesis that does not interest an organization's decision-makers and participants. An ideal research plan may not be executed if the researcher opts for problems which are not refined by practical needs.

These implementation dynamics make it difficult to replicate a study, at least much more difficult than one would have in a laboratory. Similar conditions are very hard to find where the experiment can be carried out again to enlarge on the results of the first study.

Recording Dynamics

Recording errors result from the inabilities of recording instruments to measure specific behaviors. These errors refer to artificiality of measures, inability to isolate independent variables, measurement effects, sampling biases, value judgements in quantification and an inability to replicate research questions.

There are several types of *biases introduced by the research*. First, there is a systematic bias resulting from the subject's concern to win a positive evaluation from the experimenter. This type of bias has been called "evaluation apprehension"[22] or an approval motive,[23] and expectancy effects.[24] That is, a respondent's needs for social approval could affect his/her responses, especially when the subject feels there are expectations to react or respond in a certain manner which may be different from normal reactions.

Other biases have been called demand characteristics and reactive arrangements. These include anything that alerts the subject to the purpose of the experiment, and range from special rooms, the experimenter's dress, and the testing apparatus. Instead of revealing their true behavior, subjects act like "good subjects."[25]

A researcher has difficulty conducting a field investigation without influencing (and being influenced by) the people in it, unlike a chemist who can more objectively observe the reaction of chemicals in a lab. People in experiments alter their behavior to conform to expectations of what is proper and appropriate. They react to cues in the experiment, as well as hearsay about the study, the content of the pretest, clearance forms that establish informed consent, experimental procedures, and instructions from the researcher.[26] It is equally appropriate to recognize that experimental conditions encourage people to respond in certain ways, when subjects experience more than one treatment[27] or different variations of a treatment.

Researchers can contribute a substantial amount of variance to a set of findings. They generate expectations about how research subjects should perform and sometimes provide some people with more help and encouragement.[28] Interviewees respond differently to visible cues provided by the interviewer. For instance, there may be biases from factors such as: race, age, social class, sex, and others.[29] Male interviewers obtain fewer responses than female, and fewest of all from males, while female interviewers obtain their highest response from men, except from young women talking to young men.[30] Some of the major biases, such as race, are easily controllable; other biases, such as the interaction of age and sex, are less easily handled. If we heeded all the known biases, without considering our ignorance of major interactions, there could no longer be a simple survey.

All measures are surrogates and derive their value from their approximation of the variables we wish to measure.[31] They are subject to several biases from: illusion, judgmental flaw, inconsistent processing of information, social roles, and the like.[32] Indeed, there are tendencies to see one's choices and judgments to be common and appropriate while viewing others as uncommon, deviant, and inappropriate. These biases are influenced by a host of variables with no single explanation.[33] Ratings of others are also subject to leniency and severity biases, central tendency, and halo effects,[34] which are interrelated.[35]

Reliability is difficult to recognize or control in many settings because of environmental influences from most advertised beliefs and accepted expectations. A subject's responses may be conditioned by the reality around him, and may reflect his/her aspirations or the most advertised wants and desires. Subjects reactions might be the product of free and independent judgement, but reflect mass advertising. Galbraith, for instance, suggests that some consumer expectations are created before they are satisfied.[36] In the same way, feelings may reflect those which are more predominant, such as negative feelings towards management or dissatisfaction for a certain service.

Social desirability is another form of this bias. There is a tendency of people to deny socially undesirable traits and to admit socially desirable ones. Much of the variance in personality inventories might be explained by the social desirability of a item and the probability of endorsement. The probability of bias is higher when a subject is aware of his/her subject status.[37] There is a link between awareness of being tested and the biases associated with a tendency to answer with socially desirable responses.

What people say they do may be quite different from what they actually do. People may only describe what they would hypothetically do when faced with a situation.[38] A person's behavior may be unrelated to previous statements of intention, perception, or attitude.[39]

Early research on the transfer of training encountered the threats to internal validity called *practice effects*; the exercise provided by the pre-test accounted for the gain shown on the post-test. Similarly, research on intelligence testing showed that dependable gains on test-passing ability could be traced to experience with previous tests even where no knowledge of results had been provided.[40] Similar gains have been shown in personal "adjustment" scores.[41] Indeed, there are indications that a whole range of measurement idiosyncrasies cannot be totally detected--including test anxiety, resistance to being tested--but which affect the results.[42]

TACTICS FOR DEALING WITH SYSTEMATIC ERRORS

In social settings, many problems can be described as loose, conceptless, indivisible, and difficult to categorize within conventionally accepted concepts. A Nobel prize winner, Richard Feynman provided a comment on his process of handling seemingly conceptless messes.

People say to me, "Are you looking for the ultimate laws of physics?" No, I'm not. I'm not. I'm just looking to find out more about the world. And if it turns our there is a simple ultimate law which explains everything, so be it. That would be very nice to discover. If it turns out it's like an onion with millions of layers, then that's way it is. But whatever way it comes out, its nature is there and she's going to come out the way she is. And therefore, when we go to investigate it, we shouldn't pre-decide what it is we're trying to do, except to try to find out more about it. . . and the more I find out, the better it is to find out.[43]

The action research principles in this book encourage methods for defining the problem in a creative way, generating concepts from the field, integrating concepts with real world assumptions, triangulating, verifying interpretations, and treating the research setting as a case study. The section also offers a perspective on how such methods might be used for handling systematic errors from composing, implementing, and recording. This is summarized in Table 10.1.

Being Creative in Defining the Need for the Research

Creativity in research offers an opportunity to devise something new and produce a discovery. It is an opportunity to develop new ideas or "unlock" from present ways of thinking and operating. It is the type of thinking sometimes associated with Steve Jobs of Apple computers and with the ideas associated with innovations such as lasers, satellites, FAX machines and digital watches. It is a type of thinking which may be necessary to produce environmentally efficient cars and ways to resolve the conflicting issues in the Arab-Israeli dispute.

This type of creativity is obviously more appropriate for certain types of problems, especially where traditional ideas and practices have not been working. Other less creative and more methodical research approaches will be needed to implement and verify the soundness of such ideas. Otherwise, the world would be full of creative, yet unverified, ideas.

Creativity at the beginning of a research project helps to think of problems in different ways and is a mechanism for dealing with many of the biases occurring in the composition of research. Defining a framework or theory to study a problem in a creative way allows for different ideas to break those strongly held truths or conventional wisdoms. This does not always occur at the beginning of the research and is just as necessary when one is confronted with a mess of seemingly conflictive data.

There are a variety of ways to nourish creativity including the use of metaphors and comparative examples, models, and open-ended interviews of people who have handled related problems in unusual ways.

TABLE 10.1
RESPONDING TO SYSTEMATIC ERRORS

Creativity in generating & analyzing concepts from the field	• Metaphors & models may reduce compositional errors from defining a problem prematurely. • Interviews encourage the recognition of ideas used in successful cases.
Generating concepts from the field	• Sorting may encourage the development of grounded concepts & reduce compostional errors from theories not suited to the setting • Content analysis is a way of analyzing data to indicate factors and their strengths. It can be used to support other measures.
Integrating concepts with real world assumptions	• Implementation errors can be reduced if a set of concepts and measures are based on the assumptions of the setting.
Triangulation results	• Triangulation designs offer ways to verify results & reduce recording errors.
Verifying interpretations	• Implementation and recording errors can be reduced by sampling procedures for checking the accuracy of results.
Treating each setting as a case study	• Social science requires a number of cases to verify a conclusion. • Case study research provides vivid descriptions of implementations.

Using Metaphors and Examples

Much of the analysis which is carried out in the social sciences may too quickly label an event within conventional categories already known. A quick categorization or problem description may summarize the data, but it also encourages the use of familiar categories, words, and ways of thinking.

Metaphors are one way to avoid "quick categorizations." Try saying, "if only I had two words to describe an important feature of this site, what would they be," or simply "this is like a. . . ."[44] In most cases, interaction with others is helpful, as much creative energy can be gathered in groups. Other people bring in different ideas and angles, and they can be helpful in contributing an atmosphere of playfulness or experimentation. The metaphors describe something without using words or categories. "They are rich, saturated, yet uncritical, eloquent without being unnecessarily precise."[45] Metaphors are data reducing devices making it possible to quickly summarize a lot of details while providing an opportunity to identify possible patterns underlying the data.

Comparative examples are another way to avoid "quick categorizations." Examples have some qualities of the emerging concepts, but are full of irrelevant details. It is often helpful to search for comparable cases, bearing in mind the similarity in institutions or time periods. The comparisons with other examples is an opportunity to include variations along some known dimensions. It is like an overlay that varies in its particulars but also reveals a common pattern.

The object of using examples is not to find a perfect example, but a feeling for the concepts, definitions, or themes common among them. Once there is a critical mass of these vague events or ideas, it becomes easier to see the many ways the event could have been formed.

Models

Masses of information can be put together into a more economical unit called a model or map.[46] A model, as described here, is not a causal network but is more a chain of events. It is a strategy of developing linkages between concepts, noting regularities arousing one's curiosity. It attempts to illustrate how the various pieces of an "archaeologist's" findings will fit together. The exercise involves connecting facts with other facts or events, and then grouping these into more abstract patterns. There is a need to tie the findings to other events, to other studies, and to what has happened in the past.

There are certain steps to devising a model or map: summarizing the interview or other information in an uncategorized way so that it can be used for modelling or mapping; identifying the key phrases or events; placing these phrases into common groups; and illustrating the relationship between those individual phrases or groups. This process provides a map of the whole mass of data, and draws out the clusters of constructs and relationships forming categories.

Many of the general ideas derived from interviews or other information can be categorized. Categories may change as one goes through a number of interviews and continues the research. The model or diagram illustrates the relationship of a range of phrases and categories.

Charts, diagrams, tables, and maps of a qualitative sort are ways to display work already done and to clarify categories. They are a way of searching for common denominators and for differentiating factors within and between the types. As such, the maps or models make it possible to discover the range and the full relationships of the very terms and facts underlying a category or class.

Complex and novel events provide a set of operating principles explaining these observations. "Your job is now that of an archaeologist, carefully unearthing what is there."[47] There is no obligation to test and explore the dynamics of all the model uncovered, but to provide a useful map of the whole problem.

The process of modelling or mapping can also assist clients in understanding the problems they are dealing with. Clients will have their own interpretation of the particular significance of the categories. The model might provoke more thought when clients are asked for explanations of events, and why they might be occurring.

The modelling process is a way to abstract the many interactions and relationships in a mass of data gathering from interviews and other sources. It goes beyond the questions asked, and is an opportunity to search for explanations of what is happening. This becomes a major tool for beginning an analysis.

It is not always appropriate to use models or maps for developing concepts for further analysis. Indeed, much can be done with a less labor intensive process of categorization. However, this sort of modelling might be most useful when people are "mentally stuck" and need another way to try to explain the data or get client input into it.

Open-ended Interviews

Creative ideas can be generated by open-ended interviews with people who were able to handle similar problems in unique ways. Two groups of people might be interviewed: the unusual problem-solvers who handled similar problems, and the clients or people who need the solution. Unusual problem-solvers are those people who might illustrate unique or exceptional ways they deal with problems. Clients, on the other hand, provide a user perspective and offer ways they might use new ideas.

Open-ended interviews are an opportunity for interviewees to probe and identify existing problem areas, past incidents and their outcomes, as well as suggestions they might find useful for improving communications.[48] This line of questions is thought-provoking, because it seems to asks people for details of specific events rather than opinions or comments which were unfounded. The following is an example of a question on handling critical decisions in a nuclear power plant.

> Can you describe a situation based on your experience of an upset condition in which the root cause was difficult to diagnose? How did you arrive at the correct diagnosis? Who else was involved? (Analogous to a medical doctor correctly diagnosing throat cancer).

Other related questions probed for examples of effective and ineffective communications, procedures, instruments, and skills.

These questions, especially when they are followed with further probes, yield information on what the person did. The questions ask individuals to provide data on incidents or events that people were involved with or observed. A pooling of incidents on various aspects of communication is a review of events that individuals found most important.

Metaphors, comparative examples, models and open-ended interviews are all ways to think differently about the mass of data and information summarizing a problem. These methods provide an attitude of playfulness toward the phrases and words used in forming a definition. They are the bridge to the words used to describe the events. The first concepts may be loose and undemanding, like analogies. The trap is to use known terms and phrases too quickly. Terms might be defined after looking for their synonyms in a dictionary or technical books. This provides a full range of connotations. This simple exercise encourages one to elaborate the terms and to define them in a less wordy and more precise fashion. It also makes concepts and terms more specific and concrete, based on terms emerging in the setting.

Generating Concepts from the Field

At some point, it is appropriate to begin arranging the various observations and ideas and to develop classes or categories. The concepts become the substance for devising a questionnaire or theory or ordering and tallying a mass of interview or observational data.

Developing Concepts for Theory Building

Several classical writers have used sorting procedures for forming the concepts of their theories. Sorting was used during World War II by Eric Trist, as a method of selecting officers; candidates would be faced with a complex "field," and they would have to make choices in providing some meaning through

a process of grouping and categorization. In developing a student-generated
-professor-evaluation questionnaire, Bavelas, Bavelas, and Schaefer used a four
step process: (1) dividing the total number of cards among six individual sorters,
giving each sorter fifty to sixty-five cards; (2) summarizing the individual efforts
together, and asking the group to develop a collective statement; (3) refining and
cleaning each category to ensure that it is homogeneous (this step is designed to
assure that the cards have not been accidently categorized and to allow the
experimenter to record the labels given to each card); and (4) selecting the items
that best represents the category since each category is homogeneous, and then
choosing the cards to be included and eliminated from the questionnaire.[49]

Herzberg used a method which includes (1) brainstorming, (2) eliminating
hygiene suggestions, generalities, and horizontal suggestions, and (3) developing
a job profile.[50] Whyte describes a process of card ranking for analyzing worker
reactions to the mental and physical processes in the work itself.[51] The process
consists of: (1) describing a job's characteristics on a set of note cards, (2) asking
the workers to rank order the cards in order of preference, and (3) and asking
them to explain their rankings. The explanations revealed a great deal more about
the work process than was gathered from interviews. Neely Gardner (1976)
describes a process of (1) interviewing, (2) summarizing interview statements on
cards, (3) sorting, and (4) assembling a questionnaire.

Sorting can be used for developing the logic for almost any type of
organizational data, ranging from titbits of gossip to hard scientific data and
statistical information. In some cases, ideas from group members might be
summarized through "brainstorming," and then arranged for sorting. In other
cases, open-ended interviews might be used to derive data for a sorting
procedure.

Sorters are usually the same people who carried out the exploratory analysis
or interviews, although groups of sorters might be selected from the same
population of those interviewed. Normally, two or three people can be involved
in the sorting process, although other groups might be used to verify the process.
In preparation for sorting, the interview statements should be summarized on file
cards. Groups of sorters are each given identical sets of cards. The task is to sort
these cards into homogeneous groups of cards which say the same thing.

The decision on card placement and interpretation is based on intuitive rather
than mathematical logic. Sorting is a trial and error process of trying to
understand how various items fit together. The sorters are not limited in the
number of categories they are to develop and are simply given the information to
arrange and asked to label the various interview statements into general
categories.

Each group's categories, and the items underlying them, can be recorded.[52]
Categories that are immediately similar can be identified, and those that are not
can be collapsed.

The sorters can be asked to eliminate those statements that are redundant and to refine those that are unclear. Each group can then articulate why it had chosen to refine or eliminate a statement; other groups should either modify their statements according to the suggestion or defend the position of why it should not. With the knowledge of the initial sort, a second sort can be conducted by each group. This process may be repeated several times, until a common list of categories is agreed upon by all groups.

An example of the concepts that emerged in a sorting process is presented in Table 10.2. The concepts emerged from interviews with managers who were asked to identify skills used in managing certain critical incidents. These statements were sorted into categories describing personal traits and technical and behavioral skills. Each concept was defined from the actual words used in the interviews. Examples of such definitions are presented below.

Examples of Statements Used to Describe Behavioral Skills

Organizational Communication Skills. Keeping people informed so that they can understand what is happening in the organization. Ability to organize and present data in a way which is understood by the listener. Communicating to the right people. Keeping people informed but not overloaded with irrelevant information. Ability to understand the type of information needed by people for their work and for a sense of purpose in the organization.

Organizing and Priority Setting. Ability to establish priorities. Ability to manage competing demands for one's time. Ability to organize job duties. Ability to delegate tasks to others.

Problem-sensing and Solving. Ability to identify and define a problem. Ability to differentiate between real and apparent problems. Ability to assess the impact of a problem throughout the organization. Ability to develop appropriate solutions. Ability to implement solutions.

Coaching. Guiding, motivating, and helping staff. Encouraging and assisting others to perform well in their jobs. Providing feedback on performance in a constructive manner. Helping staff to set achievable goals. Making resources available to assist staff in developing their skills and achieving their goals. Assisting staff to make their own decisions and solve their own problems.

Content Analysis

Many systematic errors of quantification and classification can never be totally satisfied with quantitative or qualitative methods. Coding different things

TABLE 10.2
PERSONAL ATTRIBUTES AND TECHNICAL SKILLS

Personal Traits	**Technical Skills**
• Attitude of service	• Technical knowledge
• Resident philosophy	• Manpower planning
• Management philosophy	• Financial analysis
• Public posture	• Written communications
• Integrity	
• Risk taking	
• Positive disposition	
• Regard for others	
• Confidence	

Behavioral Skills

Interpersonal Skills	• Working with others • Group relations • Teaching/Instructional • Interpersonal communications • Organizational communications
Decision-making Skills	• Negotiating • Resource management • Data gathering • Organizing and priority setting
Leadership Skills	• Strategic & critical thinking • Establishing a direction • Conceptual skills • Flexibility in management • Problem-sensing and solving
Team Skills	• Decision-making style • Coaching • Support/Teamness

or people into the same category inevitably alters some of the information. Categories such as old and young alter a person's age by making older people fit into a younger category, and vice versa. Classifying according to existing theoretical categories encourages the use of definitions with a different history, timing, and purpose. These theories may have originated from people who have systematically reviewed the literature, from the experiences of one articulate writer, or from those more acceptable to key academic journals.

The concepts used for content analysis might be more relevant when they emerge directly from the data.[53] This allows the researcher to get a "feel for the data" because he/she sees the data in their rawest form and works them into categories describing them. The researcher can incorporate other categories as they are needed, or add explanations and conditions for the categories.

Content analysis is unlike statistical analysis where the researcher receives a pile of responses, ships them off to a key puncher, categorizes the variables on the basis of their statistical relationship, and massages the data by eliminating items that do not fit or vary from the norm. Content analysis is a way of ordering and sorting items or statements to represent a collective view of the issue or problem.[54] It is a process of categorizing or developing a picture of how many parts of a universe fit together. It is based on the logic that, through the use of intuitive processes, it is possible to establish categories or factors of similar statements that are mutually exclusive. The statements within each category are intuitively related.

Content analysis can be used for analyzing letters, autobiographies, diaries, ethnographic materials, newspaper articles, minutes of meetings, and so on. It can be used for understanding feelings, needs, values, attitudes, stereotypes, and the like. The technique is useful for an understanding of feelings and values generated in interviews. Ideally, the analysis can be carried out alongside other types of measurement. In this way, it can be used to validate other methods and can be a source of items to develop objective tests, scales, and interview schedules.

A central problem with content analysis evolves from the data reduction problems by which the words and phrases are classified into much fewer categories. The variables are valid to the extent that the constructs measure what they are said to measure, and this is always open to question because of the ambiguity of word meanings. The best ways to substantiate the validity of the concepts, in such cases, may have to rely on other researchers, cases, and supporting studies.

The weakest form of validity is face validity, or the extent to which a category represents the investigator's representation. While expert agreement may improve the strength, face validity is often viewed skeptically by other social scientists. As a result, content analysis is often viewed with skepticism.[55]

Much stronger validity is obtained when an external criterion is used for comparing content-analytic data. In this regard, construct validity is the extent to which the category is compared with other measures of the same construct. This suggests that a construct should be generalizable across other measures and methods.[56]

Other types of validity include hypothesis, predictive, and semantic validity. Hypothesis validity relies on the correspondence among variables and the measures they represent. Predictive validity is the extent to which the forecasts about events and conditions are shown to correspond to actual events or conditions. Semantic validity exists when persons familiar with the language and texts examine lists of words (or other units) placed in the same category and agree that these words have similar meaning.[57]

Content analysis is no panacea. It is laborious, time-consuming, and expensive. In this regard, a researcher may spend a great deal of time developing and validating a question and ask each of 250 employees to spend an hour of their time filling it out. Then, the researcher still has to code the information and spend hours analyzing it.

Some of the data used for content analysis may be weak or the sample may not be representative. For example, some informants may be better than others or have more knowledge. Or,there may be a multiple indicators, some which are better than others. Thus, there may be a need to adjust the sources of data to provide more weight to certain groups or indicators.[58]

Three types of reliability are important in content analysis: stability, reproducibility, and accuracy. Stability, or the extent that a content classification varies over time, can be ascertained when the same content is coded more than once by the same coder. It may be the weakest form of reliability, because only one person is coding. Reproducibility, or the extent that more than one coder can produce the same results with the same text, offers a stronger indication of reliability. Stability measures the consistency of shared understanding, while reproducibility is an indication of personal interpretations.

Accuracy is the extent a classification of text corresponds to a standard or norm. It can be used to test the performance of human coders.[59]

Integrating Concepts with Real World Assumptions

Any set of categories is based on certain assumptions. There are patterns, themes, and logic underlying the data and categories developed. They indicate the regularities or directions. Miles and Huberman provided the following statement about the way in which this process can occur. "When one is working with text, or less well-organized displays, one will often note recurring patterns, themes, or 'Gestalts,' which will pull together a lot of separate pieces of data. Something 'jumps out' at you, suddenly making sense."[60] Most sets of data have underlying assumptions, themes or patterns underlying them. After the data are organized into various categories, clusters, or factors, what is the underlying theme? Thus, there is some need to search for the pattern or logic underlying the categories of data. This is "l'essence" of the information, without which it is just a list of factors.

Patterns of Co-occurence

Patterns of co-occurence among events are a way of displaying the systems of standards for perceiving, believing, evaluating, and acting that people are using to organize their events. Vertical co-occcurence describes events occurring at a particular moment in time and function jointly. Horizontal co-occurence describes how events recur consistently together in sequence and function in relation to one another.[61] Co-occurence patterns can be found in various levels of social organization. They can illustrate the underlying rationale for an occurrence and the rationale or set of values underlying it.

An example of co-occurence can be found in a study exploring the reading programs in elementary education.[62] A pattern of co-occurrence included (a) consistently high reading scores + (b) schoolwide emphasis on "reading and understanding" + (c) high standards and expectations for student performance + (d) organizational strategies that reduced the number of reading ability groups per teacher + (e) curriculum and staff stability over time. The study indicated that the program features (b) through (e) were routinely co-present in schools with consistently higher test scores in reading. They were not present in schools of comparable students with median and low scores on reading.

These patterns illustrate behaviors which typically go together and provide the logic for a set of concepts or categories. They reveal an underlying assumption and logic for explaining a set of actions.

Logical Relationships

All theories provide a logical set of relationships or ways of factoring concepts into certain groupings. The logic for the groups can be intuition and creativity, statistical, or systematic. Intuition relies on the use of common sense, experience, and maturity. It can be encouraged or developed by the use of groups and creative exercises. Statistical procedures such as factor analysis, discriminant analysis, and correlations have often been used for establishing statistical relationships between factors. Systemic or naturalistic procedures are often used by ethnographers to illustrate the natural relationships, based on common groupings and key interactions.

All organizational theories use some form of logic to define the assumptions which outline why the factors are related. A theory without logic is like "a fish without water." While this expression is overused, it does vividly imply that theories and the factors defining them, are based on some critical assumptions of life. A fish cannot live without water just as a set of concepts is an unrelated jumble until it interrelated within some critical assumptions. In the same way, the hierarchical relationship of Maslow's hierarchy of needs and the motivation/hygiene theme of Herzberg's motivational theory were the assumptions giving them life. These are the broader constructs that put these categories or factors together.

All such broader categorizations or theme statements are limited to some intent. Intuitive logic may sound very persuasive and "common sense" to some people, while statistical logic might sound more precise. These seemingly logical statements might be wishful thinking. In this regard, the best ways to test the logical relationship of a set of variables might be to try to combine some of these methods, and to ask other individuals or groups for verification.

Triangulating the Results

The action research process in based on the principles of gathering information from multiple perspectives. The goal is to achieve convergence where methods of data gathering and analysis complement each other. The results converge when the complement one another.

There are few guidelines to assist in ordering the various levels of data or answering some questions of whether all evidence is equally useful. The triangulating investigator searches for a logical pattern of results from a mixture of methods. When convergence is achieved and different methods illustrate the same results, confidence in the results is higher. When divergence in results occurs in the data from different methods, the first step is to look for problems with the method and design. Then, there is an opportunity to search for other reasons to illustrate the variation.

The validity of using different methods and designs often rests on the researcher's ability to organize data within a plausible framework.[63] The researcher is like an architect, piecing together the various pieces to construct a coherent picture. In this creative process, he or she relies on others' ideas, intuition, and a feel for the concepts describing the setting. The various methods are an opportunity to get closer to the data and to provide a "brighter picture" of the architectural drawing.

The triangulation strategy is not without its limitations. It is exceedingly difficult to replicate the results because it is very unlikely that two situations will allow for the same data. In addition, the strategy relies on one's ability to ask the right questions.

Verifying Interpretations

A researcher's biasing effects on a group of participants is impossible to completely control if he/she is not aware of how he/she affects the study. If one researcher is likely to get entirely different information than other, the biasing can be serious. Some of these effects can be miminized by paying attention to certain norms of gaining the respect and understanding of the clients, and by making sure that the research methods and practices address the technical needs of a sound design as well as the needs of the organization's participants. If researchers are not viewed as outsiders, and if their interests are not incompatible with participants, researcher effects might be minimized. This is an act of becoming a fuller participant in the organization, and allowing participants to gain a higher degree of respect and understanding.

At times, researchers may become so involved in a situation that they lose their objectivity and pay too much attention to a certain group of people or types of ideas. Thus, other methods--checking for representative and Q sorts--might be useful.

Checking for Representativeness

The speculative romp through selected sets of cases does not provide useful information in qualitative analysis.[64] Unrepresented samples allow certain cases to unrealistically foreshadow the others, or conclusions of one case to foreshadow the whole.

It is realistic to expect that most studies will be unrepresentative and are based on convenience sample.[65] Thus, it is safe to assume that most samples are selective and it is important to check on the representativeness of the sample. This can be accomplished in five possible methods: checking the accuracy of the findings with people in the field setting; increasing the number of cases and encourage other perspectives; carrying out other studies in similar settings; looking purposefully for contrasting cases which are extremely negative, positive, or otherwise different; and sorting the cases systematically to look for differences.[66] These methods allow the researcher to look more carefully at the data or conclusions and then check them to see if they are representative. Each method offers a different perspective in enhancing the data's representativeness. Checking the findings with field people, gathering other cases, and carrying out further studies are methods of verification. Further classifications and sortings are ways to carry out the analysis in different ways.

In a large number of cases, the researcher might choose to develop the categories for analysis based on a systematic sample of the total possible cases. In such cases, a Q sort procedure might be used for developing and understanding the representativeness of a sample. This is an effort to define valid concepts for the cases in the analysis.

Content analysis requires a sampling of the environment where the research is to be done, and for this reason, it needs to be a systematic representation. The elegance of content analysis is worthless if the setting, cases, or information sets are not representative. Ideally, this involves the selection of a sample of people or events that will illustrate the concepts.

Like any form of science, one important code is the openness to an audit. At times, this may mean that interview statements should be recorded, even though sealed so that they can not be used by indiscriminant people. In some cases, it might be possible to tape record some feelings and observations made during the process, yet, at the same time taking notes to summarize the interactions. The transcription might only be necessary, if there are reasons to question one's findings or a desire to reinvestigate parts of the data. In other cases, the researchers might want to practice a code of continually summarizing their assumptions and perceptions of difficulties, and the decisions made during various stages of the process.

The Q Sort

Q sort procedures can be useful for assuring the representativeness of a sample. Its logic centers on the sorting of decks of cards called Q sorts and in the correlations among the responses of different individuals to the Q sorts.[67] It is a ranking methodology where individuals are asked to rank a number of issues or variables according to a specified criterion. The following is an example of a rank ordering of the success levels of seven entrepreneurs using four experts. Rank order correlations could be used to compute the relationships, and illustrate if there are any clusters of ratings.[68] See Table 10.3.

Unstructured Q sorts can be used to assemble a set of items without specific regard to the variables or themes. Such unstructured procedures were used by some researchers in developing personality scales. For example, a large number of statements can be taken from various sources--personality inventories, patient interviews with therapists, researcher theories--and put together in a Q sort. They are sorted to provide a statement of various personality constructs.[69] In such studies, researchers can offer inferences on the results of therapy. Subjects can sort the cards themselves before, during and after therapy. If a neurotic person has benefitted from the therapy, so the reasoning goes, there should be a low correlation between the pre-therapy and post-therapy Q sorts, provided that measures are reliable.

The principles behind the Q sort methods--such as structured Q sorts, one-way structured Q sorts, two-way (factorial) structured Q sorts--call for the collection of items to represent or totally describe the population or items. Instruments or theories are constructed and tested to describe the theory underlying the items. Thus, the goal of the Q sort is the development and testing of theories by asking individuals to sort items according to specific criteria.

Q procedures can be used for the development of factor arrays. In this sense, factors are similar clusters of objects--persons, items, characteristics. Positive and negative statements are both used in identifying and interpreting the arrays.[70]

TABLE 10.3
RANKING THE SUCCESS LEVELS OF ENTREPRENEURS

	Expert 1	Expert 2	Expert 3	Expert 4
Entrepreneur 1	1	1	5	4
Entrepreneur 2	2	3	4	5
Entrepreneur 3	3	2	6	6
Entrepreneur 4	4	6	1	2
Entrepreneur 5	5	5	2	1
Entrepreneur 6	7	7	3	3
Entrepreneur 7	6	4	4	7

The major strength of Q methodologies is the ability to test propositions. In addition, it is possible to intensely study one individual, by giving him/her two, three, four, or more related Q sorts. One individual can sort an array many times. The data of such "sorts" can be analyzed objectively. Stephenson claims that a theory built into the Q items can be tested using the Q sort of one individual whose characteristics are known. A conservative who has sorted social attitude items should have a mean score of the conservative items which is greater than the mean of liberal items.

There are, of course, disadvantages. It is not possible to work with a large number of individuals, and if the sample of items to be sorted is not appropriately done, the resulting Q sort will be very different. Such differences in individual judgement need to be guarded.

Treating the Research Setting as a Case Study

Case Descriptions and Direct Quotations

It is obviously easier in the natural sciences to measure the chemical compositions and physical properties of bodies and materials. Social scientists have the same desire to understand the magnitude and the most interesting classes of phenomena.[71] Qualitative measures are longer, more detailed and vary in content, and the analysis cannot be presented easily in a short space. It seems much easier, on the surface, to use quantitative measures because of their succinctness, ease of aggregation for analysis, and efficiency of presentation in a minimum of space. Yet, its purpose is to provoke change rather than simply describe what has conveniently occurred. This purpose may justify the time and extra space it seems to demand.

The desire to document individualized client outcomes is one major reason why case studies may be more useful than measuring standardardized outcomes for all the program's participants. In addition, detailed case studies of extreme cases might provide examples of unusual successes, failures, or dropouts. These cases may be justified in situations where a few cases may be untypical. For example, if a new individual enters a program--a client with different background or history--it may be useful to gather in depth information on them and their experiences.

Direct quotations are the basic source or raw material for much of the qualitative measurements. They reveal respondents' levels of emotion, the way they have organized their thoughts, their ideas, experiences, and perceptions. These descriptions reveal the actual statements that people use to describe their emotions and are vivid descriptions of what people think.

There are severe limitations to open-ended data collection on questionnaires. These limitations relate to the writing skills of respondents and the impossibility of probing for further detail. In addition, people often do not take the time to answer the questions before them.

Open-ended questions and interviews provide a richer variety of information to use. Many people choose to present open-ended information in the form of cases. In this way, a selection of cases are used to illustrate a set of concepts. The task is then to analyze the cases within certain criteria.

The danger in the use of direct quotes is to end up with too much volume. Thus, some writers have chosen to use direct quotes in a more limited way. That is, they use them as an example of feelings generated with other data. In this regard, the data amplify and provide another perspective on other information.

After completing the conceptualation and analysis, the researcher faces a formidable task of presenting and condensing a mass amount of data in a easy-to-read format. Most qualitative data, especially case evidence and open interview statements, do not lend themselves to concise presentations. This is especially true if researchers are urged to illustrate how the results of one set of measures can be collaborated in others.

One partial solution is to continue to strive to condense the data so that the major findings can be presented in a minimum number of tables, frequency distributions, or pie-charts. Selected examples to represent the important findings can be included in the text, including only those most relevant statements or definitions. While the table may provide an overview of all the interactions, only the most important qualitative details will be presented. This "rule of thumb" eliminates nearly 80 percent of the bulk and it is then possible to select quotes, details, examples, which triangulate the major finding.

Integrating Knowledge Across Cases

Many behavioral sciences are generally considered to be nomothetic sciences, although this might be disputed. The science of organizational studies might be idiographic, and concerned with providing accurate descriptions of singular events or cases.[72]

Cases can be viewed as those experiences that the researchers have accumulated over the course of research in a given area. It is realistic to expect that most of the studies we carry out can be called case studies, and it would be appropriate to collect and analyze studies related to specific research questions.[73] This is not a simple process of reviewing studies and summarizing the methods or findings. The key is to use coded dependent variables, and using the same approach so that analysis can be carried out across cases.

When researchers collect and analyze their own cases, they have an opportunity to view and observe the effects of different interventions and processes of change. They have the same information on the same variables, and can provide useful and accurate data for analysis. They can also work with others in codifying the data so that it can be used for analysis.

An important aspect of external validity is whether the results generalize to some population of individuals. There are two ways of constructing a research environment comparable to some population of individuals. First, the researcher can employ random selection methods of drawing from a defined sample of individuals. Or, even though a sample in an experiment was not selected at random, it may be "judged" to be typical of some larger sample. This obliges the researcher to describe the details of a sample so that others can make an informed judgement of its representativeness.[74]

It is usually feasible in most field studies to carry out similar work in other settings, and to observe other similar cases where the intervention was not made. Such groups provide a basis for comparison of what happened, but they also are an inspiration for defining other interventions or ways to intervene.[75]

SUMMARY

There are a range of interactions and occurrences which do not easily lend themselves to our ability to weight, measure, count, and tabulate. The search for truth in the form of statistical proof occupies much time of the social scientist. Researchers can usually draw on methods which are highly sophisticated and elegant. Indeed, the statistics used are sometimes more interesting to the researchers than the subjects. Numbers are added, divided, and correlated even though they do not perfectly describe the reality. Is it really possible to measure learning style or intelligence? Can numbers be used to determine types of learning style or levels of intelligence? Some materials are not as amenable to quantification as others, and questionnaire researchers have illustrated that it is also much easier to assign numbers to surrogate measures than to real ones. It may seem easy to use numbers for a range of items, such as feelings and unique ideas, but it may not be appropriate.

A "qualitative" ideal does not reject numbers or statistical methods. Rather, it simply uses numbers to summarize concepts that have emerged inductively and naturally. Quantification relies on one's ability to be careful in determining whether or not the item should be represented by a number. Further discussion with other researcher and a better understanding of the total context makes it easier to see where these units fit later on. A high level of eclecticism in the exploratory stages of a project, when the concepts are formulated and methods constructed, may increase the operational validity of the research results.[76]

Scientific controls in action research does not mean the creation of a laboratory-like setting. Rather, it calls for mechanisms to "convince a reasonable person" that what is alleged to happen did in fact happen."[77] While it is not possible to control a setting, it is necessary to assemble evidence to illustrate a conclusion is verifiable.

NOTES

1. R. L. Ackoff, *The Second Industrial Revolution* (University of Pennsylvania Working Paper, n. d).

2. R. L. Ackoff, *The Second Industrial Revolution*; R. L. Ackoff, "The Art and Science of Mess Management," *Interfaces*, vol. 11, 1981, pp. 20-26.

3. See D. T. Campbell, "Systematic Error on the Parts of Human Links in Communications Systems," *Information and Control*, vol. 1, 1958, pp. 335-337.

4. P. Shrivastava and I. I. Mitroff, "Enhancing Organizational Research Utilization: The Role of Decision Makers' Assumptions," *Academy of Management Review*, vol. 9 1984, pp. 18-26.

5. T. S. Kuhn, *The Structure of Scientific Revolutions*, 2nd ed. (Chicago: University of Chicago Press, 1970), pp. 23-25.

6. T. S. Kuhn, *The Structure of Scientific Revolutions*. pp. 35-37.

7. T. S. Kuhn, *The Structure of Scientific Revolutions*, pp. 35-37.

8. T. D. Cook and D. T. Campbell *Quasi-experimentation: Design and Analysis Issues for Field Settings* (Boston: Houghton Mifflin, 1979), pp. 52-54.

9. M. L. Smith and G. V. Glass *Research and Evaluation in Education and the Social Sciences* (Englewood Cliffs, N. J.: Prentice Hall, 1987) p. 147; G. Morgan, *Images of Organization* (Beverly Hills, Calif.: Sage Publications, 1986), pp. 66-69.

10. J. A. Chatman, "Improving Interactional Organizational Research: a Model of Person-Organizational Fit," *Academy of Management Review*, vol. 14, 1989, pp. 333-349.

11. T. R. Mitchell, "The Evaluation of the Validity of Correlational Research Conducted in Organizations," *Academy of Management Review*, vol. 10, 1985, pp. 92-195.

12. The phrase was popularized by Marshall MacLuhan, and indicated that the way a message is delivered is as important as the content.

13. M. L. Smith and G. V. Glass, *Research and Evaluation in Education and the Social Sciences*, p. 147.

14. R. L. Rosnow and D. L. Davis, "Demand Characteristics and Psychological Experiment," ETC: *A Review of General Semantics,* vol. 34, 1977, pp. 301-313.

15. It is named after the Hawthorne studies pointing to the biases from knowledge about the study and the special attention given to subjects.

16. M. L. Smith and G. V. Glass *Research and Evaluation in Education and the Social Sciences*, p. 148.

17. D. F. Bradley and M. Calvin, "Behavior: Imbalance in a Network of Chemical Transformations," *General Systems* Yearbook of the Society for the Advancement of General System Theory, vol. 1, 1956, pp. 56-65.

18. D. Katz and R. L. Kahn, *The Social Psychology of Organizations* (New York: John Wiley, 1965, 1978), pp. 24-25.

19. R. N. Rapoport, "Three Dilemmas in Action Research," *Human Relations*, vol. 23, 1970, pp. 449-513.

20. A. Curle, "A Theoretical Approach to Action Research," *Human Relations*, vol. 2, 1949.

21. D. T. Campbell and J. C. Stanley, *Experimental and Quasi-experimental Design for Research* (Boston: Houghton Muffin, 1966), p. 31.

22. M. J. Rosenberg, "The Conditions and Consequences of Evaluation Apprehension," in R. Rosenthal and R. L. Rosnow (eds.), *Artifacts in Behavioral Research* (New York: Academic Press, 1972).

23. D. P. Crowne and D. Marlowe, *The Approval Motive: Studies in Evaluative Dependence* (New York: John Wiley, 1964).

24. R. Rosenthal, "The Volunteer Subject," *Human Relations*, vol. 18, 1965, pp. 389-406.

25. M. L. Smith and G. V. Glass, *Research and Evaluation in Education and the Social Sciences*, p. 147.

26. M. L. Smith and G. V. Glass, *Research and Evaluation in Education and the Social Sciences*, p. 147.

27. T. D. Cook and D. T Campbell *Quasi-experimentation: Design and Analysis Issues for Field Settings*, p. 67.

28. R. Rosenthal, "The Volunteer Subject," pp. 389-406.

29. See R. Hyman, *The Nature of Psychological Inquiry* (Englewood Cliffs, N. J.: Prentice Hall, 1964); R. L. Kahn and C. F. Cannell, *The Dynamics of Interviewing: Theory, Techniques and Cases* (New York: John Wiley, 1957).

30. M. Benny, D. Riesman, and S. Star, "Age and Sex in the Interview," *American Journal of Sociology*, vol. 62, 1956, p. 143.

31. T. R. Mitchell, "The Evaluation of the Validity of Correlational Research Conducted Organizations." pp. 92-195.

32. D. C. Funder, "Errors and Mistakes: Evaluating the Accuracy of Social Judgement," *Psychological Bulletin*, vol. 101, 1987, pp. 75-90.

33. G. Marks and N. Miller, "Ten Years of Research on the False-consensus Effect: An Empirical and Theoretical Review," *Psychological Bulletin*, vol. 102, 1987, pp.72-90.

34. B. D. Bannister, A. J. Kinicki, A. S. Denisi, and P. W. Hom, "A New Method for the Statistical Control of Rating Error in Performance Ratings," *Educational and Psychological Measurement*, vol. 47, 1987; W. F. Cascio, *Applied Psychology in*

Personnel Management, 3rd ed. (Englewood Cliffs, N. J. : Prentice Hall, 1987), pp. 82-85.

35. G. M. Alliger and K. J. Williams, "Confounding Amount Measures of Leniency and Halo," *Educational and Psychological Measurement*, vol.49, 1989, pp. 1-10.

36. J. K. Galbraith, *The Affluent Society*, (Boston Mass. : Houghton Mifflin, 1958).

37. D. T. Campbell, "Factors Relevant to the Validity of Experiments in Social Settings," *Psychological Bulletin*, vol. 54, 1957, pp. 297-312; D. T. Campbell and J. C. Stanley, *Experimental and Quasi-experimental Design for Research.*

38. I. Ajzen and M. Fishbein, "Factors Influencing Intentions and the Intention-Behvaior Relation," *Human Relations,* vol. 27, 1974, pp.1-15.

39. L. Festinger, "Behavioral Support for Opinion Change," *Public Opinion Quarterly*, vol. 28 1964, pp. 404-412; H. J. Ehrlich, "Attitudes, Behaviors, and Intervening Variables," *American Sociologist*, vol. 4, 1969, pp. 29-34; W. J. McGuire, "The Nature of Attitudinal Change," in G. Lindzey and E. Aronson (eds.), *The Handbook of Social Psychology*, 2nd ed., vol. 3, (Reading, Mass. : Addison-Wesley, 1969).

40. A. Anastasi, *Psychological Testing* (New York: MacMillian, 1982), pp. 41-44.

41. C. Windle, "Test-Retest Effect on Personality Questionnaires," *Educational Psychology Measurement*, vol. 14, 1954, 617-633; A. Anastasi, *Psychological Testing*, pp. 22-44.

42. A. Anastasi, *Psychological Testing,* pp. 41-44.

43. R. Feynman, "The Pleasure of Finding Things Out," (Transcript). GBH Educational Foundation for Nova (originally broadcast on PBS, January 25, 1983, as quoted in J. B. Bavelas, "Permitting Creativity in Science," in D. N. Jackson and J. P. Rushton (eds.), *Scientific Excellence: Origins and Assessment* (Beverly Hills, Calif.: Sage Publications, 1989).

44. B. M. Miles and A. M. Huberman, *Qualitative Data Analysis* (Beverly Hills, Calif.: Sage Publications, 1984), p. 222.

45. J. B. Bavelas, "Permitting Creativity in Science. " in D. N. Jackson and J. P. Rushton (eds.), *Scientific Excellence: Origins and Assessment* (Beverly Hills, Calif.: Sage Publications, 1989), pp. 307-327.

46. "Maps for action" is a term used by Chris Argyris to describe a way to help us understand and explain why human beings behave as they do. They are intended to represent the problems or causal scripts people use to inform their actions. See Chris Argyris, "Making Knowledge More Relevant to Practice: Maps for Action," in E. E. Lawler III, A. M. Mohrman, Jr. , S. A. Mohrman, G. E. Ledford, Jr. , T. G. Cummings and Associates, *Doing Research that is Useful to Theory and Practice* (San Francisco: Jossey-Bass, 1985), pp. 79-125. "Cognitive mapping" is a similar term that has been used for modelling a persons' beliefs and assist clients to explore their thinking on a particular problem. There are two elements which describe cognitive mapping: a person's concepts of ideas in the form of descriptions of what is occurring, and beliefs or theories about the relationship, shown in the map by an arrow or line. The arrows indicate the positive relationships which exist between people. See C. Eden, S. Jones, and D. Sims, *Thinking in Organizations* (London: Macmillan, 1979).

47. J. B. Bavelas, "Permitting Creativity in Science," pp. 319-320.

48. J. C. Flanagan, "Critical Requirements: A New Approach to Employee Evaluation," *Personnel Psychology*, vol. 2, 1949, pp. 419-425; T. Janz, L. Hellervik, and D. C. Gilmore, *Behavior Description Interviewing* (Newton, Mass.: Allyn and Bacon,

1968).

49. J. B. Bavelas, A. Bavelas and B. A. Schaefer, *A Method for Constructing Student-Generated Faculty-Evaluation Questionnaires* (Victoria: University of Victoria, 1978).

50. F. Herzberg, *The Managerial Choice* (Homewood Ill. : Dow Jones-Irwin, 1976).

51. W. F. Whyte, "Models for Building and Changing Organizations," *Human Organizations*, vol. 26, 1967, pp. 26-31.

52. It is usually considered sound practice to calculate the correlation between groups of sorters before they discuss or adjust differences.

53. B. Berelson, "Content Analysis," in G. Lindzey, *Handbook of Social Psychology*, vol. I, (Cambridge, Mass: Addison-Wesley, 1954), chap 13; B. Berelson, *Content Analysis in Communication Research* (New York: Free Press, 1952); R. R. Jauch, R. N. Osborn, and R. N. Martin, "Structured Content Analysis of Cases: a Complementary Method of Organizational Research," *Academy of Management Review*, vol. 5, 1980, pp. 517-525 ; F. N. Kerlinger, *Foundations of Behavioral Research* (New York: Holt, Rinehart and Winston, 1967), pp. 544-553.

54. Some of the early organizational theorists which used content analysis include Eric Trist and Alex Bavelas. E. L. Trist and V. Trist, "Discussion on the Quality of Mental Test Performances on Intellectual Deterioration," *Proceedings of the Royal Society of Medicine*, vol. 36, 1943, pp. 243-249; E. Weigl, "On the Psychology of So-Called Processes of Abstraction," translated by M. J. Rioch, *Journal of Abnormal Psychology*, vol. 36, 1941, pp. 3-31; A. Bavelas, "A Method for Investigating Individual and Group Ideology," *Sociometry*, vol. 5, 1942, pp. 371-377.

55. A discussion of the validity issue can be found in: R. P. Weber, *Basic Content Analysis* (Beverly Hills, Calif. : Sage Publications, 1985).

56. Researchers often further define construct validity by differentiating convergent from discriminant validity. High construct validity may be an indication that a construct correlates with other measures (convergent) and is uncorrelated with other measures of dissimilar constructs.

57. A discussion of the validity issue can be found in R. P. Weber, *Basic Content Analysis*.

58. M. B. Miles and A. M. Huberman, *Qualitative Data Analysis* (Newbury Park, Calif: Sage Publications, 1984), pp. 235-236.

59. K. Krippendorf, *Content Analysis: An Introduction to Its Methodology* (Beverly Hills, Calif. : Sage Publications, 1980). This monograph illustrates ways of calculating reliablities. It also indicates the need to encourage practices of calculating reliablities between raters before resolving the differences between them. Resolving the differences may produce judgments biased toward the opinion of the most verbal or senior spokesperson.

60. M. B. Miles and A. M. Huberman, *Qualitative Data Analysis*, p. 216.

61. S. E. Tripp, "On Sociolinguistic rules: Alteraction and Co-occurrence," in D. Hymes and J. Gumperz (eds.), *Direction in Sociolinguistics: The Ethnography of Communication* (New York: Holt, Rinehart and Winston, 1972), pp. 213-250.

62. For a summary of the study see D. W. Dorr-Bremme, "Ethnographic Evaluation: A Theory and Method," *Educational Evaluation and Policy Analysis*, vol. 7, 1985, pp. 65-83. The actual study can be found in D. W. Dorr-Bremme, *Higher Educational Achievement in Long Angeles Title I Elementary Schools, An Exploratory*

Study of Underlying Factors (CSE Report No. 190) (Los Angeles, Calif.: Center for the Study of Evaluation, University of California, 1981), (EDIR Document Reproduction Service No. ED 219, 1981), p. 728.

63. R. S. Weiss, "Issues in Holistic Research," in H. S. Becker, B. Geer, D. Riesman, and R. Weiss (eds.), *Institutions and the Person, Papers Presented to Everett C. Hughes* (Chicago: Aldine, 1968), pp. 342-350; T. D. Jick, "Mixing Qualitative and Quantitative Methods: Triangulation in Action," *Administrative Science Quarterly*, vol. 24, 1979, pp. 602-611.

64. R. R. Jauch, R. N. Osborn, and R. N. Martin, "Structured Content Analysis of Cases: a Complementary Method of Organizational Research," *Academy of Management Review*, vol. 5, 1980, p. 519.

65. T. R. Mitchell, "The Evaluation of the Validity of Correlational Research Conducted Organizations," pp. 92-195.

66. For a discussion of some of these methods see: M. B. Miles and A. M. Huberman, *Qualitative Data Analysis*.

67. W. Stephenson, *The Study of Behavior* (Chicago: University of Chicago Press, 1953).

68. The calculation of coefficients of correlation is summarized by: F. N. Kerlinger, *Foundations of Behavioral Research*, pp. 584-585.

69. C. Roger and R. Dymond (eds.), *Psychotherapy and Personality Change* (Chicago: University of Chicago Press, 1954).

70. In an oversimplified explanation, the procedure is to sum the responses of individuals of a cluster of any Q sort item. This can be done for every item in a Q sort, the result being a weighted sum for all items. The sums would, of course, vary; this can be rank ordered and then fitted into the original Q distribution. The "new" synthetic Q sort is really a description of the factor. Factors arrays can be calculated and prepared for each factor. See F. N. Kerlinger, *Foundations of Behavioral Research*, pp. 591-592.

71. F. N. Kerlinger, *Behavioral Research: A Conceptual Approach* (New York: John Wiley, 1979), p. 264.

72. H. Tsoukas, "The Validity of Ideologic Research Explanations," *Academy of Management Review*, vol. 14, 1989, pp. 551-561; D. P. Schwab, "Reviewing Empirically Based Manuscripts: Perspectives on Process," in L. L. Cummings and P. J. Frost (eds.), *Publishing in the Organizational Sciences* (Homewood, Ill. : Richard D. Irwin, Inc. , 1985).

73. T. R. Mitchell "The Evaluation of the Validity of Correlational Research Conducted Organizations," p. 194.

74. M. L. Smith and G. V. Glass, *Research and Evaluation in Education and the Social Sciences*.

75. B. G. Glaser and A. L. Strauss, "The Discovery of Substantive Theory: A Basic Strategy Underlying Qualitative Research," *The American Behavioral Scientist*, vol. 7, February, 1965, pp. 5-12.

76. E. Van de Vall, M. Bolas, C. Bolas, and T. S. Kang, "Applied Social Research in Industrial Organizations: An Evaluation of Functions, Theory, and Methods," *Journal of Applied Behavioral Science*, vol. 12, 1976, pp. 158-177.

77. This is akin to an assumption of British common law,which does not require

demonstration of absolute "lawlike certainty" as is obtained in a laboratory experiment in the physical sciences. British common law is based on moral certainty, which is the degree of proof which produces a conviction in an unprejudiced mind.

Part IV

The Action

11

Carrying Out the Process of Change: Some Implementation Steps

The seats on the train of progress all face backwards; you can see the past but only guess about the future.[1]

Evaluation and data collection reports most often identify the need for change and the problems or issues central to an organization. The information collected reflects issues and events people have found interesting and important. However, creating a novel and nonroutine organizational transformation is more challenging and difficult than just summarizing the need for change.[2] Such an organizational transformation relies on ideas and a vision of the future.

A home renovation metaphor illustrates how data gathering and analysis can be useful in creating a novel and nonroutine organizational transformation. In renovating a home, the builder must assess the technical features of the present structure--its foundation, bearing walls, electrical facilities, and plumbing system. The builder must pinpoint the problems to resolve and define the needs of the home owner.

An assessment of the need for change might focus on the house's structure or the customer's needs and wishes. However, this is only one set of data or perspective on renovating a home. A successful and thoughtful renovation emerges from someone's vision of what the renovation might look like based on architectural ideas, trends in construction, and new materials available. The vision, a creative idea, is "tailored" to the present structure and data. The final proposal for the change emerges from the initial sketches to the more detailed architectural plan which is submitted to the building inspectors and engineers. A plan for construction assists the builder implement the envisioned design.

Data collection and analysis are most valuable when they provide a reflection of the interests and issues to be addressed. They should not provoke resistances, embarrass people, or force people to take sides to defend their positions. The data gathering or assessment phase of any change project provides a summary of the problems, perspectives, and opportunities. It provides a definition of the need for change and an important baseline to start.

Most organizational changes are not new constructions where one can completely define the goals and methods that fit the newest technology. Even if a builder is successful in doing a major demolition before the construction, there are always questions of the needs of the participants, clientele, and community.

The data collection and analysis process can inhibit rather than enhance the potential for creative thinking and change. It encourages the use of existing standards, procedures, and predefined categories to describe data to be gathered. The results may not illustrate innovative solutions to problems or unique ideas for change. They provide an assessment of levels of satisfaction and effectiveness within known criteria. This is a perspective on "what is" rather than "what might be."[3] People's impressions, perceptions, and a priori concepts are largely based on their past experience. When asked questions about the future and visions of it, individuals are most often provoked by past experiences.

This chapter describes how action research principles can be used for thinking creatively about change. It outlines steps for focusing a change and implementing.

A PROCEDURAL MODEL FOR FOCUSING AND IMPLEMENTING

The success of most change efforts hinges on the shared culture of those people in the organization who are seeking to carrying out the plan. Thus, an initial goal is to create a climate for planning and problem-solving where ideas are encouraged and valued. An organization's managers can begin such a process by their commitment and identification with the process and the importance they attach to the participation of others.

Planned change is a process where employees are jointly responsible for engaging the process through a steering committee or (A. R.) group which has defined terms of reference. It consists of two stages: focusing a direction and developing a commitment to the changes, and implementing the plan.

Focusing the Change

How does a manager begin to conceive and focus a process of change? The initial steps in a planning process can be undertaken during a conference or series of workshops attended by a diversity of the organization's participants. In such a conference, task groups can meet and discuss the various topics within each of the planning steps. Subsequent steps of the planning process are undertaken after subgroups report their results to the total group. The steps are: identifying environmental trends, opportunities and threats; outlining strengths and weaknesses within the organization; defining values and philosophies (defining the mission and philosophy; and identifying a vision.

Environmental Trends, Opportunities, and Threats

A planning conference provides an opportunity to pull together a vast amount of information related to the need for change and the opportunities and threats an organization might have to encounter. The data collected provide one perspective on these issues. Most importantly, the process of data collection involves people and seeks to gain their commitment and enthusiasm. The larger environment affecting the organization can potentially affect the way the plan is developed and carried out. In analyzing the environment, prior research can assist participants to become aware of the current and potential actions of competitors, economic trends, government policies and legislation, demographic changes, changes in market influences and so forth. It is important to distinguish between existing or known threats and those which are more uncertain. Some of the negative or threatening aspects can be summarized as PESTs, an acronym for (P)olitical, (E)conomic, (S)ocial, and (T)echnological forces.[4] Table 11.1 is an example of environmental trends.

Conference participants can prioritize these trends in terms of their (p)robability, (i)mpact, and the organization's ability to (c)ontrol or manage them. This PIC analysis may indicate that certain events are highly probable and have a great impact, and that the organization can take action to control them. As a rule of thumb, managers need be concerned with only those events which they have some possibility to control and have some probability of happening.[5]

Organizations need to focus on their opportunities and threats as well as the environmental events which threaten them. Opportunities provide a way to expand the organization's activities in new directions. Threats indicate those which may be most troublesome.[6]

The understanding and imagination of conference participants is particularly useful in identifying the opportunities and threats impacting an organization. Brainstorming and other idea-generation activities are useful in identifying opportunities and trends that the organization will have to respond to in the short and long term. The brainstorming sessions can assist in the establishment of an atmosphere where ideas are encouraged.

The Organization's Strengths and Weaknesses

A conference can also be effective in identifying the usefulness of the resources and procedures the organization is currently using. A statement of the organization's "strengths and weaknesses" is one way to review the organization's current resources and procedures.

TABLE 11.1
ENVIRONMENTAL TRENDS *External Environment*

1. *Technological Change.* The rapidly changing technological environment will hasten and aid the decentralization process. Technology improvements will provide the means for less direct centralized operational control and will permit decentralized control, while enabling senior management to obtain timely and usable financial iformation for decision-making.

2. *Intergovernmental.* Changes to Federal income tax legislation and regulations will affect our work and there will be increased requests for statistical information which will increase workloads.

3. *Demographic.* The "baby boom" bulge will slow down the rate of career progression and increase the need for "career development," i.e., changes in work assignment through lateral transfers.

4. *Economy.* Free trade will result in increased competitiveness in the Canadian economy. This will increase the rate of change in the economy. Government structural deficits have not yet been eliminated, so resource constraints will continue for the foreseeable future.

5. *Privatization.* There is likely to be a continued shift in service delivery to the private sector. More and more, the public service will become contract administrators rather than direct deliverers of service. This will result in a shrinking and stabilization in the size of the public sector.

6. *Decentralization.* Several of our branch functions could be affected by decentralization, including accountable advances, payroll corrections, chart of accounts and accounts payable. The implementation schedule is uncertain but the end result is that some clerical tasks will be eliminated in our organization.

TABLE 11.1 (Continued)
ENVIRONMENTAL TRENDS *Internal Environment*

7. *Political.* Any change in government resulting from an election or reorganization of the political party in power could completely alter the current priorities, trends and requirements of the branch. Flexibility must be incorporated into any developments to permit prompt response to such challenges.

Internal Environment

1. *Technological.* The focus of technology implementation will continue to shift from automating what we are currently doing to developing new and better ways of doing things and to improving the range and quality of services provided. Additional staff training in the use of computer technology will be required if we are to realize the full potential of existing and future computer hardware and software.

2. *Human Resources.* The shift from clerical to professional should continue but at a reduced rate. The branch has a good mix of age groups and should not be faced with a sudden turnover due to retirements. It will be an ongoing challenge to keep performance and morale up in a climate of increasing workloads, change, and uncertainty.

3. *Budgets.* There will probably not be a significant increase in resources unless there is an increase in governmental revenues. There is a risk of additional cutbacks and freezes particularly if there is a downturn in the economy.

4. *Workload.* The workload will continue to increase. The work will become more ad hoc and less routinized.

More often than not, organizations have a great deal of information to describe activities, and are well acquainted with the inputs--resources, equipment, and so forth--and their adequacy. They have less information on the outputs and their worth or effectiveness. For example, universities can measure students satisfaction with courses and instructors, but are less able to measure student learning or achievement based on the classes they take. Health organizations can measure the number of patients treated and the types of ailments, but they are less able to construct a health system for preventing many of society's illnesses. "If the organization cannot demonstrate its effectiveness against the stakeholders' criteria, then regardless of any inherent worth of the organization, stakeholders are likely to withdraw their support."[7]

The above two steps are often called a SWOT analysis. SWOT is an acronym that stands for (S)trengths, (W)eaknesses, (O)pportunities, and (T)hreats. Together, these provide a perspective on the organization's internal and external environment. See Table 11.2.

A Mission Statement

An organization's mission statement describes its justification for existence.[8] A mission statement requires the identification of the organization's stakeholders, or the persons or groups that place a claim on the organization's resources, time, or outputs. The key to success in most organizations is the satisfaction of stakeholders. A complete understanding of the stakeholders' needs is a basis for judging and evaluating success. It illustrates what resources are in most demand and what are most needed. The analysis will help clarify "whether the organization should have a different mission and set of strategies for different stakeholders."[9]

The mission statement can evolve after staff and group members respond to a number of questions which can be summarized by What, Who, Where, and Why and How.

What-	"What makes the organization distinct?"
Who-	"Who are the customers or client groups?"
Why-	"Why do we have the goals and motivators we have?"
Where-	"Where are the facilities and markets?"
How-	"How are we carrying out the production, marketing, sales distribution?"

What does the organization produce or do? This can be expressed in terms of the needs it meets and what makes the organization distinctive. It is not stated by the products or services supplied. This method of stating what is done allows the organization to look for new ways of meeting the needs; it expands the range of possibilities.

Who are the organization's clients, customers, or stakeholders? This

TABLE 11.2
**EXAMPLES OF OPPORTUNITIES AND THREATS,
STRENGTHS AND WEAKNESS, AND PROJECTS**

Opportunities

- There is a whole gamut of change taking place in the society.

- We need to find a focus & direction.

Threats

- Funding is inadequate.

- The physical location of the programs can foster isolation.

Strengths

- Sophisticated, timely & well organized system for budgeting.

- Staff are skilled and dedicated.

- The organization is dynamic. Everyone likes what we do, including the clients.

Weaknesses

- Government has little interest or funds for our clients

- Staff are expected to do more with less.

- Diversity may cause resources to be spread too thinly.

Project ideas

- Use building for other things
- Improve communications-- newsletter
- Retreats & planning sessions
- Develop a plan and direction
- Professional development opportunities
- Funding tactics

- Begin interest-based bargaining
- Improve staff morale
- Access volunteers
- Develop service philosophy
- Employees evaluations
- Job descriptions
- Staff benefits
- Find out what our clients need

provides a description of the existing or desired groups of clients and customers.

Why does the organization do what it does? *Why* the organization does what it does may be related to return on investment, profit for shareholders, provision of service, market domination, public image, technological leadership or some other broad objective. This part of the mission statement provides qualitative criteria for assessing of the organization's success.

Where does the organization do its business?

How and *Where* production occurs are statements of the mechanical aspects of production. This provides a description of the facilities and equipment. It also indicates how the organization responds to key stakeholders. An organization's mission statement describe the unique aim setting it apart from others. The statement refers to what the organization is in "business" for, or the purpose of existence. It is the "raison d'être." Table 11.3 includes examples of missions statements from a government department, a bank, and a forest product firm.

Developing a Philosophy Statement

A philosophy statement describes individual values, or the broad, general beliefs people feel are desirable or preferable. They are the underlying values and beliefs such as those reflected in the family like values of Japanese organizations. The following is an example of a philosophy statement from a religious organization.

- Of all the environmental influences in our lives, the most powerful ones are personal relationships.
- Of all relationships, it is the family relationship which leaves the deepest impressions and has the greatest effect on us.
- Fundamental to the work of society is an honouring and a respect for each person: adults and children needing our services; staff and volunteers working in our programs; board and society members providing direction for the organization;professional colleagues in other agencies and in government departments;benefactors who donate money, and goods and services in support of the centre's work.

A philosophy statement is just one tool for developing a "culture," which is described by groups of people who share values, history, and so forth. Like societies, organizations are said to have cultures. For example, there may be a service culture, an accounting culture, or a sales culture, depending on the organization or department. A philosophy statement evolves from the values people feel are most important. It articulates a view of realistic, credible, attractive, and desirable values and preferences. It can be described in terms of: client orientation, operational and decision-making philosophy, importance and responsibilities of employees. That is,

TABLE 11.3
EXAMPLES OF MISSION STATEMENTS

The Government Branch of Accounting and Reporting

The objectives of the Accounting and Reporting Branch are to achieve goals of excellence in service, accounting, and financial reporting and to create the working environment that will accomplish these goals.

Excellence in service is striving to meet the needs of our clients--taxpayers, Treasury Board, ministries, suppliers to government, etc.,--in an efficient, effective, and friendly manner.

Excellence in accounting and financial reporting is ensuring that there is an effective system for accurately recording government expenditures, revenues, assets, and liabilities on a timely basis, and ensuring that financial information produced from those records is accurate, timely, understandable, and useful to the reader.

The skills, abilities, and dedication of our staff are our most valuable resources. This belief is supported by our commitment to enhancing the knowledge, skills, and experience of our people and by encouraging risk taking, greater two way communications, more decision-making, a greater sense of trust at all levels and a better work environment overall.

We want our clients, as well as each staff member, to regard the Accounting and Reporting Branch as professional, innovative, fair, efficient and responsive, and providing leadership in the areas of our accountability, expertise, and responsibility.

Our objective is to promote consultation, teamwork and cooperation with our clients and with each other.

Our goal is to become the Canadian model for service, accounting and reporting in public sector financial administration.

TABLE 11.3 (continued)
EXAMPLES OF MISSION STATEMENTS

The Bank

To enhance our position as the Northwest's top provider of Financial Services and dominate the 1990's through Teamwork, Technology, Quality Service and Pride.

The Forest Firm

We (in this organization) will be the highest quality, lowest cost producer of Japanese wood products in the Pacific Northwest.

Bringing together innovative people, raw material and technology to produce a product that meets our customer requirements every time.

What are our desired values and beliefs for serving our client?

What are our values and beliefs about working together and making decisions which affect us?

What are our values and beliefs that describe how this organization should treat employees?

What are our responsibilities as employees?

The process of planned change assumes that planning is ineffective if the resulting plans do not correspond with the values and culture of the organization. The organization may or may not have a formal statement of "What we believe in." If the organization does not have a shared statement of values, the planning group needs to clarify the importance of such elements as profit, employee satisfaction, location, identity of preferred or unacceptable suppliers, clients or customers, avoidance of unionization, community relations and so on.

Mission and philosophy statements should be much more than just a statement of words and ideas. The process of articulating these statements is probably more important than the resulting words. The process should provide an opportunity to build a consensus of the most important values and beliefs. The discussions and debate clarify values of what staff feel are important and unimportant. They provide a signal to staff of the values others think are important, and a forum for people to debate issues. So, the resulting statements should, ideally, reflect the mission and values that people are committed to.

The Vision

Some organizations have articulated their vision of the future. There has been a growing recognition of the importance of such visions in developing commitment and in coordinating an organization's activities.[10] A vision is no more than an idea or a direction in the minds of people associated with it. For example, some managers commit their organizations to values outlined for "Excellence" organizations. Such values are described in Table 11.4.

A vision evolves from an understanding the possible and desired directions of participants. It is based on an understanding of the forces propelling and resisting new directions and the political and psychological climate. It integrates the values of people and the opportunities available.

Developing a vision can be an interactive experience where organizational participants become aware of others' ideas and directions. Such a process can increase the range of possible ideas and provides an understanding of how others in the organization think and feel. An interactive process for outlining a vision allows people to contribute their ideas and develop an understanding of what others are thinking. The process assumes that: (1) the relevant information for visioning is available and understandable, (2) the information is usable and manipulable, (3) the cost of obtaining, understanding, and using the information is not beyond one's capacity, (4) the vision encourages a style where members are constructively aiding its implementation, and (5) a process of adapting the vision can be accomplished without damaging the implementing process.[11]

It is conceivable that a visioning process might produce unrealistic ideas. There are a number of pitfalls: it may seem idealistic and a wish-list; the temptation arises to design the future for resolving issues addressed rather than recognizing new ideas; it may not reflect the values that people are committed to and may just be one person's ideals; it may divert energy into unproductive activities and create unrealistic expectations.[12]

Defining a vision is both an art and a science. It is a skill of provoking an innovative direction to respond to the needs of people and the resources available. The implementation of a vision will evoke new thoughts and understandings by focusing on those aspects of the situation that are most familiar and similar to previous experiences.[13] We attempt to answer questions such as: What is the

TABLE 11.4
VALUES OF EXCELLENT ORGANIZATIONS

Peters and Waterman's have suggested that excellent companies display general characteristics reflecting a culture of excellence.

A bias for action. This reflects a bias for getting things done rather than spending time analyzing the problem. This is described by developing "can-do" attitudes.

Closeness to the customer. Often, learning the customer's problems, preferences, and needs provides a very different way to develop an organization's structure. Instead of achieving production goals, the organization seeks to achieve goals which are important to customers.

Autonomy and entrepreneurship. Creating small units will provide a sense of ownership and control. People are more likely to feel that their efforts are essential and important in small, autonomous units.

Productivity through people. The involvement of people is important because they can provide more input and can more easily see how they can be rewarded for their work.

Hands-on, value drive. If managers keep in touch with the organization's mission, philosophy, and values, they can develop goals, structures, and procedures which are less likely to be resisted.

Stick to the knitting. All organizations have a more important mandate, mission, or business that they should stay in close contact with.

Simple form, lean staff. Organizations can be top heavy and more concerned with analysis and auditing. However, holding down administrative layers and top-level managers increases the focus on output rather than analysis.

Simultaneous loose-tight. Organizations should be "tight" in that they should have a common set of values that are widely understood to guide action. Organizations can be "loose" in allowing people a great deal of freedom to operate within these values.

probability that the organization will achieve its vision? Do we think that we can invest successfully in the new market? In answering these questions, we force the new problem or situation to be representative of things we already know.

Implementing a vision is an iterative and a trial and error process. Successive definitions of the vision have to respond to constraints such as cost, an inability to change the existing structure, and so forth. The home renovator has a similar problem. He/she has a vision of what is ideal, but is faced with data describing the way the present house is designed, the cost of renovation, values, and future plans.

The focusing process provides a way to identify many of the threats and opportunities affecting the organization's environment. It assists the participants to articulate values and beliefs they want the organization to realize. The most important strategic directions, therefore, are those responding to opportunities and threats within agreed-upon values. The process has also assisted in identifying a number of operational strengths and weaknesses of the organization. Operational issues which are important, therefore, are those responding to these strengths and weaknesses within agreed-upon values.

Developing and Implementing Action Plans

The initial planning conference can create a great deal of enthusiasm and commitment to the philosophy and mission. Such a conference can also provide a statement of the strategic direction, although it is just as feasible to do this after the conference is over. At the very least, an initial conference should provide a draft philosophy, a mission statement, and a general vision of how to achieve it. Subsequent conferences might be planned for developing strategic objectives and projects.

The implementation sequence is usually undertaken after the initial conference. Five steps are part of the implementation sequence: (1) identifying strategic issues, (2) formulating strategies and directions to focus these issues, (3) developing an action plan, (4) monitoring and evaluating, and (5) developing a commitment plan.

Developing Strategic Issues

The manager can use various kinds of knowledge in his/her prescription of an organization's direction.[14] First, there are the concepts, variables, and propositions from the basic disciplines of the social sciences. These could allow the manager or researcher to search for key concepts uniting the field. It could encourage the manager to search for examples of successful interventions used elsewhere. Managers might develop issues from ideas in popular books or articles. In some cases, it may be appropriate to make comparisons with similar ideas, rather than simply accepting the most popular. This might involve a content analysis of other relevant ideas, theories, or examples which have been used elsewhere. This is a dissection of the techniques and propositions of various approaches. Table 11.5 summarizes a number of the statements that are within the Canadian government's "Public Service 2000" strategy or vision for improving the level of satisfaction in the federal public service. Such a vision can be used in developing strategic directions and objectives.

The manager can also rely on data collected from the organizational system, as it is exhibited within the terminology of the organization's actors. This second type of data has more presence in common-sense interpretations, phrases, and modes of behavior. A strategic direction might be an individual's personal theory of management, as it has developed from years of experience and interaction. In this sense, the concepts useful to the direction are those which are most cherished by the manager.

To avoid overcommitting the organization to one set of strategies, participants can identify strategies within four functional areas: adaptive/regulative, coordinative, productive, and maintenance or problem-solving. Strategies concerned with designing how the organization relates to its environment are called adaptive functions. Coordinative strategies are concerned with directing, coordinating, and assuring that inputs are utilized appropriately for producing outputs. The strategies concerned with the production of outputs might be called the production function; those concerned with repairing and helping are labelled maintenance or problem-solving strategies.

Adaptive or regulative strategies start with the assumption that routine or problem-solving strategies only resolve immediate issues. Problem-solving might be a necessary step in keeping the regular level of objectives at a safe and comfortable level. However, adaptive strategies provoke new ideas from outside the firm.

Coordinative or managerial strategies focus on improving the administrative system to keep up with the changes which have occurred. These strategies are ways to improve the administrative system to keep up with new technologies and with changes of staff. *Productive strategies* focus on the regular, ordinary requirements for the survival of the organization. Such strategies may be further defined by stating the requirements needed to keep the organization stable. These strategies are usually introduced by the phrases "to produce" or "to provide a service," and represent a realistic statement of the organization's need or requirements during the period covered in the plan.

Maintenance or problem-solving strategies are designed to help the organization raise questions about its strengths and weaknesses. The purpose of collecting and analyzing strengths and weaknesses is to identify and interpret present directions and those possible with a more organized and deliberate plan. These strategies will usually be introduced after a thorough definition of the problems or needs.

TABLE 11.5
STATEMENTS FROM "THE PUBLIC SERVICE 2000:
THE RENEWAL OF THE PUBLIC SERVICE OF CANADA"

Selected Statements Summarizing Public Service 2000

The framework of Public Service 2000 - problem definition, values, mission and broad directions for the future - is the result of extensive work and thinking over the last decade. During this period, many Deputy Ministers have launched departmental initiatives to improve the way in which they do business. . . .

The findings and recommendations of the task forces were made available to all members of the Public Service, to Public Service unions and to the Consultative Committees before the Government made decisions about the matters covered in the reports and the broader issues at stake in Public Service 2000. . . .

Improving service to Canada and Canadians is the central theme of Public Service 2000. This means improving services to Ministers, the general public, and individual Canadians. . . .

Overall Strategies

From these broad statements, the Public Service 2000 identified strategic issues which related to:

1. Creating a client-oriented Public Service and setting out clear standards of service.
2. Developing consultation strategies to ensure that consultative skills are a key criterion in hiring staff, in their training and development and in the design of program activities.
3. Ensuring that regional people are involved in decision-making.
4. Ensuring that budgetary incentives are controlled at local levels, and not controlling budgets within fixed person-years.
5. Attracting and retaining Canadians of talent and providing training where appropriate.
6. Reducing the number of layers of senior management.
7. Encouraging mechanisms for encouraging "excellence" and not tolerating sub-standard performance.
8. By focusing more on results and clients, the importance of accountability based on shared values is going to be greater.
9. Emphasizing the importance of leadership in the public service.

Different and often conflicting needs and values are inherent in each of these strategies. In a typical manufacturing organization, these differences manifest themselves in interdepartmental "warfare." Production fails to understand and appreciate the constant modification of products and plans of the adaptive research and development department. The management subsystem is commonly perceived as intrusive and top heavy. These differences are a reflection of the conflict inherent in the tasks acted out by the different subsystems.

Strategic issues respond to the unique needs of the organization at a particular time. At certain times in an organization's life, it may be necessary to highlight certain strategies over others. This indicates that it may be inappropriate to think of strategic issues as responding only to the adaptive needs the organization might face. Changes in one functional area (in one subsystem) will affect other areas. Thus, after a major change, it might be appropriate to emphasize managerial or problem-solving issues.

The value of defining strategies in the four areas gradually becomes apparent as individuals learn more about the difficulties of implementation. For example, many people begin the process with idealistic visions of what the organization should be doing. If nothing else, the areas encourage people to recognize that organizations have different needs. It also encourages people to deal with some real and immediate issues identified as strengths and weaknesses of the organization.

Strategy identification can be a process of continually dividing strategies into actions and resources needed. The formulation of strategies can be a process of redefining strategies into more specific ones. This includes establishing the general strategy issue to be achieved, discovering a general set of means for accomplishing this goal, taking each of these means, in turn, as a new sub-strategy and discovering a more detailed set of means for achieving this. However, there is a danger of creating a difficult to administer and complicated process.

Alternatively, it is possible to use the following criteria for defining strategic issues:

1. The issue can be framed as a question that responds to participants' interests, as well as one which the organization can do something about. If the organization can not do anything about a threat or a weakness, it is not an issue.[15]
2. The issue can be defined from the point of view of those forces making it difficult to implement, as well as those enhancing its implementation. The force field analysis framework discussed in the following chapter can be useful for doing this.
3. The issue can be defined from the consequences of addressing and not addressing it. This will list just how important or strategic the issue really is.

That is, if there are no real positive consequences of addressing the issue, then, it is probably less important to carry out. The goal is to focus on adaptive, coordinative or managerial, productive, and maintenance strategies.[16]

Once strategies or objectives are set, people in organizations expect things to happen. When expectations fall through, the credibility of the whole process is threatened. One very important rule of thumb, then, is to pad the time requirements of each strategy so that the managers of the process can be assured of its achievement. Any strategy or objective which is not realized is worse than having no objective at all.

Formulating Strategic Directions to Focus the Issues[17]

A strategy is a "pattern of purposes, policies, programs, actions, decisions, or resource allocations that define what the organization is, what it does, and why it does it."[18] This usually involves, at least at the outset, a commitment to consider and adopt some significant variations to present activities. The srategic direction can be defined by the following steps: identifying practical alternatives for resolving the issues, enumerating the implementation requirements and barriers to achieving these alternatives outlining the major proposals, identifying actions and resources needed, and assessing the accomplishment of objectives.[19]

Practical alternatives provide a range of possible ways for resolving an issue. The alternatives are realistic possibilities requiring further research and understanding. It is also useful to identify stategic objectives much as those listed in table 11.6.

It is useful to identify *potential difficulties* or roadblocks detracting from the organization's ability to alter the desirable future. These are ideas and concerns about what may be more difficult to do. It is important to avoid associating those weaknesses with a particular person or group of people. Lack of training, low morale, poor management skills and other people-related deficiencies can be remedied. The weaknesses can be seen as problems to be solved, not failures to be punished.

There are also several *opportunities* or "avenues" strengthening the organization's pursuit of its desirable future. The strengths of an organization can be tangible (plant, inventory, market share, salary levels, patents) or intangible (quality of management, employee loyalty, public support). The qualities of certain people might be important strengths. In general, *proposals* are possible projects. They suggest possible actions and objectives needed to implement them. The selection and development of possibilities are simplified by listing numerous proposals. The choice of the most feasible action possibilities is an opportunity to "flesh the project out."

The initial proposals are probably vague and much larger in scope than is necessary. It is useful to find some experiences where it is possible to check these

TABLE 11.6
**EXAMPLES OF STRATEGIC OBJECTIVES FROM A
PROVINCIAL GOVERNMENT MINISTRY**

1. Develop and implement accounting policies to effectively address emerging issues in government including: fixed assets; determination of government reporting entity; accounting for pensions; guaranteed debt.

2. Ensure the Public Accounts are meaningful and relevant to the readers, especially the general public.

3. Automate the financial analysis function and the preparation of reports through the integrated use of the main frame and micro data bases to improve the accuracy and timeliness of financial reports, e.g., have the Public Accounts ready for presentation to the Legislature by September 30.

4. Develop and implement systems to improve accounts receivable administration, including the development and implementation of: (1) a coherent and comprehensive policy framework; (2) a government wide accounts receivable system; and (3) an integrated government wide system of credit management.

5. Continue decentralization of payroll adjustment functions allowing ministries to: (1) finalize statutory deduction adjustments, (2) have direct adjustment inputs to the MSA systems, (3) deposit recoveries from employees; (4) initiate cheque vouchers for payroll underpayment, and (5) initiate journal vouchers for some payroll deductions.

6. Develop and implement new methods of communication to meet the needs of clients not fully served by existing reports.

7. Provide staff with developmental training opportunities to help make them more effective in their current position and help prepare for future positions.

ideas out. This is a kind of "pilot work," as used by nautical people when a pilot is taken on board a ship to guide it through unchartered waters. This kind of pilot work is not the scientific firming up of procedures before one carries out research. Rather, this piloting process seeks to guide the ideas and principles into other waters. This is the process of talking to others, looking for examples in other settings, and seeing if the idea is relevant in the "sea."

After the proposals and projects are outlined, it is useful to begin outlining certain *actions* to be taken and the resources (money, people, and equipment) needed to carry them out. The task is to first align actions needed to responsible groups of people. These selected people can then identify the means to accomplish the actions.

One final step involves the identification of *criteria* to judge the accomplishment of the strategic objectives. This is not a rigid definition of the level of change expected based on measures currently existing. Rather, the criteria identify the standards people can use to focus their development. It is a way of articulating what one really wants to obtain when the change has been implemented for determining salaries or for constructing a rigid set of standards for career progress. That is, what will the complete project look like when it is finished?

Developing the Action Plan

A plan is a list of actions to follow in reaching objectives. It allows you to evaluate the activities before you commit yourself to them. While it does not guarantee that the best means will be selected, it offers a chance to improve one's batting average. Furthermore, the very act of planning may reveal that the original objectives have to be adjusted.

The planning also requires a statement of action goals. These goals, derived out of the previous phase, should be defined so that they are likely to get the organization's commitment of time, effort, and logistical support. Under normal circumstances, a well-defined objective is:

1. Specific: General goals are less useful than specific ones; the specific ones imply next steps or behaviors that need to be changed.
2. Performance-oriented: It guides what the person will do.
3. Realistic: The goal is obtainable.
4. Observable: People can see the result.

These goals can directly affect the way that resources are currently allocated. It can directly affect operational departments, in terms of resources needed, results expected and desired. Thus, it is important to asses their impact on finances, products and services, marketing, human resources and facilities. This should identify points at which the plans are to be reviewed with respect to of quantitative targets and contribution to overall strategy. The overall resources needed to effect the tactical plan will be determined at this point, and opportunities for cooperative work or coordinated efforts among departments can be examined carefully by the action research (A. R.) group or committee.

The A. R. group might analyze environmental reactions, envisioning circumstances likely to occur or affect the organization as a whole. Legislation, market changes due to economic conditions or consumer tastes, actions or reactions by competitors and other variables might affect the planning efforts.

The action plan is a tentative course of action, plotted in a sequence of logical steps. Indication of how the plan is to be pursued is drawn not only from statements of objectives, which reveal causes, but also from a re-evaluation of the research phase.

The word planning has many different meanings, ranging from military plans to sequential steps. In conventional planning, defining goals or objectives is usually performed at the beginning of the process; it is the step on which all other steps are based, not the product of those steps. It the crucial point of the whole process.

Many effective change processes use plans which are incremental and recognize people's needs at the time. These plans illustrate a grand design and the steps along the way. This form of planning might be compared to a sports analogy of identifying tangible actions which get the "ball rolling." It is a sports strategy of winning "one point at a time, one game at a time." The idea is compatible with studies on technological innovation indicating that small, rather than large, organizational changes play a key role in reducing production costs.[20] Small steps form the basis for a consistent pattern which attracts people who want to be allied with the venture. They deter opposition because it is difficult to argue with success. Also, grand designs incite opposition because people can not defend them properly, partially because they are vague. Small wins build confidence levels and provide an indication of success. This can be developed in the following manner:

1. The year may be divided into time segments;
2. The group should name each segment as they would the chapters of a book. Each segment may be outlined in terms of the activities to be done during implementation (i.e., Segment I--Introduction of Plan to the Organization: Segment II--Implementation);
3. Each segment may be outlined in terms of assigning responsibilities, costs, time;
4. Each segment may be outlined in terms of the resistance expected.

The major responsibility of the action research consultant, at this stage, is to facilitate the transfer of information and decisions of the action research group to the membership of the organization. He/she must encourage the group to develop different ways of communicating their results, particularly when they involve changes in one part of the organization. This "watchdog" or "conscience" function is often the most difficult role that the action research consultant must play.

Action may take the form of individual or group training, procedural changes, or policy changes, as dictated by the action plan. The pattern and pace of specific actions will vary according to the sequence in the general action plan.

Monitoring and Evaluating

In many cases, managers do not want to carry out a formal evaluation because the effects are so obviously positive or because of the perception that new information might be critical. Indeed, it is usually not possible to experimentally evaluate the impact of most organizational changes, as the original intervention has normally been revised and adapted so that it is very unlike its original definition. As a result, evaluations are not a normal part of many organizational changes.

At some stage in the change process, it may be appropriate to summarize the major outcomes and results of the change effort. Such an evaluation would be similar to the initial assessment, in that it provides a definition of the problems perceived and the need for change. What are some of the problems within the present system of operations? What are some the positive aspects within the present system of operations? In what areas are further changes required? Formative evaluations are conducted for the purpose of improving programs in contrast to making basic decisions about whether or not the program is effective. They might be thought of as systematic information-gathering activities providing a perspective on the implications of the new change. Such information gathering is a planned activity to facilitate the change rather than to evaluate the implications. In this sense, evaluation is not a separate activity which takes place after the change has been implemented. Rather, it occurs at various stages of the intervention, as an effort to provide information.

Formative evaluations can be planned at various stages of the change process. With this in mind, certain questions are appropriate to ask?

1. How will we know that the implementation is "on track?" What indicators do we have for monitoring the progress of the change? What should be evaluated? Which organizational variables are of most concern? (attitudes, outcomes, administrative processes, structures, operations)
2. How will we know whether our expectations or goals are "on track" with those in organization's culture? How have we assured commitment to our goals? What data collection methods should be used? How valid and reliable does the information have to appear?
3. What fears or resistances have been expressed? How will we know whether or not to respond? How will you respond? Who will we listen to? Who will we ask? When will we make adaptations? Who provides the most valuable

perspective and who might provide alternative perspectives?
4.   When will we initiate our plan? When should evaluations be carried out? How should information be reported? Is there a plan to feed back the data provided to the sources?
5.   How will we know that the change is worthwhile? What are the positive implications? What are some of the negative implications? What recommendations are useful for modifying the process?
6.   How can we make sure enthusiasm is maintained?

During the ongoing life of an organization, it is usually appropriate to monitor the impact of unique interventions. In this sense, specific operations of a project may have far reaching effects. Many actions are like "pebbles" thrown into the water of a lake. "A small intervention (a pebble) in a large system (a lake) can have far reaching effects (sending ripples to the far shore)."[21] A small operation may have effects which reverberate to other aspects of the program of change. Thus, on-going monitoring should be able to identify problems before they affect other operations.

Information gathering is a systematic process and there are many short-cuts. The short-cuts reduce the size of the samples and breadth of the variables covered. They should, however, provide data from multiple perspectives presented in an economical way. In the same way, the evaluation should not interrupt the change or provide data which are tangential to it. The prime purpose of evaluation is to monitor and assist the change.

An important element of any evaluation is the summary and feedback of results to those who originally asked the questions. When people are asked for their views, they are usually interested in seeing how others responded.

Developing a Commitment Plan

Not all change projects require that those affected be involved in the design in order for it to gain acceptance. For example, although a new telephone system may affect a number of people, staff may trust the manager to design an acceptable system without their involvement. For other changes, no amount of involvement may seem to encourage communication such as trying to introduce a non-smoking policy among a group of smokers. Involvement is important when it can:

1.   Increase the ability of employees to understand the future,
2.   Increase the ideas which may help respond to the future,
3.   Increase the employees' ability to operate within the new changes,
4.   Reduce unnecessary fears or anxieties.

Commitment to the research may not always be guaranteed through involvement. This is an issue graphically illustrated by Maruyama's description of the attitudes of prison inmates to being interviewed by people who were psychologists, sociologists, students, and reporters. The interviewers were trying to prove a theory, write a book, or get a degree, such purposes were irrelevant to the inmates. So, the prisoners felt exploited by the researchers and responded by developing phoney answers to minimize the intrusion.[22] Such projects, thought to be irrelevant to one's interests, cannot be salvaged by involvement.

There is nothing more insulting than being asked to participate just for the sake of participation. The single criterion of a commitment plan is to involve people when they are needed, and to use them on assignments assisting the organization's and individuals' objectives. Commitment requires objectives and goals which allow individual to articulate them in relation to their roles and responsibilities.

In any change process, a critical mass of people is necessary to assure implementation. This may mean two of nine participants who are the strongest informal leaders. In this sense, the critical mass includes "those individuals or groups whose active support will ensure that the change will take place.[23] "A commitment plan is a strategy described by a series of action steps devised to secure the support of those subsystems which are vital to the change effort."[24] Various questions could be part of such a plan:

1. Who are individuals or groups whose commitment is needed? What do they contribute?
    *   who is committed to the idea?
    *   who is able and willing to provide resources?
    *   who is willing to carry out and persevere with the new process?
2. Who are the people who form the critical mass?
    *   who can provide useful idea and insight?
    *   who are they?
    *   how have you assured commitment?
3. How will you know whether your expectations are "on track" with those in organization's culture?
    *   who are they?
    *   how have you assured commitment?
4. What contingency plans are possible for adapting the plan?
    *   What schedules be changed?
    *   What operations can be changed?

Various strategies or tactics can be used for implementing this commitment plan. These include problem-solving activities, educational and training activities, communications and briefings, changing the structure and reward system, listening, and problem identification activities. Generally, these are activities to manage the process of change.

SUMMARY

Organizational change involves an understanding of who in the organization must be committed to the change and to carrying it out. This is an understanding of the politics of the change. As a result, most change agents have suggested such terms as: "getting the executive's approval," "getting key people on board," "making sure the union is committed," and "having the membership understand it."

Implementation should also involve a systematic analysis to determine who is committed to the idea, who is able and willing to provide resources, and who is willing to carry out and persevere with the new process.

Action research seeks to encourage participants to take a direct part in planning the future of their organization. Such a research process will not naturally improve the level of worker satisfaction as this often hinges on the level of trust, openness, communications, problem-solving strategies, and role conflict experienced. However, there is oftento be some marked influence on decision-making at all levels, and especially at the supervisory and middle-management levels. Participating individuals also feel more comfortable with their relationship to others in the organizations.

Action research is normally a protracted set of activities. It cannot be completed in a matter of days but requires attention over a long period of time. This evolutionary planning approach seeks to encourage people to develop and activate mechanisms for communication and internalize the resulting changes in the culture. As the organization becomes more familiar and comfortable with the process, it should begin to take less time and less energy.

It would be unrealistic to maintain that action research will work in all organizations. There will be circumstances where the process will be unusable. For example, action research is not suitable in an organization whose senior executives refuse to consider the input of organizational participants or where a union forbids its members to participate. This approach is built on participation.

NOTES

1. E. G. Boring, "History, Psychology, and Science," in R. I. Watson and D. T. Campbell (eds.),(New York: John Wiley, 1963).

2. Compatibility is the degree to which an innovation is perceived as consistent with existing values, past experiences, and needs of the receivers. In this sense, a novel innovation can be either compatible or incompatible with the needs and values of the adopter.

3. E. Van de Vall, M. Bolas, C. Bolas, and T. S. Kang, "Applied Social Research in Industrial Organizations: A Evaluation of Functions, Theory and Methods," *Journal of Applied Behavioral Science*, vol. 12, 1976, pp. 158-177.

4. J. M. Bryson, *Strategic Planning for Public and Nonprofit Organizations* (San

Francisco: Jossey-Bass, 1988), pp. 52-53.

5. As part of the PIC analysis, participants can be asked to rate the probability, impact, and capacity to control. Those actions which are rather high on the following dimensions are those where action is needed.

6. J. Pfeffer and G. R. Salancik, *The External Control of Organizations: A Resource Dependence Perspective* (New York: Harper and Row, 1978).

7. J. M. Bryson, *Strategic Planning for Public and Nonprofit Organizations*, p. 55.

8. J. M. Bryson, *Strategic Planning for Public and Nonprofit Organizations*, p. 48.

9. J. M. Bryson, *Strategic Planning for Public and Nonprofit Organizations*, p. 52.

10. W. G. Ouchi, *Theory Z Organisation: How American Business Can Meet the Japanese Challenge* (Menlo Park, Calif.: Addison Wesley, 1981); T. J. Peters and R. H. Waterman, Jr., *In Search of Excellence: Lessons for America's Best-run Companies* (New York: Harper and Row, 1982); J. M. Bryson, *Strategic Planning for Public and Nonprofit Organizations*, pp. 60-61.

11. Chris Argyris uses the first three criteria for assessing a systems competence. See C. Argyris, *Intervention Theory and Method* (Reading, Mass: Addison Wesley, 1970).

12. Vision statements often neglect many pertinent factors in the systems they represent. There is a tendency to leave many factors out because they are difficult to define or are unknown. To omit a factor suggests it has zero effect--probably the only value that is known to be incorrect. On the other hand, some people may lose sight of the data and the mechanics of the data.

13. The process often relies on heuristics. It turns out that, to make even the most trivial decisions, we rely on "heuristics," a term which has been used to describe rules of thumb or tricks of the trade.

14. Three approaches can be used for developing strategic directions: a problem-solving, goal orientation, and visions of success. See J. M. Bryson, *Strategic Planning for Public and Nonprofit Organizations*, p. 59.

15. A. Wildavsky, *Speaking Truth to Power* (Boston: Little Brown, 1979).

16. J. M. Bryson, *Strategic Planning for Public and Nonprofit Organizations*, p. 59.

17. J. M. Bryson, *Strategic Planning for Public and Nonprofit Organizations*, p. 59.

18. J. M. Bryson, *Strategic Planning for Public and Nonprofit Organizations*, p. 59.

19. These steps are adapted from J. M. Bryson, *Strategic Planning for Public and Nonprofit Organizations*, pp. 59-60.

20. S. Hollander, *The Success of Increased Efficiency: A Study of Du Pont Rayon Plants* (Cambridge, Mass. : MIT Press, 1965).

21. R. Beckhard, and R. T. Harris, *Organizational Transitions: Managing Complex Change* (Menlo Park, Calif. : Addison Wesley, 1977), p. 88.

22. M. Maruyama, "Endogenous Research: Rationale" in P. Reason and J. Rowan (eds.), *Human Inquiry: A Source Book of New Paradigm Research* (Chichester, England: Wiley, 1981).

23. R. Beckhard, and R. T. Harris, *Organizational Transitions: Managing Complex Change*, p. 53.

24. R. Beckhard, and R. T. Harris, *Organizational Transitions: Managing Complex Change*, p. 54.

12

Managing the Process of Change

Eighty percent of success is showing up. Woody Allen[1]

Organizations are not usually purposeful, except as we try to explain their activities after the fact. Rather, organizational systems evolve in response to events and individual interests and values. Effectiveness, as a result, depends on the degree to which organizational members are able to work together within common values and respond cooperatively to emerging threats and opportunities. Otherwise, the organization's purposefulness can be lost in haphazard, seat-of-the-pants management reactions.

Implementation strategies and programs can be designed to respond to people's values and beliefs as well as issues strategic to the organization's development. Such issues are dealt with more effectively when groups and organizational members are pulling together. Thus, rather than expend membership energy on negotiating and manoeuvring to fulfil one's personal self-interest, the energy and common values are directed at common strategies, issues, and problems.[2] Such implementation strategies, it is argued, might be superior because they create longer lasting changes, and receive more employee commitment. Participative plans are more implementable because they respond to what employees can best do.

In this chapter, the major concern is the management of the process of change, or the conscious use of information for modifying practice. It is based on an assumption that no universal strategies exist for introducing, processing, and having change accepted. Rather, strategies are usually developed, either formally or intuitively, to respond to particular needs. A necessary prerequisite of a successful change may involve immobilizing the forces against it. Individuals have their defences to fight off threat, maintain integrity, and protect themselves against unwarranted intrusions of other demands. In addition, they may seek ways to defend themselves against ill-considered and overly prescriptive innovations.[3]

The implementation of change, both in terms of its acceptance and its impact requires an understanding of why people resist. This chapter outlines some of the characteristics of successful change projects and then outlines skills and principles to assist the process. The principles and skills are not irrefutable rules of management. Rather, they are this author's view of a process for managing change.

CHARACTERISTICS OF SUCCESSFUL AND UNSUCCESSFUL CHANGE

Why do we have so much difficulty implementing our plans when there seems to be so much information about the process? So often, well-conceived ideas and plans do not get implemented, and only temporarily provide a direction for change. It seems that many implementation difficulties, unforeseen events, and unrepresented perspectives are not represented.

A review of studies on the implementation process leads one to question how ideas, plans, and theories are used in practice. This questioning comes from various perspectives and illustrates the character of successful and unsuccessful change.

Theories of organizational behavior do not unite the field. Many of the most important organizational behavior theories have been judged by researchers to be of little importance for providing a consensus for the field.[4] Traditionally, research aims to increase our understanding and ability to predict. The underlying hope is that if enough research in conducted, social scientists will have theory on which to provide a better understanding of behavior. However, the increased levels of research have not provided any consistent understanding of the relationship of known variables, and each new research seems to provoke more variables which could be of interest. The numerous studies in organizational behavior have not brought us any closer to more integrative theories.[5] Few traditional theories appear to account for more than a small fraction of the variance in dependent variables. In addition, there is no reason to believe that a strong relationship found in one study will be confirmed in later studies.[6]

Grounded concepts tend to assist practice. Many academic theories are accused of having a low level of application, and having little use for solving organizational or social problems. With some exceptions, theories do little more than support the status quo. In fact, they may even play a negative role in the change process.[7] In one study, a team of American and Dutch social scientists studied 120 projects of applied social research in The Netherlands. These included projects in industrial and labor relations (40), regional and urban planning (40), and social welfare and public health (40). Most of the conclusions were drawn from interviews because the researchers felt that they could not reliably judge the range of projects. They found that the projects which used grounded concepts and qualitative methods had a higher level of utilization. These projects used theories developed to provide relevant information for feedback to the organization and for focusing an organization's direction.[8]

Managers use their own frameworks. Managers do not seem to want to use academic theories, even those which are most practical. They do not seem to have the time to theorize, as they spend most of their time with others in performing a large number and variety of activities.[9] As a result, a manager's theories emerge from practice, as they attempt to understand various problems and focus organizational change. Managers claim that many books and articles about management have little to do with what they consider important and relevant for real-world problems.[10] They argue that the many theories are contradicting and any attempt to construct an integrative theory leads to unusual complexity.[11]

Change relies on changing people's beliefs. The road to implementation does not rest on ingenious models, advanced procedures, mathematical and statistical schemes, new concepts, precise quantitative techniques, or an adherence to the canons of experimental principles. Implementation relies on informal processes, such as contacts between researchers and practitioners. In settings where contacts are more frequent over the course of the research, there may be more application of the findings and collaboration transcending the impact of the study. Several factors seem important to these contacts: getting interim feedback on study findings, establishing "personal" contacts with researchers, having several people in the unit involved early on with this study, having substantive exchanges with researchers prior to dissemination, overcoming initial suspiciousness toward the researcher and research, and having contact between supervisors/directors and the research team. The key component in implementation may be the amount and quality of the contact between the change agents and clients.[12]

Organizational change seems to evolve from what participants perceive.[13] Systems of meaning develop through the repetition of behavior and socialization. These serve as the foundation for the construction of beliefs, attitudes, and perceptions. Changes in organizations are usually associated with changes in participant's belief systems and systems of meaning.[14] These disruptions are usually uncomfortable because they challenge and question a view of reality. Thus, change will be unlikely unless there is a compelling reason to do so.[15]

There are no easy solutions to these problems. Our present theories of change do not seem adequate to use confidently in changing organizations. At best, the theories can be used as blueprints or guides. We might encourage the development of grounded theories and concepts to assist our work in organizations.

PRINCIPLES AND SKILLS FOR MANAGING CHANGE

The previous chapters have outlined an action research approach to organizational development. They outline strategies for gathering research and information, defining an organization's direction which recognizes possibilities and obstacles, and implementating changes by relying on a process of change which is managed by groups and individuals.

The principles and ideas in this book do not offer a "cookbook" approach for implementation. They offer a framework for managing organizational change. Certain skills or principles are useful for facilitating the change process. These principles refer to: developing a collaborative relationship; conceptualizing the impact of the changes to be made; recognizing the sociotechnical criterion; using participation and groups appropriately; changing behavior through problem-solving discussions; and recognizing that expectations amplify or reduce resistances.

The Relationship Issue in Changing Organizations

Certain people may be more successful in using the principles and suggestions offered in the previous chapters. A major reason for the lack of success of organizational development efforts may be due to the assumptions researchers and clients share about the organizations they are working in.[16]

The successful implementation of an action research design depends to some extent on the relationship between the researcher and those being researched. Traditionally, researchers tend to focus on the technical aspects of research such as developing a sound research design, developing reliable questions to ask, and collecting and analyzing data. Managers and researchers, on the other hand, may be more concerned with the change and implementation. The relationship issue is concerned with designing research and change to respond to both the technical needs of the researcher and the social needs of organizational participants.[17]

The relationship between researchers and organizational members can be characterized as a transactional process. It is a complex sociotechnical system composed of: the researcher's needs and perceptions and those who are being researched, and the technical demands of the research design. It is the researcher who assigns the "role descriptions" of researcher and subject, and determines what will be considered research results. Similar dynamics are also found in relationships involving the consultant and the consulting process, the teacher and the educational process, and the manager and the managerial process.

The sequence of encounters between the researcher and participants might be characterized as a sophisticated game where there are plausible and explainable outcomes.[18] The ingredients of the game, according to Frank Friedlander, are based on the transactions between people as revealed in their motivations and payoffs.[19] Both "the researcher and subject cooperate, each with unexpressed (and frequently different) motivations, and each expecting and receiving some payoff."[20] The game has a number of rules, which are determined by the researcher's purpose and instructions. Table 12.1 illustrates the various roles and levels of interaction between the researchers and participants.

In transaction 1 (RP-SP), the researcher hopes that the subject will perceive the experimental stimuli and researcher in an authentic manner and the subject will respond within the constraints of the research.

Transaction 2 (RR-SS) is the most likely research/subject relationship. Here, the subject acts according to the rules of the game and plays the make-believe role assigned. This is the role of the "good subject."

Transaction 3 (RR-SU) is a game which cannot be predicted or understood. The subject may not understand, be aware of, or may resist the researcher's cues.

The transaction model suggests that difficulties arise when the researcher and subject are not playing the same game. It is the angular or cross-transactions causing difficulty, particularly in regard to unknown quantities in the research. When the two parties are reacting at different levels, results may be misleading and the transaction may be nonconstructive.

The bottom parallel transaction (RP-SP) might provide more valid data in a research relationship. Such strategies are more inclusive and involve communications, attitudes towards others, and ways of defining issues.

1. *Communications.* An inclusive research process is fostered by open and honest communication of relevant information between researcher and subject, while an exclusive strategy results from techniques used for obtaining information about others who may be unwilling to communicate.

2. *Attitude toward one another.* An inclusive research process is aided by a trusting, friendly attitude and a willingness to respond helpfully to the other's needs and requests, while an exclusive strategy is encouraged by methods which exploit the other's needs.

3. *Concern with issues.* An inclusive research process is fostered by a definition of mutual interests between researcher and participants, while an exclusive process is stimulated by the view that the solutions to problems meets only one party's interests.[21]

Friedlander's model suggests the researcher might draw not only upon a set of highly developed research skills, but also upon basic managerial skills for understanding participants' interests and needs.

Conceptualizing the Impact of the Changes to Be Made

Changes can be both disrupting and nondisrupting, positive and negative, and driving and restraining. That is, whenever one introduces a change, there is the potential that there will be a number of factors to enhance or assist the

**TABLE 12.1
RESEARCH/SUBJECT TRANSACTIONS IN THE
CONVENTIONAL RESEARCH PARADIGM**

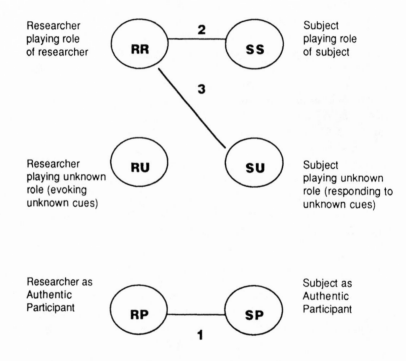

implementation. There will also be a number of factors or events inhibiting the change from becoming a reality.

There is some compelling logic that all organizational changes enter into a field of interacting forces, much like a force field. The interacting positive and negative forces are in a state of equilibrium, and they are relatively stable within themselves. There are a range of positive and negative forces, each restraining each other.

Certain laws from physics might be used to explain this. For example: *A body will remain at rest when the sum of all the forces operating upon it is zero. A body in motion will remain in motion until it is acted upon by another force.*

As changes are introduced, they create stresses and strains, disrupting the normal equilibrium. External or internal factors (stimulus) disrupting this equilibrium are countered by forces restoring it as closely as possible to its previous state. There is a tendency for systems to adjust, to seek balance in the light of change.

This equilibrium principle is best exemplified in observing the physiological functioning of the body, as adrenalin and white corpuscles are immediate responses to injury or illness. Or, the body's internal thermostat assists in helping to adjust to changes in temperature through shivering or sweating. In organizations, there is a constant inertia or resistance to new changes affecting individual habits and group norms. This does not mean that organizational systems are never modified by change, but they continually try to adjust to it.

Suppose for example, that a manager wished to introduce a new performance evaluation system, one which is based on assessments by peers. In this system, peer groups of managers would evaluate each other and be responsive to goal setting and providing mutual support and feedback.

The forces in Table 12.2 illustrate a force field which this new change may have to enter into. Among the forces tending to improve the chances of the implementation of the new peer group system are: supportive peer group relationships; an opportunity to work in a team; and an opportunity to be recognized for what we do. These forces, and any like them, are called *facilitating forces.*

Among the forces that tend to lower the chances of implementation (which might be called *impeding forces*) might be: not wanting to be evaluated by certain people in groups; not wanting to be evaluated at all; wanting the manager to evaluate us individually instead; lacking experience and inability to provide constructive feedback; the Board of Directors may not approve (they are a bunch of controlling people).

As in the case of the movement of bodies in physics, the balance of *facilitating* and *impeding* forces determines the possibilities of implementation, even though the "body" being acted upon is a human thing (the behavior of a group of people). As in physics, the forces need not be of the same magnitude. The result, illustrated in Table 12.2, is a series of opposing forces of varying

---

TABLE 12.2
A FORCE FIELD EXAMPLE

The change is: Introducing a new peer evaluation system.

FACILITATIVE FORCES	IMPEDING FORCES

Supportive peers | Not liking some people in group

------> | <----------------

Stimulation of working as a team | Do not want evaluations at all

--------------> | <--------------------

Recognition | Want manager's evaluation

------------------------> | <----------------------------

| Lack of experience
| <--------------

| Board of Director's approval
| <------------

(Present)
(State)

---

strengths (represented by varying lengths). Attempts to induce change by removing or diminishing opposing forces will generally result in a lower degree of tension. An important restraining force that requires removal in our example is the managers' lack of experience and skills in dealing with conflict. As the managers acquire new skills, a key restraining force could be removed.

Changes accomplished by overcoming counter-forces are likely to be more stable than changes induced by additional or stronger driving forces. Restraining forces which have been removed will not push for a return to old behaviors and ways of doing things. If changes come about only through the strengthening of driving forces, the forces supporting the new level must be stable. For example, many work groups are stimulated toward new ways of working together, only to find the former behaviors and habits re-emerging shortly after return to the day-to-day job. If the change started by the learning and enthusiasm of working together is to continue after the session, some other driving force must be ready to take the place of the initial stimulation.

One efficient way to enhance change is to alter the direction of one of the forces. If the managers in our example can be persuaded to "encourage" the board of directors to support a peer system, they might find more encouragement than they previously thought existed. Thus, the removal of a powerful restraining force (expected board disapproval) becomes an additional, strong driving force (actual board support) in the direction of change.

A group or organization stabilizes its behavior when the forces pushing for change are equal to the forces resisting change. Lewin called the result of this dynamic balance of forces the "quasi-stationary equilibrium." In our example, the equilibrium is represented in Table 12.2 by the mid-point between the two arrows.

The management team is interacting at its present level because of a balance of organizational and individual needs and forces. Thus, change will only occur if the forces are modified so that the system can move to and establish itself at a different level where the driving and restraining forces are again equal. The equilibrium can be changed in the direction of establishing a peer system by: (1) strengthening or adding forces in the direction of change, (2) reducing or removing some of the restraining forces, or (3) changing the direction of the forces.[22]

Essential Tasks and the Sociotechnical Requirement

All systems have to focus on a range of tasks--adaptive/regulative, coordinative, productive, and maintenance--in order to survive. Tasks concerned with designing how the organization relates to its environment are called regulative or adaptive; they assure that the organization is structured to respond to the needs of its clientele. Coordinative functions are concerned with directing, coordinating, and assuring the inputs are used appropriately for producing outputs and are focused on administrative objectives of supporting other subsystems. The tasks concerned with the production of outputs--goods or services--might be called the production function. The maintenance subsystem seeks to use its reserve of resources to maintain and repair any parts that wear out, and to provide staff services and support for other subsystems.

Systems problems often emerge from certain parts of the system disrupting the equilibrium of other parts. Essentially, disruptions take the form of incompatibilities between the components of the larger system. Each subsystem performs tasks so that it can grow and serve itself and the organization as a whole.

The above principles describe the characteristics of a technical system. Every technical system is embedded in a social system and is influenced by its culture and values, by a set of generally acceptable practices, and by the roles the culture permits for its members. The tasks of the social system are generally concerned with the individual's growth and achievement within the norms defined by those involved, as well as the stimulation of these norms through new challenges and information. The task is oriented toward gaining commitment and morale.

The incompatibility between the technical and social systems is one of the potentially most vivid systems interactions. The history of organizations illustrates how "time and motion" study engineers sought to design the most efficient technical systems. In terms of technical criteria, these designs have emphasized: efficiency, specialization, unity of command, and so forth. These and other technical interventions have interfered with individuals who have needs for independence.

Underlying these technical systems is a social system, which is made up of the values, beliefs, and interests of the participants. In terms of organizational change, certain social criteria might be important: if participants in any change see it as reducing rather than increasing their current burdens; if the change accords with the values and beliefs which are acknowledged by participants; if the change offers an opportunity to learn and grow, and support is there to assist this; and if the change allows people to participate in how it will affect them, and so forth.

Getting Commitment Through Participation and Groups

There is often controversy over whether or not participative methods should be used in organizational decision-making. Participation is often risky; there is a risk of collecting information and perceptions that the manager may not really want, and hence raising expectations about issues unwanted. In addition, participation has long been argued, ever since the Hawthorne experiments, to interfere with or invalidate scientific results.

Those who argue for participative methods suggest that it is an important element in the derivation of information. That is, effective change is more likely if organizational members discover for themselves the various factors affecting a problem. In addition, effectiveness may be enhanced if the parties have been able to perceive and understand how the solution affects them.[23] It is generally conceded that people support their own ideas more enthusiastically than if they were imposed by others.

The intrinsic rightness or quality of a decision and its acceptance are not always separate factors. Sometimes, organizational problems cannot be achieved if individuals act independently. Certain artistic endeavors, such as the creation of the Mona Lisa, are best left to individual artists who have the instinct and intuition to provide an artistic interpretation. However, many organizational and societal endeavors are usually social rather than individual experiences. They are expressions of what an assortment of individuals can accomplish by using their collective creativity. Organizational problem-solving is not a unique individual experience. People usually need the help of others to carry out most organizational tasks. While Leonardo da Vinci could have used a committee of artists in creating the Mona Lisa, he certainly did not need them. On the other hand, a committee could have easily created a grotesque art form which we would have hidden away in some remote place. Organizations require the assistance of others in order to accomplish certain tasks. If a problem is of concern to many people, or if it is likely that the experiment will affect many people, the action research should involve these people.

Participation does not mean that people should be encouraged to be needlessly involved in the sharing of information. There is nothing that angers some people more than "tokenistic involvement." Participation does not mean that managers need to encourage individual autonomy or "shop floor" democracy. It does not assume that individuals will have the ultimate control for managing their own work-place. It does not replace autocratic management with "laissez-faire" and directionless styles.

A participative philosophy recognizes that different levels of participation may be appropriate at different stages of the change endeavor. Many problems in organizations require creative solutions and are complex. These solutions to these problems are interconnected to other issues and are more easily resolved through concerted rather than individual action. There are times when participative processes might not be as appropriate. Several conditions--the maturity of the subordinates, the creativity required in the decisions, the structure of the task--dictate how successful participative processes might be.

1. A participative philosophy assumes that subordinates have the technical expertise and personal maturity to be a constructive asset in participative decisions. Technical competence of the decision might be improved if contributing individuals have the knowledge and skill that might add to the decision. In addition, a participative philosophy assumes that individuals are willing to take on the responsibility for the decision and have the maturity to provide input in a constructive manner.

2. Creative or discovery oriented tasks require participative processes more than standardized tasks. Creativity requires unique and diverse perspectives, intuition, and energy, which can be attained when people work together in a

participative manner. Standardized and routine problems require defined solutions, and therefore might be completed by individuals acting alone.

3. Certain interconnected tasks are sometimes more difficult to implement if they do not involve other participants or groups. Piecing divergent pieces of a task together suggests that one person's solution may be the source of inspiration for another. Such tasks may require different ways to work together: pooled; sequential; and reciprocal. Being a member of a "track" team is a pooled task where the combination of individual outputs produce a team output. Being a participant on a "relay" team is a sequential task where one person's output will directly affect the next sequence of operations. A reciprocal task, such as being a member on a "hockey" team requires the dynamic interaction of people working together.

The culture of the organization, among other things, influences employee expectations. A democratic pattern of leadership may be seen as a sign of weakness in organizations where management has traditionally exercised absolute authority. Where it is the rule rather than the exception that the leaders in organizations rule by orders, a sudden change in the principle of leadership towards a democratic pattern may be taken as a sign of weakness, or lack of knowledge and confidence.

Other basic considerations guide whether or not one shares problems with subordinates, or gives a group some responsibility for decisions. These describe the importance of: quality or rationality; acceptance or commitment needed by employees in implementing a decision; and time required to make the decision.[24]

Using Groups

One of the more successful ways to change people might be to change groups. Individual change is slow and labor intensive, even in small organizations. When the focus is group change, there is a stronger compulsion for the new behavior to be reinforced by other group members.[25]

The findings of Lewin and his associates illustrate how powerfully social forces affect group decisions and actions. Group discussions generate pressures for action much more effectively than when decisions are made by the individuals alone. The group's impact can be felt in several ways:

1. Findings can be examined in a broader perspective, because the group brings together a rich variety of experience.
2. Groups provide a psychological situation in which superiors and subordinates can work together without wide role differences.
3. Improved interpersonal relations in cohesive groups leads to more acceptance, trust, and confidence among members. Each member develops a sense of security and personal worth by being involved in a cohesive group.
4. Groups, if trust is properly developed, are helpful for the open discussion of problems and frustrations.

5.   Group decisions put powerful pressure, in the form of reciprocal expectations, on each member to carry out what the group has agreed on.[26]

Through groups discussions, findings can be examined in a broader perspective because a group brings experience that is much richer and more varied than any one individual. Group discussions, by allowing the pooling and exchange of a wider range of information, allow supervisors and subordinates, at all levels, to work on developing possible solutions. Also, group discussions help supervisors to understand what members in the organization expect of them concerning their relationship with their subordinates and association with their supervisors.

Group methods are often useful for obtaining information and feelings about how well the organization is functioning and the problems they are experiencing. This type of diagnosis is valuable where the dimensions of organizational life can best be determined by those directly concerned. It is often only the members of the group who can decide which factors are likely to have the greatest impact on its effectiveness.

Group norms discourage individuals from deviating from the group and conform to the ways the group has chosen to operate. There is a greater chance of change if new norms are introduced to groups rather than to individuals alone. Changes to new procedures and methods are more easily introduced if members feel that they have devised them.[27]

Group forces can assist in facilitating changes and redefining issues. Participation in group discussions and decisions concerning the future can set in motion pressures for action which are more effective than when individuals act alone. Groups can lose effectiveness in certain situations where there are forces which bolster lower standards. These situations occur when groups become insulated from their environments or try to bolster their internal morale at the expense of critical thinking. One of the common norms appears to be remaining loyal to the group by sticking to its policies even when the policies are working badly. Other symptoms can be observed when members of decision-making groups avoid being critical in their judgements, and adopt a soft, non-confronting line of criticism. These are cases of "concurrence--seeking" behaviors over providing realistic and honest appraisals. In some cases, more cohesive groups can adopt this self-protecting behavior, although this need not always be the case. This simply suggests that the advantages of groups can be lost if they develop powerful psychological pressures to be protective rather than honest and positively critical.

TABLE 12.3
ASSUMPTIONS OF CHANGE

Communicate & Control	Problem-solving	Laissez-faire
Description		
Employees are told about change in a timely & efficient manner.	Managers & employees are seeking to respond to mutual interests.	Researchers or managers respond to requests of others & pay no attention to mutual interests or rational methods.
Assumption		
The best solution is efficiently implemented by a technical plan.	The best solution responds to mutual interests of all all parties.	The best solution to a problem is one that responds to employee needs & frustrations.
Relationship		
Manager's role is to manage & control deviations & problems.	Relationship between parties is valued as much as each party's goals.	Manager's task is to understand employees'needs.
Power and responsibility		
Manager has power and responsibility for change.	Managers and others parties share responsibility for change.	Management may have the the power, but it is delegated to employees.
Outcome criteria		
Quickness & efficiency.	Understanding, commitment, responsibility.	Satisfaction.

Changing Behavior through Problem-solving Discussions

Managers and researchers spend a great deal of time laying out plans, making decisions, and implementing. They are constantly involved in information exchanges, briefings, and related exchanges relaying instructions, explaining plans or decisions, and motivating individuals to follow through on decisions and directions. The function of many such meetings is to assure that organizational procedures are "communicated" and to check to see that they are appropriately carried out or "controlled," as illustrated in Table 12.3. In such a "communication and control" strategy, the task is to communicate one's wishes and gain obedience and loyalty from group members.

A "communication and control" strategy assumes that each party has a position to be communicated. However, many such communications never get implemented because they produce resistance to change. Placing the person in a spotlight encourages him/her to hide defects, and become defensive in justifying old behaviors. If the communication is threatening, it may induce frustration, hostility, and stubbornness. When a person seeks to defend a behavior, he/she seeks to justify a position rather than search for new or better ways of working.[28]

"Laissez-faire" change practices are those where the managers and change agents are conciliatory when faced with disagreements, even at the expense of objectivity or fairness. The goal is to fulfil personal interests or the needs of specific groups. It is a change approach which is "unfocused," and directionless, but is often assumed to parallel participation and consultation.

There is a third strategy called "problem-solving." It seeks to recognize that communication and change need to respond to the mutual needs of each party. An entirely different objective is implied when a manager calls a group together to develop ideas or make discoveries. The manager's role is to state objectives and directions, act as coordinator, facilitator, and chairperson of the group. The strategy assumes that organizational members are better able than anyone else to define their problems and propose solutions.

The objective of problem-solving is to stimulate employee growth and development, and create enthusiasm for research and change. Problem-solving strategies assume that certain alternatives are not yet apparent and they can best be discovered through the combined problem solving efforts. Such strategies seek to identify alternatives by first examining the interests and concerns underlying each party's respective position.

In some cases, trust can be manufactured by technique. For example, certain verbal behaviors such as "Mhm," and "Good," and nods of one's head tend to reinforce certain responses.[29] The technique of problem-solving includes: (1) active listening--phrasing or trying to understand the thoughts, attitudes and feelings, (2) using pauses--or waiting patiently for others to investigate their own inner feelings, (3) reflecting feelings--or showing that one understands, and (4) summarizing feelings--or updating the progress of the interview. Certain practices assist in establishing joint responsibility for an issue. These include: verbally acknowledging with positive attention to issues, actively working with the contribution by summarizing and rephrasing it, synthesizing and coordinating contributions with other ideas, stating the issues fully, and observing rules to control the participation and tension.

However, problem-solving relies on much more than technique. It involves gaining respect, genuineness, understanding, and acceptance and empathy. Genuineness in thoughts and feelings reduces a person's ambivalence and uncertainty about exposing oneself. Curiosity and exploration is more likely to be aroused in a free and secure environment; exploration is likely to cease when danger or threats of punishment are introduced.

Using Supportive Language in Communicating a Message

Most of the more important data we receive from others comes from the personal communications and feedback of others. The competence for structuring a message is also important for communicating research results and providing feedback to employees after new organizational changes have been introduced. Table 12.4 summarizes characteristics of communications evoking supportive and defensive behaviors.[30]

Communications describing a person's behaviors vs. personal traits is less likely to produce resistances. This implies that it is more useful to use adverbs relating to actions rather than adjectives relating to personal qualities.

Feedback reflecting observations vs. inferences refers to what the communicator sees or hears in another's behavior rather than what one interprets and concludes. This implies that feedback should relate to specific situations directly observed in the "here and now," rather than those in the abstract "there and then." Feedback is generally more meaningful if given as soon as appropriate after the observation. Certain aspects of the feedback--the what, how, when, where, and what is said--are more likely observable characteristics. The "why" of what is said takes us from the observed to the inferred, and involves questions of motive and intent.

Feedback which describes rather than judges whether behaviors are good or bad provokes less resistance. Evaluative communications can also be made by expressions, manner of speech, tone of voice, as well as verbal content. Descriptive communications, by contrast, tend to arouse a minimum of judgement.

Problem-solving vs. persuasive language is less controlling and directing. In persuasive communication, there is often an implicit attempt to control and redirect the other person. Methods of control include: legalistic insistence on detail, gestures and facial expressions, and the use of examples to persuade another person. A problem-solving orientation seeks to identify issues of mutual

TABLE 12.4
CHARACTERISTICS OF THE
MESSAGE ENHANCING COMMUNICATION

Supportive Characteristics in Message	Defensive Characteristics in Message
Focused on Behavior	Focused on Person
Focus Feedback on Observations	Focus Feedback on Inferences
Focus Feedback on Description	Focus Feedback on Judgement
Focus on Problem-solving	Focus on Persuasion and Control
Focus on Provisional Information	Focus Feedback on Certainty
Focus on Mutuality	Focus on Strategy
Focus on Equality	Focus on Superiority
Focus on Conditions	Focus on Total Information

concern to both communicator and listener. It allows the receiver to define theissue from his/her own perspective, to set goals, to make one's own decision, and evaluate one's progress.

Provisional vs. certain language may be perceived as more compromising and less dogmatic. One reduces resistances when there is the opportunity to correct or supply new information. There is a difference between those who are seeking to search for new information as opposed to those who are wishing to assure it is accepted. A problem-solving meeting is a mechanism for exploring alternatives rather than providing answers or solutions. In this sense, feedback is given as a method of sharing ideas and information rather than giving advice. This leaves room for people to decide how to use the ideas and information.

Communication which serves mutual vs. strategic interests provides a context for the definition of goals. One of the adverse reactions to some of the human relations techniques is the feeling that they are gimmicks and tricks to involve others or to persuade them to change their behavior. In contrast, communications which seeks to define mutual interests in problem-solving is more likely to recognize another person for the information he/she brings.

Superiority vs. equality in communications is evoked when one person expresses more power, wealth, knowledge, and control. These characteristics can arouse feelings of inadequacy and can provoke reactions such as jealousy, competition, and rightness. They imply that a person is not willing to enter into a problem-solving relationship and that the feedback is one way. In contrast, communication seeking to define equality may provoke less resistance. It encourages participation, mutual problem-identification, and teamness.

Supplying the total information vs. needed information may overload a recipient's ability to receive the communication. When more information is given than is needed, the communicator may be satisfying his/her own needs rather than those of the recipient. One reduces resistances when feedback and communication is adjusted to take into account the needs or the capacity of individuals to absorb the new information as well as the "value" it has. Since feedback often involves emotional reactions, it is important to be sensitive to when it is given. Feedback is more relevant when it is adjusted to what the recipients needs for their decisions at that time. The way the message is communicated is as important as the content of the message.

Recognizing that Expectations Amplify or Reduce Resistances

Individuals and groups are often motivated by beliefs about themselves and goals about what they can achieve. Some beliefs emerge from initial judgments or biases. A person's belief may, in the beginning, be based on incorrect or scanty information. They provide the concepts of how an individual operates and are powerful in personal goal setting.

Beliefs are like irrefutable truths such as those held about blue collar workers, union members, women, and certain racial groups. The beliefs might suggest that blue collar workers are lazy and are motivated only by money and self-interest. They might suggest that union members do not want to work with management or that certain racial groups do not have the intelligence to carry out managerial tasks. People who hold such beliefs may unconsciously collect facts and information to fit their thinking.

Under experimental conditions, Bruner and Postman asked subjects to identify a series of playing cards; most of the cards were normal, but some were unconventionally unique. For example, there was a red six of spades and a black four of hearts. After each set of exposures, the subject was asked what was seen; a second set of exposures followed where the subject was allowed to see the cards for a slightly longer period of time. The subjects were able to identify most of the normal cards, even with the shortest exposures. The anomalous cards were almost always identified without hesitation as normal. The four of hearts might be called the four of either spades or hearts. That is, the subjects fell back on the categories they previously used based on their prior experience.

With further increases of exposure to the anomalous cards, subjects did begin to hesitate and to display an awareness of an anomaly. When exposed to the red six of spades, subjects were able to identify it, but they did hesitate. Some said: "There is something wrong with it. The black has a red border."

Further increases in exposure resulted in more confusion and hesitation. Then, finally, and sometimes quite suddenly, most subjects would produce the correct identification. After doing this with two or three anomalous cards, they would have little difficulty with the others. A few subjects were never able to recognize the anomalous cards. Even at forty times the average exposure required to recognize the normal cards, more than ten percent of the anomalous cards were never correctly identified.[31]

A second set of classical studies, on selecting employees, suggests that interviewers make early judgements on a candidate's suitability. Most interviewer decisions changed very little after the first four or five minutes of the interview. That is, interviewers make their judgements very early and held to them, letting new information reinforce the initial decision. Studies in the Canadian Army concluded that personnel interviewers develop a stereotype of the good applicant.[32]

A third set of experiments illustrates how expectations and belief systems affect performance among school children. Teachers were given lists of pupils, designating 20 percent as late bloomers. In fact, they were randomly assigned, and were no different than other groups of students. Over the course of the term, these students did illustrate the predefined suggestion that they were, in fact, gifted. The teachers, although they were not aware of it, had a concept of these children's superior intelligence and this became true.[33] Later studies have illustrated that the Pygmalion effect (or self-fulfilling prophecy) has implications for training adults. Trainees whose instructors were led to expect more did indeed learn more.[34] The heart of the Pygmalion question is that teachers' beliefs influence student performance. In these experiments, it seems that teachers favored pupils for whom they expect more by giving them more attention, expressing more satisfaction, encouragement, and praise, by giving more extreme levels of both rewards and punishments, and by communicating with them more.

The conclusions to be drawn from the above research are that: individuals often make judgements about people on the basis of very little information, and individuals derive their knowledge partially from their beliefs and expectations rather than what they perceive and perceive selectively.

SUMMARY

A major factor in unsuccessful changes has been the use of unilateral power by those in higher positions. Failure also results when top managers totally delegate the responsibility for change to lower levels and remains uninvolved.

Successful change relies on participation of those who will be affected by it. This, in many cases, is the sharing of power and information. However, it does not imply that workers should make managerial decisions or managers should become involved in the decisions of their supervisors. Rather, it suggests that various perspectives need to be recognized in making decisions.

This chapter suggests that people have more influence and power in making decisions on those matters affecting their work. This usually means a shift in the style of management and leadership based on a belief that worker input in valuable. Workers provide ideas, feedback, and relevant information in the problem-solving process, in addition to gaining independence and responsibility in their work lives. The skills and principles in the chapter are simply one person's view of the process for managing change.

NOTES

1. J. M. Bryson, *Strategic Planning for Public and Nonprofit Organizations* (San Francisco: Jossey-Bass, 1988), p. 1984.

2. E. Trist, "Action Research and Adaptive Planning," in A. Clark, (ed.), *Experimenting with Organizational Life* (New York: Plenum, 1976) ; M. Emery and F. Emery, "Searching for New Directions in New Ways . . . For New Times," in J. W. Sutherland (ed.), *Management Handbook for Public Administrators*, (Toronto: Van Nostrand, 1978); F. C. Clark, *The Search Conference: How to Conduct It* (Downsview, Ontario: York University Co-operative Future Directions Project, 1982); R. H. Hayes and W. J. Abernathy, "Managing Our Way to Economic Decline," *Harvard Business Review*, vol. 58, 1980, pp. 67-77; A. Rock, "Strategy vs. Tactics from a Venture Capitalist," *Harvard Business Review*, vol. 65, 1987, pp. 63-67; R. F. Ackoff, *A Concept of Corporate Planning* (New York: John Wiley, 1970); R. L. Ackoff, "The Art and Science of Mess Management, " *Interfaces*, vol. 11, no. 1, 1981, pp. 20-26.

3. D. Klein, "Some Notes on the Dynamics of Resistance to Change: The Defender Role," reprinted in W. G. Bennis, K. D. Benne and R. Chin, (eds.), *The Planning of Change*, (New York: Holt, Rinehart and Winston, 1969).

4. The "data provide no evidence that the validity of a theory, and thus its goodness, has anything to do with the forming of a consensus regarding its importance at this time in the field." The feedback is at least sufficiently negative to encourage a readjustment of goals, paradigms, and basic processes of a what is an organizational science and how it is taught. John B. Miner, "The Validity and Usefulness of Theories in an Emerging Organizational Science," *Academy of Management Review*, vol. 9, 1984, p. 299.

5. C. Argyris, *Inner Contradictions of Rigorous Research* (New York: Academic Press, 1980); I. I. Mitroff and R. H. Kilmann, *Methodological Approaches to Social Science: Integrating Divergent Concepts and Theories* (San Francisco: Jossey-Bass, 1978); L. B. Mohr, *Explaining Organizational Behavior: The Limits and Possibilities of Theory and Research* (San Francisco: Jossey-Bass, 1982).

6. T. G. Cummings, "Designing Effective Work Groups," in P. C. Nystrom and W. H. Starbuck (eds.), *Handbook of Organizational Design*, vol. 2 (New York: Oxford University Press, 1981); L. B. Mohr, *Explaining Organizational Behavior: The Limits and*

Possibilities of Theory and Research; K. S. Cameron and D. A. Whetten, *Organizational Effectiveness: A Comparison of Multiple Models* (New York: Academic Press, 1983).

7. E. Van de Vall, M. Bolas, C. Bolas, and T. S. Kang, "Applied Social Research in Industrial Organizations: An Evaluation of Functions, Theory and Methods," *Journal of Applied Behavioral Science*, vol. 12, 1976, pp. 158-177.

8. E. Van de Vall, M. Bolas, C. Bolas, and T. S. Kang, "Applied Social Research in Industrial Organizations: An Evaluation of Functions, Theory and Methods," pp. 158-177.

9. H. Mintzberg, *The Nature of Managerial Work* (New York, Harper and Row, 1973); L. R. Sayles, *Managerial Behavior: Administration in Complex Organizations* (New York: McGraw Hill, 1964).

10. B. M. Oviatt, "Irrelevance, Intransigence and Business Professors," *The Academy of Management Executive*, vol. 3, 1989, pp. 304-312; L. B. Mohr *Explaining Organizational Behavior: The Limits and Possibilities of Theory and Research.*

11. E. E. Lawler, A. M. Mohrman, Jr., S. A. Mohrman, G. E. Ledford. Jr., and T. G. Cummings and Associates, *Doing Research That is Useful for Theory and Practice* (San Francisco: Jossey-Bass, 1985), p. 283.

12. M. Huberman, "Linkage Between Researchers and Practitioners: A Qualitative Study." *American Educational Research Journal*, vol, 27, 1990, pp. 363-391.

13. These have been called paradigms, frames of reference, learning models, myths, sagas, cognitive maps, or organizational cultures. See E. E. Lawler, A. M. Mohrman, Jr., S. A. Mohrman, G. E. Ledford. Jr., and T. G. Cummings and Associates, *Doing Research That is Useful for Theory and Practice.*

14. The relationship between belief systems and changes in behavior is not causal. A. M. Mohrman, Jr., and E. E. Lawler, III, " The Diffusion of QWL as a Paradigm Shift," G81-13(18), Center for Effective Organizations, University of Southern California Press, 1983.

15. E. E. Lawler, A. M. Mohrman, Jr., S. A. Mohrman, G. E. Ledford. Jr., and T. G. Cummings and Associates, *Doing Research That Is Useful for Theory and Practice,* p. 281.

16. P. Shrivastava, and I. I. Mitroff, "Enhancing Organizational Research Utilization: The Role of Decision-makers' Assumptions," *Academy of Management Review*, vol. 9, 1984, pp. 18-26.

17. H. Mintzberg, *The Nature of Managerial Work* (New York: Harper and Row, 1973).

18. F. Friedlander, "Behavioral Research as a Transactional Process," *Human Organization*, vol. 27, no. 4, 1968, pp. 369-379; Table 12.1 is taken from *Human Organization* and used with permission of the publisher.

19. The model is based on E. Berne, *Games People Play* (New York: Grove Press, 1964), p. 48.

20. F. Friedlander, "Behavioral Research as a Transactional Process," pp. 369-379.

21. F. Friedlander, "Behavioral Research as a Transactional Process," pp. 369-379.

22. D. H. Jenkins, "Force Field Analysis Applied to a School Situation," in W. G. Bennis, K. D. Benne, and R. Chin (eds.), *The Planning of Change* (New York: Holt, Rinehart Winston, 1969), pp. 238-244; K. Lewin, "Quasi-stationary Social Equilibria and the Problem of Permanent Change," in W. G. Bennis, K. D. Benne, and R. Chin (eds.), *The Planning of Change*, pp. 235-238.

23. N. Maier, *Principles of Human Relations: Applications to Management* (New York: John Wiley, 1952), p. 31.

24. V. A. Vroom, "A New Look at Managerial Decision Making," *Organizational Dynamics,* Spring 1973, p. 70.

25. K. Lewin, "Frontiers in Group Dynamics," *Human Relations*, vol. 1, 1947, pp. 5-40.

26. K. Lewin, *Field Theory and Social Science* (New York: Harper and Brothers,1951).

27. K. Lewin, "Frontiers in group Dynamics," *Human Relations*, vol. 1, 1947, pp. 5-40.

28. See N. R. F. Maier, *The Appraisal Interview* (New York: John Wiley, 1958).

29. W. S. Verplanck, "The Control of the Content of Conversation: Reinforcement of Statements of Opinion," *Journal of Abnormal and Social Psychology*, vol. 51, 1955, pp. 668-676; J. Greenspoon, "The Reinforcing Effect of Two Spoken Sounds on the Frequency of Two Responses," *American Journal of Psychology*, vol. 68, 1955, pp. 409-416.

30. J. R. Gibb, " A Research Perspective of the Laboratory Method," in K. D. Benne, L. P. Bradford, J. R. Gibb, and R. O. Lippitt, (eds.), *The Laboratory Method of Changing and Learning* (Palo Alto, Calif: Science and Behavior Books, 1975).

31. See J. S. Bruner and Leo Postman, "On the Perception of Incongruity: A Paradigm," *Journal of Personality*, vol. 18, 1949, pp. 206-223.

32. See E. C. Webster, *Decision-making in the Employment Interview* (Montreal: Industrial Relations Center, 1964). Other studies have tended to confirm these results. See L. H. Peters and J. R. Terborg, "The Effects of Temporal Placement of Unfavorable Information and of Attitude Similarity on Personnel Selection Decisions," *Organizational Behavior and Human Performance*, April, 1975, pp. 279-293.

33. During subsequent debriefings, most of the sixteen teachers said they paid little attention to the lists. They were only able to recall the names of eighteen of seventy two children designated as special; they falsely identified 18 control-group children as having been listed. This lead the researchers to conclude that the effect was most apparent among primary-grade pupils. See R. A. Rosenthal, and L. Jacobson, "Pygmalion in the Classroom: Teacher Expectation and Pupils," *Intellectual Development* (New York: Holt, Rinehart and Winston, 1968).

34. D. Eden and B. S. Abraham, "Pygmalion goes to Boot Camp: Expectancy, Leadership, and Trainee Performance," *Journal of Applied Psychology*, vol. 67, no. 2. 1982, pp. 194-100.

13

Different Stages
of the Change Process

Organizational change is a disorderly, highly dynamic process. It typically entails shifting goals and surprising events. The chaotic nature even occurs in organizations with the best laid plans.[1] Goals and activities shift as they are modified by managers and other organizational participants, reflecting previously unvoiced or even unknown needs and aspirations.[2]

Managing organizational change is much like trying to cure a cancerous person. The condition may arise from a bad diet, excessive smoking, or a range of life style conditions. In many cases, no single variable accounts for the cancerous conditions, and there is rarely "one" certain cure.

There are probably thousands of situational variables affecting whether a change is successfully implemented or not. As a result, we cannot have a precise cause and effect knowledge of implementation, as there are numerous interacting variables to consider. Introducing change in organizations is much like cancer research where there is no single variable or event responsible for a successful implementation. In this sense, smoking may cause cancer if other situations are also present. In the same way, an organizational pay system or compressed work week will not stand on its own, but will depend on a range of resistances people manifest at different stages of an intervention.

During the stages of the implementation of a change, different reactions occur making it necessary for managers to respond in unique ways. This chapter outlines how people feel during various stages of a change. It then provides a perspective on the tactics and strategies at each of these stages.

INTERPRETATIONS OF THE STAGES OF A CHANGE

Table 13.1 illustrates how stages of a change have been defined by various theories. Change, at its most basic level consists of events of unfreezing, moving, and refreezing, although the movement through these sequences is rather unclear.[3] When a change is introduced, existing patterns and values are disrupted producing a period of uncertainty and conflict. The degree of personal trauma is often associated with how people adjust to the uncertainties they face. Reactions during a period of change range from rejection and withdrawal to fundamental shifts in thinking and behavior.[4]

People seem to have different emotional reactions during different stages of a change. Facilitators or managers develop an initial view of the change during an *anticipation* stage, based on rumors and other titbits of information. This initial view is *confirmed* or disconfirmed based on conventional explanations and comparison to past events. During an *action* stage, people compare conditions before and after the event and attempt to explain them. They then take action. The *aftermath* is characterized by reviews and explanations.[5]

The *anticipation* stage is characterized by a period of uncertainty and unfreezing, and participants strive to develop a view of how an event will affect them. The fragments of information about the change are analogous "to randomly arranged pieces of a puzzle for which managers possess neither a final picture as a construction guide nor a specific indication of whether the final picture will contain some, all, or none of the pieces."[6] Organizational members spend much of their time searching for information. Ideas and hunches about what might happen provide the nourishment for further speculation and conjecture. Organizational members use the titbits of information available to try to explain what will happen.

At a certain stages of a change, more complete information becomes available and people learn how the change it will affect them personally. This may mean that the whole truth comes out as management *confirms* plans not revealed before. This does not mean that managers intentionally withheld information from employees. It is just as likely that new information became available as buyers completed their financing of a takeover or as banks or government agencies provide financial or legal verification of an impending deal. What is most interesting during this stage is a sense of relief as people finally know what will happen to them. While the affect of the change may not be pleasant, it seems to be a relief to begin planning for a new future.

During the *action* stage, people are actively reconstructing their environment and deciding on the new directions they will take. This is a process of sorting out things to be saved or retained and those to be discarded. It is like preparing for a move to a new country. Once the decisions have been made and people are aware of the move, unneeded items or clothing and furniture can be discarded. Then, those items needed in the new country can be arranged and packed.

TABLE 13.1
STAGES OF A CHANGE

INITIATION

ANTICIPATION
UNCERTAINTY
UNFREEZING

CONFIRMATION
RECOGNITION

ACTION
PARADIGM SHIFT
MOVING

AFTERMATH
ROUTINIZATION
REFREEZING

People have voiced different feelings during stages of anticipation, confirmation, action, and aftermath. *The transformational cycle has been defined as stages of initiation, uncertainty, recognition, paradigm shift, and routinization.* Lewin's model of unfreezing, refreezing, and moving has been associated with stages of the change and learning process.

More accurate information is available during a decision or action stage. Interpretations are no longer presumptions, aspirations, or conjectures. New views or frames of reference are being constructed as each new mini-event brings with it the need to create the need to develop new norms and behaviors. Old norms and behaviors are no longer useful and are slowly discarded. "New working procedures or relationships, new facilities and interaction patterns, new and unfamiliar surroundings, or new rules and dictates make the development of new realities instrumental."[7]

The new reality consists of two elements, and is like a "double exposure" containing images of before and after. People point to old behaviors that are not working and new ways of interacting which will be required. Some confusion exists because of the lack of understanding of why old behaviors were not working. They may also not understand why the new changes are occurring, even though they are aware of their affects.

The *aftermath* describes what happens after the change has been in play for a while. During this time, the change is evaluated and people become aware of its permanence. There is a growing realization of the new norms and behaviors required, and the adjustments needed. The most prominent feature of this stage is the subjective evaluation of what happened. This involves the identification of winners and losers and of positive and negative features of a change. People will make direct reference to those who benefitted and others who did not, and to advantages and disadvantages. It is very likely that people who benefitted will more readily identify the positive features while others will more readily point to the negative features. Even when the change seems to be positive overall, those who lost their political or financial advantage will not readily be willing supporters. Fairer or more justifiable ways of working do not satisfy those who are gaining the most (even if unjustified).

During the aftermath of a change, it is easy to point to some of the new behaviors or features of the change, such as jobs lost, new attitudes, and so forth. These are much like a "Monday morning quarter-back, who can identify the mistakes made during a weekend football game." Looking back offers a tremendous perspective.

It is much more difficult to stop or "go back" to the previous system at this stage, even if it has more advantages over the one in existence. Even when proponents introduce a change on an experimental basis, they are setting in motion a range of forces to change procedures, behaviors, and ways of working. People have a tendency to want to go forward, while going back may be perceived as an admission of failure.

ILLUSTRATION OF THE STAGES

This section provides examples of the stages of a change occurring during the sale of a community sports center to a university. It illustrates the events occurring and some of the statements made by individuals as they moved from one stage to another. In this example, a university sought to purchase a community recreational facility which included gymnasiums, class rooms, a hockey arena, tennis and squash courts, and other facilities. The club, known as the Racket Club, included over 500 members and had a staff of fifty people who were in charge of running and maintaining the facilities and restaurants.

Background. The Racket Club was initially a private club, where volunteer members were elected to the Board of Directors with overall responsibility for directing and operating the facilities. They initiated membership drives, made decisions on expansions, and were responsible for directing the staff. A network of volunteers members served on committees which related to squash, tennis, and other sports.

The vision during the 1970s and early 1980s was to construct and operate a club modelled on those "esteemed and private clubs which operated in large metropolitan centers." In meeting this vision, there were people who won world championships in curling, and national or provincial championships in squash and tennis. The members often used the bar and restaurant facilities as a gathering place to socialize, dance, or relax.

It is not clear why the social activities at the Racket Club began to disintegrate. Some members indicated that some members became too friendly, and relationships evolved to challenge marital norms. Others indicated that disagreements occurred over expansions, and strategic mistakes were made. The Racket Club constructed a curling facility, and many people suggested that this introduced a different culture of people, those interested in drinking, socializing, and smoking, rather than fitness. There were also strategic mistakes in the construction of a new squash facilities. The Board agreed to construct five new American size courts and five racket ball courts, and they later learned that the international size courts were to become most popular in North America, and racket ball did not ever receive any interest among members.

The financial viability of the Racket Club was called into question in the late 1970s. The club went into receivership. It was later sold to a developer who then took on the task of reestablishing a viable club.

The new owner soon fell into receivership, as a depressed real estate market challenged the financial viability of other investments. Interest rates almost doubled in the early 1980s, and the increased costs for loans on developments forced the new owner into receivership. Following this period, the receiver appointed an interim manager.

In the late 1980s, the Racket Club was purchased by a private school named the Saint Michael's University (SMU) School, and the new club became known as the SMU Racket Club. The new owners quickly applied to have the club rezoned so that they could convert it into a school. Racket Club members responded by signing petitions and organizing phone campaigns to the city's council members. To the Racket Club members, the takeover would destroy the tradition of a sport facility which was unique in the community. Some members offered the following statements:

> We have been in existence for years. And there is no other facility of its kind in the area. Look at those trophies. They illustrate the role that the club has played in the community. It has developed younger athletes. . . . And now it will be owned by a private school for Yuppies and their children.

The opposing voices against the rezoning were very vocal and organized. As a result, the city council decided against the rezoning.

The new owners (SMU) then worked out a compromise strategy with the members and council allowing the School to construct a set of classrooms on the site and to use the facilities during specified times. The club would continue to operate and members would enjoy the same privileges as before. The school would schedule their events during certain day-time hours, which were also less peak hours for Racket Club members.

SMU took a very positive approach to improving the facilities of the Racket Club, badly in need of maintenance because of years of operation under receivers. This involved painting the club, establishing a fitness centre and dance studio, reconstructing the curling arena into more tennis facilities, constructing meeting rooms, improving the restaurant and bar facilities, constructing a pro shop, and reconstructing many of the racket ball courts so they could be used for squash. They also devised a set of plans to improve the club's ambiance by tying in the open air swimming area to the tennis courts with a set of patios, fountains, and gardens. In most members's eyes, SMU was doing an excellent job at improving the facilities.

However, after a few years of operation, SMU directors began to realize that students were not as interested in using the facilities as they had hoped. Students were not developing into championship swimmers or tennis or squash players, either because of lack of interest or because of the inability of the school's teacher to encourage them. The school was no longer asking the club for specified times to handle their athletic and recreational needs. It was also obvious that the community would not positively endorse the club's vision of enlarging the school's facilities to a campus-like atmosphere where all their students could be housed and schooled. In addition, the school subsidized the club. Thus, the school's directors began to look elsewhere for a location to construct a new campus.

During the four year period of the school's ownership, there were several attempts to sell, trade, or redevelop the facility to make it respond to the School's vision. Most of the information on these potential deals was circulated after the events had surfaced and failed. So, rumors and the possible anxiety from them were minimal and information could be easily corrected with the actual decisions made.

During these periods of change, the managers seemed to operate within a style of supplying minimal information and only upon request. There was no communication of plans, known information, intensions, and no attempts to dispel the rumors that were surfacing. Because the events were short-lived from anticipating the change to the aftermath, this strategy seemed appropriate. Why get the members all excited unless something is really happening?

TABLE 13.2
VIEWS EXPRESSED DURING STAGES OF A CHANGE

STAGE CHANGE	STATEMENTS	CHARACTERISTICS
Anticipation	"I'll bet the university takes a bulldozer to the whole place."	• Rumors • Invalid information
Confirmation	"The club has never been financially viable."	• More valid information • Sense of relief
Action	"I've got my membership & I've taken up a new membership downtown."	• Rationalizations • Actions
Aftermath	"It is too bad they had to handle it so badly."	• Interpretations

Views Expressed During Stages of the Change

Anticipation. Rumors of the university's plan to purchase the Racket Club came from one member of the university staff who had heard about it unofficially from some secretaries in another office, July 1991. The information had also been circulated at an in-camera meeting of the University's Board of Governors. See Table 13.2.

Don't tell anyone, but insider knowledge says that the University has agreed to purchase the Racket Club. It is only a matter of days.

When asked what the university plans to do with the Racket Club, this university staff member said.

No one knows. The Director of Athletics and Recreation does not know. The

Manager of the Recreational Facilities for the University has not been consulted. .
. . Who knows? The faculty do not know anything about it. . . . This kind of stuff
is typical of the way that this University does business. No one is ever told anything,
so you lose your motivation to help.

Within days, news had circulated to a very large number of club members.
There was no official announcement from the club's manager and staff were left
to fend off members who were in search of information and who, at times,
openly displayed their anger. One conversation went as follows:

Club Member: What have you heard about the university's plan to purchase the
Club?
Front Desk Supervisor: We do not have a lot of information at this time. The
newspaper reported that the university was planning to buy it, but we do not know
anything else. We're just waiting to hear.

Club Member: I've asked my son, who is a lawyer to place a judgement against the
Club. There is no way that I'm going to be stuck for a loss of fees.
Front Desk Supervisor: The Club would never take your money. All fees will be
reimbursed. There is no need to worry. SMU would never cancel your membership
and not return your fees.

Club Member: Well, I'm going to have him draft a letter to you. The members
should not lose out. You people just do not think of others in times like this.
Front Desk Supervisor: If you feel you have to do this. . . But, the club will be very
honorable about the memberships. We just don't have any information at this time.
. . .The member walked away.

Front Desk Supervisor: How can he be so concerned about himself? There are over
fifty staff members who may be losing their jobs. You think that he might also think
we are concerned.

During the next few months, club members found out that the sale had not
been completed and that the university still had to convince government officials
of its merit. During this period, university and government officials toured the
building, while inspections were made on the physical soundness of the structure.
Members took a range of actions such as visiting the university president, signing
petitions, and phoning political representatives.

Staff in the recreational department at the university still had no information
about the impending sale. They would be asked to supervise its operations and to
use it for their athletic programs, yet they were not asked for their comments nor
given any information about future plans. The following is a sampling of the
comments which came from university staff, club staff, and members.

Comments from University Staff: This is very typical of our administration. No input and no information. I think this purchase is completely silly. The Club has over 20 tennis courts, 12 squash courts, an arena, a bar and restaurant, and a swimming pool. The only facilities we can possibly use are the classrooms and gyms and they are so far away from the main campus that most staff and students will be reluctant to use them.

It looks like the V.P. is trying to save face because of the screw-ups he made in trying to get the Commonwealth Games people to construct new buildings on campus. Building which were supposed to go on campus have gone elsewhere just because of him. Now, the university has got nothing. This purchase is the V.P's way of salvaging something.

Comments from Club Members: I'll bet that the university takes a bulldozer to the whole place. There is no reason for them to keep it. They do not need the swimming pool, especially one which is this small. They do not need many of the other facilities, unless they want to start a tennis program.

They wouldn't just terminate our memberships, would they? Surely, they would allow us to continue on. . . . Maybe, we'll have to enroll in a course. That would be cheap membership. We could attend one class and then drop it. We could do this every semester.

Comments from Staff Members: I have to look for a new job after 15 years of working here. The Club has not told us anything. The university will probably not need us because they are unionized.

I don't want to cause a stir. If we do, they will probably not help us if there is a chance for a job.

I told them one month ago that I was planning to take out a mortgage to buy a home. I wanted to make sure that I would have a job here. You think they would have said something.

Comments such as the above were very common during this period. Club members heard that the government money for the building was late in coming and that SMU managers were meeting to discuss their actions should the sale fall through. During this two month period, there was only one two-line comment from the club manager indicating the university was planning to purchase the club and the sale had not been finalized. "The Club would honor the memberships and return membership fee."

During this stage of anticipation, the absence of information from those who had responsibility for the change seemed to be the breeding ground for hunches and rumors. Several statements pointed to mistrusts of management motives, fears of job losses, or concerns about how the changes would affect individuals. Negative feelings about the change seemed to be associated with the lack of information about it. During this phase, personal concerns were identified as individuals were seeking to explain what was happening and what it meant for them personally.

In the absence of complete information, most people tend to feel ambiguous and uncertain. Such feelings are unusually unpleasant. The absence of information and understanding will seldom be accompanied by a lack of curiosity. Rather, gossip and half truths may emerge in the form of rumors and these may be far less flattering to the perpetrator than the truth would be. Resistance may be reduced if it is recognized that innovations are likely to be misunderstood and misinterpreted and if provision is made for feedback of perceptions of the project and for further clarification if needed.

During this phase, the most common personal concerns were addressed, and individuals sought to understand how the change would affect them. Individuals were seeking to explain what was happening and what it meant for them. Negative feelings about the change usually are associated with no information about it.[8]

Confirmation. The sale to the university was confirmed when the local newspaper reported that the Racket Club sale had been finalized. One type of comment was a sense of relief. During the anticipation stage, it was not actually clear what would happen. Even though people might have feared the worst, it is only after the confirmation of the change that new plans could be set in motion. The comments included:

> The Club has never been financially viable. For the last 10 years, no one had been able to make a go of it. . . . So, we have been lucky to be here.
> I have no idea what will happen. I doubt that the university will lay us all off. They would be too much community pressure.

While denial, rumors, and invalid information were characteristics of the anticipation stage, the confirmation stage was typified by a period of more valid information and initial shock. However, there was also a feeling of relief as the period of uncertainty was over and people felt they could plan their future.

During these times, members made such statements which begin as:

> We used to be able to. . . .
> I am planning to move to the new. . . .

The endings to such statements usually point to what the people are planning to do in responding to the change.

Some people are overly willing to cast off old norms and behaviors. They tend to be groups of people who are the proponents of the change, or who have some personal interest in it. They tend to offer statements such as:

> I'm looking forward to the. . . .

Feelings during the anticipation and confirmation stages are similar to those people express after the death of an ailing loved one. During the anticipation stage, there is often denial and high hopes for almost any alternative offering a cure or improvement. The confirmation of the disease or imminent death is shocking and disturbing. However, the period of uncertainty and anxiety is over and a person can begin to make the last days of life most comforting while taking steps to "get one's house in order."

Action. During the confirmation stage, it became clear what would happen. Plans are set in motion to respond to the changes. It is only after the confirmation of the change that new plans are set into motion. This is the stage where the change become a reality and certain adjustments are necessary. These adjustments begin to occur as people take into account certain unanticipated needs. These episodes of adjustment continue to occur from this period on.

Shortly after learning about the sale, individuals began to focus on their future and take action. Many club members asked for refunds on their memberships. Others simply indicated they would wait it out. During the initial months, no staff left as the job market was not promising. Even though people expressed concerns about losing a job, they still waited for word about what would happen from their employer.

At this stage, some of the anxiety from not knowing about one's future had disappeared. Individuals were now aware that the Club would be sold although they were not sure of their futures. Many members quietly asked others of their plans while some employees offered a statement similar to the following:

> "I'm looking elsewhere for a job, but I'm not hopeful."
> "I'm just going to wait to see what happens. What choice do I have. There are not other jobs."
> "I've got my membership dues out and I've taken up a membership downtown."

On November 1, the club's managers indicated that they would no longer require the service of the employees after December 31, and would be providing them with two months severance pay. The reactions among club members now ranged from bitterness to resigned disbelief.

> "I never thought this school or the university would be so unfeeling."
> "I cannot believe that a publicly funded university would be part of such actions."
> "I will never send my children to the school."

The case highlights the stages of a change as perceived by employees and members. It is still too early to assess the full implications of this change. The club closed and many individuals found jobs elsewhere. At this stage, people were disillusioned and shocked, and found it hard to interpret the events.

The action stage provides the setting where decisions have to be made. Some people refused to accept the decision and continued to lobby political officials claiming the public funds of a university should not be used to create unemployment. These reactions were bitter and angry and illustrated an unwillingness to accept the change. Like a relative who lost a loved one, these are reactions of unwillingness to accept and adjust but to continue the fight to preserve what was.

During the action stage, some staff and members illustrated "transformations" or "paradigm shifts." They made adjustments and got new jobs or joined other clubs. They offered statements illustrating:

> "The closing of the Racket Club was the best thing that ever happened to me. . . . I have a much better job now."
> "I joined another club and this provided me with many stimulating people to play with. I've made several important business contacts."

Aftermath. The case highlights the stages of a change as perceived by employees and members. The change had both positive and negative effects for different people. The effects seemed to be related to the way people reacted. Many who reacted with anger and bitterness never did respond positively, but continued to try to preserve what had previously existed. Others were able to assess one's strengths, weaknesses, and opportunities. They seemed to be better able to put aside their difficulties and respond to their opportunities.

Epilogue. The Racket Club closed its doors on January 1, 1992. On January 13, the University's newspaper printed a story indicating that the Racket Club purchase was "on hold." Disappointed university officials had to delay plans to expand the university's recreational programs by purchasing the Racket Club. The Racket Club's Minor Hockey Association, which used the center's rink facilities, would not release its five-year renewal option for further ice time after 1994. The purchasing agreement between the university and the Racket Club stipulated that the Racket Club was to obtain a release of the five-year renewal.

University officials offered a letter of intent to the association proposing to negotiate further ice time should the university decide to maintain the rink facilities past 1994. The Racket Club believed, when it announced the sale of the center to the University in July 1991, that the association would release its five-year renewal option in exchange for a cash settlement, equipment and existing ice time up until April 1994. On December 20, 1991, the university was informed that the association voted to reject the July agreement with the university.

During the following months, the university and the Racket Club negotiated with the Hockey Association. The dispute was finally settled in the early spring and the university finalized their purchase. They also were able to offer employment to some of their staff to take effect after they had completed some required renovations. During this time, many staff left and only a few were finally hired by the university.

Many of the former members of the Racket Club have memberships in the newly renovated facility. The university's staff is also rather positive, thus, many of their fears did not come to pass.

This case illustrates how change was perceived when managers provided little direction and assistance. The following section outlines the possible reasons for resistance and appropriate steps for responding. It is based on the assumption that change, even when it has seriously repercussions for employees, can be more effectively managed. Managers and change agents have the responsibility for assisting people and providing them with information so that can make decisions relating to their work and lives.

STRATEGIES FOR IMPLEMENTING CHANGES

To be successful, there is a need for strategies to neutralize or at least contain people who delay making essential commitments or protect turf. There is also a need to recognize more effective strategies for assisting people with a change and its repercussions.

If there are more successful strategies for implementation, what are they? This section outlines five implementation strategies and illustrates their appropriateness for certain stages of a change.[9] The strategies include intervention, participation, persuasion, edict, and support.

Implementation by intervention: This tactic included steps such as acquiring the authority to manage the change process, creating a need for change by appraising performance inadequacies and the need for change, identifying comparable organizations with more acceptable norms and performance, and carrying out an ongoing assessment of progress. Many such interventions include task forces made up of users to identify inefficient and ill-advised procedures. In the intervention strategy, the manager is a strong protagonists in all steps of the process.

Implementation by participation: Managers initiate changes by stipulating needs or opportunities, and then assigning decisions for developmental activities. Task force members represent certain points of view or have the responsibility for guiding the projects within certain constraints and expectations.

Implementation by persuasion: With persuasion tactics, there is little, if any, involvement and participation. Managers identify the needs and opportunities identified by experts. Persuasion is the key tactic used to sell the ideas.

Some communication strategies may be seen as a form of persuasion, especially when it concerns prospective organizational changes. Resistance can be reduced by communicating with employees and explaining the rationale and logic behind the change. This tactic assumes that if employees receive the full facts and clear up misunderstandings, then change will be more easily facilitated.[10]

Implementation by edict: Managers can use control and personal power and avoid the use of participation. In such a strategy, managers might identify needs and opportunities and prescribe expected behaviors with memoranda, formal presentations, or on-the-job instructions. Experts and users have little power and managers do not discuss changes with users or attempt to rationalize the need for changes.

This "edict" strategy might be implemented with certain tactics such as: negotiation, manipulation and cooptation, or coercion. When resistance is high, negotiation tactics are directed at providing something of value to compensate for the resistance felt. In some cases, reward packages--such as expense accounts, company car, and adjustments for moving--are given to executives to ease the transition of a move.

"Manipulation and cooptation" tactics can be used for implementing edicts, although they are, hopefully, not associated with an action research approach. They range from twisting or distorting of the facts to making the information appear more attractive. For example, withholding undesirable information or communicating selected information might be used for gaining acceptance where managers want to cut jobs or reduce salaries.

"Cooptation" is a tactic where the advice and support of key people is sought. However, the advice is not sought for its decisional value. Such tactics, once exposed, result in a loss of credibility and trust which may be so severe that people will not wish to be involved in similar ventures. Some change tactics amount to coercion, direct threats or force. Managers might find the need to cut pay and might use a range of coercive tactics such as threats of cutting jobs or closing the plant.

Facilitation and support: Supportive strategies are necessary when employee fears and anxieties are high. They are akin to listening, employee counselling and therapy. In some cases, this support might include training or short paid leaves of absence to facilitate adjustments. The tactic illustrates that managers are willing to listen to the concerns raised during a period of adjustment.

The Appropriateness of Different Change Strategies

Different change processes are more appropriate for different situations. For instance, a supportive strategy could be used during the initial stages of a crisis when all parties are unaware of the possible problems or implications of the change. We can also be supportive when the implications of a change are well known and there is a human interest of assisting people to deal with the changes. Participation and intervention strategies might be used for other situations which encourage individuals to respond and plan for the changes. The following paragraphs offer suggestions on the strategies to be used during different stages of a change as illustrated in Table 13.3.

Anticipation. The initial stages of a change are often associated with feelings or concerns from not knowing the full story, or whether or not the change will actually happen. During this stage, the overriding cause of resistance may be fears and anxieties from not knowing what will happen. There are obvious fears of dislocation, loss of a jobs and income, and an inability to carry out the work. However, there is also an added set of emotions from the ambiguity of not knowing what is going to happen. "If only I knew what was going to happen, then I could plan my life." One of the worst maladies during this stage is the rumor mill, which seems to feed itself even when there is unreliable information.

The most appropriate change approaches during the anticipation stage might be communication and support. Information which may not be a total picture may be better than no information at all, especially if managers take steps to correct it when more reliable information is available. Mechanisms for the distribution of information can be developed so that the rumor mills is not supplied with erroneous information.

Confirmation. The confirmation stage usually involves initial feelings of disbelief, but later statements that: "thank god it is over; now I can get on planning my life." It is like waiting for the decisions to be made about a job in a foreign country. The anxiety from not knowing is over only after a decision has been confirmed. Once the decision has been made, family members have to plan for the move and take care of other important matters.

The confirmation stage requires the most attention, as there is still the need for some support and counselling. The overriding cause of resistance is the lack of awareness of opportunities which may be present elsewhere. But once the change has been confirmed, people need to be aware of the directions they can take. Thus, any strategy which promotes awareness is appropriate.

Action. During this stage, people are aware of some of the opportunities they might pursue. It is now time to take action or begin working within the new conditions. This is the time when people begin new jobs, take on new procedures, or begin a new life after a traumatic event.

The action stage requires mechanisms to give people a new direction and increase their comfort with their new roles. In most cases, strategies relying on participation or intervention are more likely to get commitment to the new direction. In some cases, such as the termination of employees, a range of edict strategies may be called upon. That is, employers might have to negotiate a solution or resolve a difficult situation.

Aftermath. What are the after-effects of a traumatic change? In some cases, people feel angry or bitter at the loss of something valued. Most of this feelings might result from the way the change is handled and administered. "It is not losing the job that bothers me, it is the insensitivity and callousness by which they dealt with me." or "At least, they could have told me."

The "death" of an organization, like the Racket Club, may be like the death of a person. Death is inevitable when we know that the organization or the person is terminally ill. Of course, these feelings are harder to forget when the process was unfair. Losing one's life is unfair if a person lived an honorable and wholesome life. Similarly, losing one's job is unfair if people were treated in an

TABLE 13.3
**METHODS FOR DEALING WITH RESISTANCE
TO CHANGE**

Stage & Feelings Generated	Key Reason	Methods of Facilitation
Anticipation		
"Anxiety from not knowing."	• Lack of direction • Lack of openness & experience with previous changes • Lack of support	• Support & information • Persuasion (Communicative)
Confirmation		
"Initial Shock & disbelief; Later, relief from knowing."	• Pressures for change • Lack of support • Lack of direction & power	• Persuasion (Communicative) • Intervention • Participation
Action		
"Anxiety from no direction."	• Lack of direction & power • Lack of support	• Intervention • Participation • Edict
Aftermath		
"Bitterness from treatment."	• Lack of trust, support & information	• Support • Intervention • Participation

unfair and unhonorable manner. During the aftermath, there are still times when people are searching for explanations, and mechanisms for support can assist people in dealing with these difficulties.

SUMMARY

In any change process, it is usually necessary to construct relationships outside one's formal realm of authority to generate commitment. The change strategies selected have to respond to the needs of key interest groups -- top managers, informal leaders, union executives, and the like. Or, if only one interest group feel strongly about an issue, it might be necessary to ripen the circumstances surrounding the need by heightening awareness of the need and fuelling dissatisfaction with the status quo.

Various change strategies are appropriate. The include: re-articulating needs based on conversations with strong interest groups, having interest groups involved in the definition of vision and objectives, assuring that they are involved on the design team, and the like.

As a basic element, the choice of the most effective strategy involves meeting individually with peers, managers of related functions, and potential collaborators before bringing them together in a group. The meeting, held ostensibly to discuss strategies, in fact, demonstrates support. The strategy to build a coalition of people who support the idea, as opposed to a coalition of people who support other people.

NOTES

1. R. M. Cyert and J. G. March, *A Behavioral Theory of the Firm* (Englewood Cliffs, N. J. : Prentice-Hall, 1963).

2. E. E. Lawler III, A. M. Mohrman, Jr., S. A. Mohrman, G. E. Ledford, Jr., T. G. Cummings and Associates, *Doing Research that is Useful for Theory and Practice* (San Francisco: Jossey-Bass, 1985).

3. K. Lewin, "Frontiers in Group Dynamics," *Human Relations*, vol. 1, 1947, pp. 5-41.

4. R. E. Quinn, and J. R. Kimberly, "Paradox, Planning and Perseverance: Guidelines for Managerial Practice," In J. Kimberly and R. Quinn (eds.), *New Futures: The Challenge of Managing Organizational Transitions* (Homewood, Ill. : Dow Jones-Irwin, 1984), pp. 295-314.

5. These stages on based on a model of how managers construe organizational events as a change unfolds. The model was constructed from in-depth interviews with 40 managers. See L. Isabella, "Evolving Interpretations as a Change Unfolds: How Managers Construe Key Organizational Events," *Academy of Management Journal*, vol. 33, 1990, pp. 7-41. In this book, the action stage is similar to Isabella's culmination phase. The

word "action" seemed to better describe the changes we witnessed. In addition, it may
have a broader meaning.

6. L. Isabella, "Evolving Interpretations as a Change Unfolds: How Managers
Construe Key Organizational Events," p. 16.

7. L. Isabella, "Evolving Interpretations as a Change Unfolds: How Managers
Construe Key Organizational Events," p. 23.

8. J. B. Cunningham, J. Farquharson, and D. Hull, "A Profile of Human Fears of
Technological Change," *Technolgical Forecasting and Social Change,* vol. 40, 1991, pp.
335-370.

9. Four strategies--intervention, participation, persuasion, and edict--are based on
a study of ninety one implementation cases. See P. C. Nutt, "Tactics of Implementation,"
Academy of Management Journal, vol. 29, 1986, pp. 230-261. This study suggested that
there was a 100 percent success rate for managers who used intervention tactics, although
this tactic was used in less than 20 percent of the cases. Both the persuasion and
participation tactics had 75 percent success rates;   persuasion had the highest frequency
of use (42 percent) and participation the lowest (17 percent). Implementation by edits had
a 43 percent success rate and a 23 percent frequency of use. It seemed that intervention
tactics and their variations were effective for all types of changes and under varying levels
of time pressure and importance. The facilitation and support strategy is based on an
article by J. P. Kotter and L. A. Schlesinger, "Choosing Strategies for Change," *Harvard
Business Review*, March-April, 1979, pp. 106-114.

10. See J. P. Kotter and L. A. Schlesinger, "Choosing Strategies for Change. "

Part V

Final Considerations

14

Action Research and Organizational Development: A Conclusion

The previous chapters have outlined an action research approach to organizational development. They outline strategies for gathering data and information, defining an organization's direction and implementating changes. The action research approach does not rely on the application of traditional humanistic assumptions or traditional assumptions.[1]

Those who criticize traditional scientific assumptions suggest that "there is a crisis in the field of organizational science. The principal symptom of this crisis is that research methods are becoming more sophisticated and increasingly less useful for solving the practical problems that members of organizations face."[2] Those who comment on traditional organizational development practices suggest that the term itself "remains a convenient label for a variety of activities, and that the organizational development (O.D.) literature, as a whole, is more autobiographical than organizational in focus and scope."[3]

This book offers an approach to action research and organizational development and a number of principles for gathering data and implementing changes. The research principles suggest the need for: being creative in defining the real research question; generating theoretical concepts from the field; integrating concepts with real life assumptions; "triangulating" and using multiple perspectives; verifying interpretations with perspectives in the field; and treating the research setting as a case study. The change principles refer to: developing a collaborative relationship; conceptualizing the impact of the changes to be made; recognizing the sociotechnical criterion; using participation and groups appropriately; changing behavior through problem-solving discussions; and recognizing that expectations amplify or reduce resistances. Together, these principles provide a perspective on carrying out action research and organizational development.

This chapter describes a number of action research and organizational development practices. It then summarizes a number of issues affecting the process of change.

ACTION RESEARCH PRACTICES

What makes action research different are the practices encouraging an understanding of real life problems, involving people in a collaborative relationship, and using grounded concepts.[4]

Real life problems. Action research projects spring from opportunities to provide solutions to actual social problems. These projects are conducted by researchers who are committed in a professional way to assist those concerned. The support and cooperation of those studied, in most cases, provides a greater access to a wider variety of relevant data. This makes it easier to test the findings and concepts in field settings.

The collaborative relationship. Human beings, whether individuals, families or larger groups, do not usually like to be scrutinized, and might tend to mistrust how information about them will be used. They are often unwilling to provide the researcher with access to crucial data about themselves. They may, however, be less unwilling if they believe the researcher is able to help solve a problem concerning them. Organizational researchers resemble those in medicine who are trying to assist their clients. Many such medical investigations are possible because patients feel assured that the experimental treatments are intended to benefit them. In organizations, the need for the subject's collaboration is even greater, since much of the relevant data concern feelings and motives. Subjects tend to guard much of this information. These feelings and motives are only likely to be understood and communicated when a researcher is well-known and trusted.

It is often argued that involvement will introduce a Hawthorne-type effect where the research process can affect the results as much as the change. These same effects have been noted in the medical field, where people's expectation and attitudes affect the health of a patient. There are many well known cases where the positive changes in a patient's condition can be attributed to attitudes alone.

Attitudes and expectations need to be monitored in the same way as the effects of the change. These expectations might be arranged on a scale defining being: unaware, uninterested, opposed, interested, involved, and committed.

Unaware	Uninterested	Opposed	Interested	Involved	Committed
	_____	_____	_____	_____	_____	

Most interactions in life might find a place in the above categorization, from standing in a bank line, choosing a neighbor, and being involved in a laboratory-like scientific experiment. The most rigorous scientific designs suggest that subjects are either unaware or at least neutral about the changes occurring. In some medical experiments, and in some organizational experiments, it would not be ethical to introduce a change without patient awareness. Thus, such experimentation requires different set of controls, ways to define degrees of interest in the change, and the interactions.

The action research approach to organizational development offered in this book does not reject the use of controls. Science, of all kinds, requires the use of some controlled conditions. As Campbell notes: "It is not failure-to-control in general that bothers us, but only those failures of control which permit truly plausible rival hypotheses, laws with a degree of scientific establishment comparable to or exceeding that of the law our experiment is designed to test."[5]
The controls may not require statistics and control group designs. They merely require methods for ruling out sources of invalidity that might be thought to exist. In some cases, this will require that the setting is more adequately defined and clearly described. In most cases, it requires an systematic imagination about carrying out the process of research and change.

Grounded concepts. Because of its interdisciplinary approach to understanding real social problems, a premium is placed on theory that is empirically based and practically relevant. External theories are not normally used, except when they provide a background of experience and concepts.

SUCCESSFUL CHANGE PROJECTS

Various types of resistances occur during the process of a change. These resistances may manifest themselves in the form of anger or hostility expressed toward the change and its initiators. Individuals refuse to cooperate, organize boycotts or petitions, take direct action to sabotage the implementation, or deliberately try to show the change will be unsuccessful. People will not react to the change experience in the same way. Some people may passively resist, while others might be more aggressive in organizing opposition to it. Even changes which are viewed as positive will produce some level of uncertainty and the possibility of resistance.

There are a range of issues associated with resistance to change. Resistance might be less when the environment--the market and social climate--is most receptive. There might be characteristics within the organization itself, stemming from the availability of resources or the attitudes of the people toward the change or management. In addition, certain tactics might be more successful, such as the initial contact between development/research personnel and members of the organization, the formal entry procedures and commitment, data gathering activities and posture of organizational members toward them, and so forth. Although some such characteristics are associated more strongly with either successful and unsuccessful change, only rarely will they predict success.[6]

There are lists of "rules of thumb" to explain why planned changes are not successful. These failures might be attributed to inabilities to manage the process of change, the unwillingness of certain individuals to relinquish control of their activities, and misunderstandings of disagreements about the change and its benefits and costs. Managers need to be aware of the reasons why people resist if they are to respond appropriately. The research literature offers a range of suggestions on activities which facilitate the process of change.[7] People may feel less resistance to a change when there is: a clear direction; an organization which is accustomed to change; pressures for change; skilled facilitators; and support from credible people.

The direction and commitment to it. There seems to be a growing body of evidence pointing to the need to understand the relationship between goal commitment and performance. There are many determinants of commitment, including external influences (authority, peer influence, and external rewards), interactive influences (participation and competition), and internal factors (expectancy and internal rewards).[8]

Gaining commitment to a direction is no easy task. In a classic study of workers in a pajama factory, workers routinely showed lower productivity after products were changed and they had to perform with new standards and piece rates. The workers resisted, even though supervisors exercised their authority and used an incentive bonus system.[9] The researchers observed that workers felt that they could not attain the new standards and banded together to restrict production. There seemed to be a lack of trust and support.

Commitment to directions and goals is a key activity for managers and leaders.[10] When people publicly understand the need for change and publicly announce their goals and directions, there is greater commitment and more persistence.[11]

The self-renewing organization. Organizations that are more stable and status quo oriented may be less likely to adopt changes than those more open to change.[12] An innovative organization is one continually learning and adapting to changes within itself and its environment. These are organizations and groups whose principles and operations may be different from conventional stereotypes of the bureaucratic form. Rather, these organizations have an open capacity, they explore alternatives to problems rather than solutions already defined.

The pressure for change. It may be difficult to motivate people to change when they are satisfied with the status quo. On the other hand, dissatisfactions, tensions, or pressures to change may enhance the possibility a change will be successful.[13] Resistance will be less if people perceive that a change will lead to desirable outcomes. What motivates people to accept or resist change is self-interest. This includes the desire for personal power, prestige, income, or security. Before people react to any change, they may consciously or unconsciously make a calculation of how their interests are affected.[14]

People in organizations are more ready for change when there are external pressures such as a loss of competitiveness or internal pressures from high rates of turnover or absenteeism, high grievance rates, sabotage, complaints and hostility, and so forth. External pressures for change can also be characterized by economic condition, government regulations, and the influence of interest groups. The economic pressures felt by Chrysler in the 1980s led to a labor contract where workers reduced their salaries in an effort to save jobs and to increase the marketability of the cars. The need for change becomes more apparent when a crisis highlights the failure of some aspect of the organization to function. A feeling of pain with an existing state of affairs will likely generate energy assisting the change. The key problem, then, is to manage and build momentum so that there is some pressure or need for change.

Skilled facilitators. A skilled leader, consultant, or internal facilitator is often necessary to assist in bringing about a change. Not all change agents are equally acceptable to a given client, and initial feelings of mistrust and incompatibility are likely to result in strained relationships.[15] Credibility depends on a number of variables such as past experiences within that system, customs, values, norms, and expectations. This is not always related to the formal leadership, nor whether a person is an insider or an outsider.

Successful changes might be more likely if internal resource people are carefully selected who possess assessment-prescriptive skills and if groups are involved in the process of change.[16] Some studies have emphasized the importance of contacts between the researcher and practitioners at all stages of a study. This translates into more energetic methods of contact and to more consequential use of the findings.[17]

Support of credible people. The staying power of an idea needs the support of credible people, even though most innovative ideas are usually sparked off from events occurring elsewhere, or from external persons. The investment in the change and its direction must ultimately be felt by those involved in the process of change.

Most commitment strategies indicate the importance of participation and involvement of organizational participants in reexamining problems and practices. A collaborative change strategy helps managers learn about the needs of the people involved and allows such needs to be reflected in the final changes. Employees affected by the change should be involved in its design and the final implementation should take into account the needs of the people who are going to make it work.

STRATEGIC CONSIDERATION IN MANAGING CHANGE

Certain strategic questions may need to be answered in introducing change in an organization. What will be the target of the change effort? What division of the organization should be focused on? What should be the pace of the change? Should the change effort start at the top? Should we respond to individuals or work with people in groups? These and many other questions will occur in the process of managing change. Often, these questions are outlined as a series of choices.

This section presents a series of dilemmas that managers might have to confront in the implementation of a change. The dilemmas are presented as extremes, but a strategy will obviously not be so "black and white." However, a manager or change agent will confront most of these dilemmas in some form, and it may be useful to use them as a tool for assessment.[18]

1. Total Organizational versus Departmental or Group Change. The size of a change may need to correspond to the available resources for carrying it out. Important resources are money and materials to see the project through. However, the most important resources include a talent of people to facilitate the project and the time they have to carry it out. A change project probably needs to be more limited in scope if managers, facilitators, or organizational participants do not have the time or energy to carry it through. Above all, changes take time for facilitators and managers to provide support and ideas, and encourage people to be involved.

Change might also be more limited in scope if groups of people in an organization are not supportive or are opposing a change. Such might be the case when introducing new technologies, and members may be resistant because of fears of job loss or because of lack of interest. Change programs usually provide certain people with more or less authority, and this struggle has to be dealt with. In cases where there is a great deal of opposition, it is sometimes more prudent to focus an experimental or pilot project until a critical mass of supporters forms. Alternatively, the project might introduced more slowly to recognize and respond to opposing viewpoints.

2. Changing People versus Changing Structures. How does one go about the process of changing people. One approach is to focus on changing individuals through group sessions, training, and education. A second approach is to change organizational structures and allow change to occur from the new interactions between new people who are working together on tasks. This might involve the design of new jobs, applications of new technologies, or the creation of new reporting relationships.

Both of these approaches are probably needed in changing organizations, although neither should be viewed as a pure strategy. That is, traditional forms of classroom learning may be just as inappropriate as new job designs which have no concept or vision of how they affect the interactions of people. Traditional forms of classroom learning often offer a diversity of materials and ideas not directly useful to the job. While structural change can create changes in behavior, it can also create uncertainty, insecurity, anger, and frustration when people do not deem the change useful and appropriate.

An appropriate strategy which involves people in the design of the structural change, while slower, can result in building more commitment. For example, action training and action learning are based on action research principles where people are involved in a learning process of designing a change. Action training ideas suggest that the training of individuals should be based on data generated from the organization or from people who are going to be involved in the training experience. Action learning requires the creation of "sets" of organizational people who take on the responsibility for developing knowledge in a specific area and then facilitating the training to other organizational members.

Learning and education, it might be argued, should be focused on the concepts people in an organization find useful. Organizational systems for providing rewards, training, and performance appraisal can enhance the educational experience if they are keyed into the important skills that people need to know. This suggests that it is necessary to develop a profile of the important skills to focus training.

Changes in an organization's structure can also assist the educational process when the designs are created by groups of people who are given the problem of creating the new design. People working together in groups will have the opportunity to discuss ideas, just as they would in a graduate seminar. However, these ideas are focused on real problems and people can learn a great deal about the new structures they are implementing. They should also be able to learn about how the newly designed jobs will affect their quality of working lives.

The facilitator's role and responsibility is key in the above process of change. This is a role of providing people with the experiences, ideas, knowledge, and the process for working together.

3. Power versus Integrative Strategies. Typical power tactics include the use of power and formal authority to make sure a change is implemented. Alternatively, the strategy might rely on working together in gathering information to resolve problems.

Generally, an action research approach relies on a strategy altering the power structure in an organization, and providing individuals with greater access to information. It is a problem-solving strategy seeking to encourage people to work together in the resolution of a problem. Rather than having people stretch their muscles in confrontative approaches, the goal is to encourage the parties to work together in jointly gathering information and defining a mutually acceptable solution. This requires the identification of the issue, each party's interest, brainstorming ideas or alternatives, and then gathering information to develop a resolution which is mutually acceptable.

In some settings, it might be argued, parties may feel that a traditional model of exercising control is necessary. It might be argued that unions, employees, or other interest groups might "bankrupt" a company if they were given more input into the authority. Two safequards are important in this practice of integrative problem-solving: (1) When entering into a integrative relationship, each party should define its BATNA (Best Alternative to a Negotiated Agreement). Each party should, in other words, define its "bottom-line" or the solution it would find acceptable if it were not pushed or coerced. When an integrative relationship challenges one party's values, it is appropriate to "walk away" or abandon this mode of problem-solving. (2) A most effective way to resolve difficulties when negotiations get difficult is to begin a process of research and information gathering. Ideally, parties would work together in this process, and seek to be as open as possible in the gathering of information while recognizing that information gathering should represent different perspectives. Such information gathering is not a political process of sampling those people who support one's point of view.

   4. Resolving Technical versus People Problems. Is it more appropriate to focus on resolving technical or people problems? Organizational problems are sometimes more technical and involve the way the work is designed and the structures and processes for managing (such as performance appraisals, planning, compensation). People problems involve conflicts, feelings of frustration and anger, miscommunications, and so forth.

   Many managers and change agents spend a great deal of time dealing with a range of people problems concerned with lack of communication, dissatisfaction with the work, lack of input into decision-making. These problems, in poorly designed systems, can consume the "lion's share" of energy, and can make it difficult to focus on technical issues such as providing the organization with a new design. In fact, it is sometimes strategic to not get involved with specific people issues such as counselling, correcting miscommunications, and listening except when it involves information gathering or responding to issues of a new design. A change agent who is overly eager to get involved in counselling may create a set of expectations of the key roles of the project.

   Action research is a sociotechnical experience of responding to both technical and people needs. It is judged on its ability to implement a new technical design--the new jobs, structures for reporting, or management systems, but to do so in a way which allows people to exercise their input. A new technical system may need to be created which responds to technical criteria of efficiency, cost effectiveness, or productivity. However, certain social efficiencies need to be recognized such as individual and group needs to have input into decision-making, variety, learning, and so forth.

   This does not imply that change agents should not get involved in counselling or providing support for frustrated employees. "Listening," conflict resolution, understanding, and being a person is important in developing a trusting relationship. However, if these activities are not focused within the overall task of a technical design, these activities can build a dependence. This change agent serves as a social worker or Roman Catholic priest of listening and helping, but of not being effective in altering structures which might assist the change.

At certain points in a technical design, it is obviously appropriate to act like a counsellor or social worker. Listening is the only posture to take in crisis situations, where new designs are experiencing difficulty, or when employees need an avenue to emotionally let off steam. As a principle of listening in such situations, it is important that all perspectives are heard, ideally in the presence of each other. However, after the listening is over, it is important to focus on the technical issues or reasons people are expressing these problems.

The sociotechnical principle suggests that the process of creating the new design should contribute to the individual's and organization's capacity to deal with similar problems in the future. In addition, the design should prevent future problems from occuring, while improving the quality of working life in an organization.

5. Information Gathering versus Facilitation. Many change agents act as academic researchers in gathering scientifically precise information. The information gathering strategy often requires a sizable expenditure of time and energy, and sometimes appears rather slow. Alternatively, other change agents provide little theory and research, but do an excellent job in facilitating others by holding problem-solving discussions and setting goals. This is the role of the process facilitator who works with the belief system that new solutions and actions are not brought from outside, but are developed from people within the organization. The facilitator is a catalyst.

The action research strategy attempts to combine both information gathering and facilitation. The goal is to carry out information gathering within the system being studied, and ideally with the assistance of organizational participants. Once the information is collected, there is a important responsibility to use it to resolve organizational problems. And once the project is completed, there is an important responsibility to use the results to assist other projects. This involves combining the results of this study with other similar studies in furthering the social sciences.

6. Top-Down versus Bottom-up. Change can be centrally planned from the top or allowed to flow from ideas and initiatives of people at the bottom or middle parts of the organization. Several considerations might point out the dilemma of top-down or bottom-up change. However, when the change is initiated from management, there is the need to sell it to organizational participants. If ideas come from employees, then, managers have to be convinced of the value.

Top-down change may provoke less resistance if: members of the organization are homogeneous and have common goals and values; if people do not desire interaction and involvement; if there are serious costs from inaction; when tasks are simple, similar, and defined; when the changes do not threaten the basic values of people in power; and if the change agents are unwilling or unable to handle change or diversity.[19]

An action research approach recognizes the needs of those in power positions, but it also assumes a leader's position is much stronger if people at lower levels are committed to the change. This usually means that managers and workers are more effective in joint problem-solving.

7. Rapid versus Slow Change. The pace of the change has a great deal to do with the energy, time, and resources which people are willing to expend. There is an implication that the pace of a change might be increased by more centralized and top-down strategies. However, while the change may be introduced in such a fashion, such strategies do not guarantee a quicker implementation.

The pace of a change depends on the ability of people in an organization to accept the change and to integrate it within their working lives. Acceptance is based on understanding and the ability of the change agents to assist in doing this. At times, the pace of change may have to be slowed to adjust for people's needs, energy, time, and ability to understand.

SUMMARY

This book began by recognizing that research and organizational development have been accused of being increasingly incompatible. It concludes by suggesting that research and practical organizational development need not be separate processes, as the separation increases their detachment from the activities they both rely on. Effective action research requires real life problems, collaborative relationships, and grounded concepts. Effective organizational development requires a clear direction, an organization accustomed to change, pressures for change, skilled facilitators, and support from credible people. In this sense, research is the "seed" for change, and the eventual roots to sustain it. Organizational development, on the other hand, provides an environment for this to flourish in a productive way.

NOTES

1. P. E. Connor, "A Critical Inquiry Into Some Assumptions and Values Characterizing Organizational Development," *Academy of Management Review*, vol. 2, no. 4, 1977, pp. 635-644; W. G. Bennis, *Organizational Development: Its Nature, Origins, and Prospects* (Reading, Mass. : Addison Wesley, 1969); W. L. French, and C. H. Bell, Jr. , *Organizational Development* (Englewood Cliffs, N. J. : Prentice Hall, 1973).

2. G. I. Susman, and R. D. Evered, "An Assessment of the Scientific Merits of Action Research," *Administrative Science Quarterly*, vol. 23, 1978, pp. 582-603.

3. R. L. Kahn, "Organizational Development: Some Problems and Proposals," *Journal of Applied Behavioral Science*, vol. 10, 1974, pp. 484-502. This may be a dated quote. Organizational development practices have certainly improved since this time, although many can still be accurately summarized by this quote. Recent reviews indicate that the methods and designs are certainly more rigorous, although reporting practices are still judged to be inadequate. See J. M. Nicholas and M. Katz, "Research Methods and Reporting Practices in Organizational Development: A Review and Some Guidelines," *Academy of Management Review*, vol. 10, 1985, pp. 737-749. See also P. E. Connor, "A Critical Inquiry Into Some Assumptions and Values Characterizing Organizational Development. "

4. These practices are similar to those defined in the some of the early work carried out at the Tavistock Institute of Human Relations.

5. D. T. Campbell, "Prospective: Artifact and Control," In R. Rosenthal and R. L. Rosnow (eds.), *Artifact in Behavioral Research* (New York: Academic Press, 1969), p. 356.

6. J. N. Franklin, "Characteristics of Successful or Unsuccessful Organizational Development," *Journal of Applied Behaviorial Science*, vol 12, no. 4, 1976, pp. 471-491. This study compares eleven organizations with successful OD efforts and fourteen with unsuccessful efforts.

7. L. Isabella, "Evolving Interpretations as a Change Unfolds: How Managers Construe Key Organizational Events," *Academy of Management Journal,* vol. 33, 1990, pp. 7-41; J. Hage and M. Aiken, *Social Change in Complex Organizations* (New York: Random House, 1970); R. Lippitt, J. Watson, and B. Westley, *The Dynamics of Planned Change* (New York: Harcourt Brace and World, 1958); J. P. Kotter and L. A. Schlesinger, "Choosing Strategies for Change," in J. B. Ritchie and P. Thompson (eds.), *Organization and People: Readings, Cases, and Exercises in Organizational Behavior* (New York: West Publishing Company, 1984), pp. 388-402.

8. E. A. Locke, G. P. Latham, and M. Erez, "The Determinants of Goal Commitment," *Academy of Management Review*, vol. 13, 1988, pp. 23-39.

9. L. Coch, and J. R. P. French, "Overcoming Resistance to Change," *Human Relations*, vol. 34, 1948, pp. 555-566.

10. W. Bennis and B. Nanus, *Leaders* (New York: Harper and Row, 1985); T. J. Peters and R. H. Waterman, *In Search of Excellence* (New York: Harper and Row, 1982).

11. E. A. Locke, G. P. Latham, and M. Erez, "The Determinants of Goal Commitment," *Academy of Management Review*, vol. 13, 1988, pp. 23-39; See also K. Lewin, "Group Decision and Social Change," in T. Newcomb and E. Hartley (eds.), *Readings in Social Psychology* (New York: Holt, Rinehart and Winston, 1952), pp. 330-344.

12. J. N. Franklin, "Characteristics of Successful or Unsuccessful Organizational Development," pp. 471-491.

13. L. B. Mohr, " Determinants of Innovation in Organizations," *American Political Science Review*, vol. 62, 1969, pp. 111-126.

14. V. H. Vroom, *Work and Motivation* (New York: John Wiley, 1964); E. E. Lawler, *Motivation in Work Organizations,* (Monterey, Calif. : Brooks/Cole), 1973.

15. R. Lippitt, R. Watson, and B. Westley, *Planned Change: A comprehensive Study of Principles and Techniques* (New York: Harcourt Brace and World, 1958), p. 85.

16. J. N. Franklin, "Characteristics of Successful or Unsuccessful Organizational

Development," pp. 471-491.

17. M. Huberman, "Linkage Between Researchers and Practitioners: A Qualitative Study," *American Educational Research Journal.* vol. 27, 1990, pp. 363-391.

18. These strategies are based on M. Beer, and J. W. Driscoll, "Strategies for Change," in J. R. Hackman and J. L. Suttle (eds.), *Improving Life at Work: Behaviourial Science Approaches to Organizational Change* (Santa Monica: Goodyear Publishing Company, 1977), pp. 364-409.

19. These points are summarized by M. Beer and J. W. Driscoll, "Strategies for Change."

Selected Bibliography

Ackoff, R. L. "The Art and Science of Mess Management." *Interfaces*, 11:20-26, 1981.

Andrews, J. D. W. "The Verbal Structure of Teacher Questions: Its Impact on Discussion." *POD Quarterly*, 3(4):129-163, 1980.

Argyris, C. *Intervention Theory and Method*. Reading, Mass.: Addison Wesley, 1970.

Argyris, C. *Inner Contradictions of Rigorous Research*. New York: Academic Press, 1980.

Argyris, C., Putman R., and Smith, D. M. *Action Science*. San Francisco, Calif.: Jossey-Bass, 1985.

Argyris, C. "Making Knowledge More Relevant to Practice: Maps for Action." In E. E. Lawler III, A. M. Mohrman, Jr., S. A. Mohrman, G. E. Ledford, Jr., T. G. Cummings and Associates, *Doing Research That Is Useful to Theory and Practice*. San Francisco: Jossey-Bass, 1985.

Barko, W., and Pasmore, W. "Special Issue: Sociotechnical Systems: Innovations in Designing High-Performing Systems." *Journal of Applied Behavioral Science*, 22:195-360, 1986.

Bartunek, J. M., Gordon, J. R., and Weatherby, R. P. "Developing 'Complicated' Understanding in Administrators." *Academy of Management Review*, 8:273-284, 1983.

Bavelas, A. "A Method for Investigating Individual and Group Ideology." *Sociometry*, 5:371- 377, 1942.

Bavelas, J. B. "Permitting Creativity in Science." in D. N. Jackson and J. P. Rushton (eds.), *Scientific Excellence: Origins and Assessment*. Beverley Hills, Calif.: Sage Publications, 1989.

Beckhard, R., and Harris, R. T. *Organizational Transitions: Managing Complex Change*. Menlo Park, Calif.: Addison Wesley, 1977.

Beekun, R. I. "Assessing the Effectiveness of Sociotechnical Interventions : Antidote or Fad?" *Human Relations,* 42:877-897, 1989.

Beer, M., and Driscoll, J. W. "Strategies for Change." In J. R. Hackman and J. L. Suttle (eds.), *Improving Life at Work: Behaviourial Science Approaches to Organizational Change* Santa Monica: Goodyear, 1977.

Berelson, B. "Content Analysis." In G. Lindzey, *Handbook of Social Psychology*, vol. I, Cambridge, Mass: Addison Wesley, 1954.

Bloom, B. S. et al. (eds.). *Taxonomy of Educational Objectives: Cognitive Domain*. New York: David McKay, 1956.

Bridger, H. "The Northfield Experiment." *Bulletin of the Menninger Clinic*. 6:71-76, 1946.

Bryson, J. M. *Strategic Planning for Public and Nonprofit Organizations*. San Francisco: Jossey-Bass, 1988.

Burns, T., and Stalker, G. M. *The Management of Innovation*. London: Tavistock, 1961.

Campbell, D. T. , and Stanley, J. C. *Experimental and Quasi-Experimental Designs for Research*. Chicago: Rand McNally, 1966.

Campbell, D. T. , and Fiske, D. W. "Convergent and Discriminant Validation by the Multitrait-Multimethod Matrix." *Psychological Bulletin*, 56:81-105, 1959.

Chein, I., Cook, S. W. and Harding J. "The Field of Action Research." *American Psychologist*, 3:43-50, 1948.

Clark, A. W., (ed.). *Experimenting with Organizational Life: The Action Research Approach*. New York: Plenum Press, 1976.

Coch, L., and French, J. R. P. "Overcoming Resistance to Change." *Human Relations*, 34:555-566, 1948.

Connor, P. E. "A Critical Inquiry into Some Assumptions and Values Characterizing Organizational Development." *Academy of Management Review*, 2:635-644, 1977.

Cook, T. D., and Campbell, D. T. Quasi-experimentation: Design and Analysis Issues for Field Settings. Boston: Houghton Mifflin, 1979.

Corey, S. M. *Action Research to Improve School Practices*. New York: Teachers College, Columbia University, 1953.

Cummings, T. G. and Huse, E. *Organizational Development and Change*. St. Paul, Minn: West Publications, 1989.

Cunningham, J. B. "Gathering Data In A Changing Organization." *Human Relations*, 36:403-420, 1983.

Cunningham, J. B. "Action Research: Toward a Procedural Model." *Human Relations*, 29:215-238, 1976.

Daft, R. L. "Learning the Craft of Organizational Research." *Academy of Management Review*, 8:539-546, 1983.

Daft, R. L. , and Wiginton, J."Language and Organization." *Academy of Management Review*, 4:179-191, 1979.

de Bono, E. *The Use of Lateral Thinking*. London: Jonathan Cape, 1967.

de Bono, E. *Lateral Thinking: Creativity Step by Step*. New York: Harper and Row, 1970.

Dorr-Bremme, D. W. "Ethnographic Evaluation: A Theory and Method." *Educational Evaluation and Policy Analysis*. 7:65-83, 1985.

Dubin, R. *Theory Building*. New York: Free Press, 1978.

Emery, F. E., and Thorsrud, E. *Form and Content of Industrial Democracy*. London: Tavistock 1969. (Published in Norway in 1964.)

Emery, F. "Educational Paradigms: An Epistemological Revolution." In E. L. Trist and H. Murray (eds.), *The Social Engagement of Social Science: Selected Writings*. By Members of the Tavistock Institute. Included in Volume II, 1989.

Emery, M. and Emery, F."Searching for New Directions in New Ways . . . For New Times." In J. W. Sutherland (ed.), Management Handbook for Public

Administrators. Toronto: Van Nostrand, 1978.

Fisher, R., and Ury, W. *Getting to Yes: Negotiating Agreement Without Giving In.* New York: Penguin Books, 1981.

Flanagan, J. C. "Critical Requirements: A New Approach to Employee Evaluation." *Personnel Psychology*, 2:419-425, 1949.

Foster, M. "The Theory and Practice of Action Research in Work Organizations." *Human Relations*, 25:529-556, 1972.

Foy, N. "Action Learning Comes to Industry." *Harvard Business Review.* 55:158-168, 1977.

Friedlander, F. "Behavioral Research as a Transactional Process." *Human Organization*, 27:369-379, 1968.

Friend, J. K., and Jessop, W. N. *Local Government and Strategic Choice.* London: Tavistock, 1969.

Gardner, N. "Training as a Framework for Action." *Public Personnel Review.* Jan:39-44, 1957.

Glaser, B. G. and Strauss, A. L. *The Discovery of Grounded Theory: Strategies for Qualitative Research.* New York: Aldine, 1967.

Gordon, M. E., Slade, L. A., and Schmitt, N. "The 'Science of the Sophomore' Revisited: From Conjecture to Empiricism." *Academy of Management Review*, 11:191-207, 1986.

Guba, E. G., and Lincoln, Y. S. *Effective Evaluation: Improving the Usefulness of Evaluation Results Through Responsive and Naturalistic Approaches.* San Francisco: Jossey-Bass, 1981.

Homans, C. G. "Social Behavior as Exchange." *American Journal of Sociology,* 63:597-606, 1958.

Huberman, M. "Linkage Between Researchers and Practitioners: A Qualitative Study." *American Educational Research Journal*, 27:363-391, 1990.

Isabella, L. "Evolving Interpretations as a Change Unfolds: How Managers Construe Key Organizational Events" *Academy of Management Journal,* 33:7-41, 1990.

Jantz, T., Hellervik, L., and Gilmour, D. C. *Behaviour Description Interviewing: New, Accurate, Cost Effective.* Toronto: Allyn and Bacon, 1986.

Jaques, E. *The Changing Culture of the Factory.* Londn: Tavistock, 1951.

Jauch, R. R., Osborn, R. N, and Martin, R. N. "Structured Content Analysis of Cases: A Complementary Method of Organizational Research." *Academy of Management Review*, 5:517-526, 1980.

Jenkins, D. H. "Force Field Analysis Applied to a School Situation." in W. G. Bennis, K. D. Benne, and R. Chin, (eds.), *The Planning of Change.* New York: Holt, Rinehart and Winston, 1969.

Jick, T. D. "Mixing Qualitative and Quantitative Methods: Triangulation in Action." *Administrative Science Quarterly*, 24:602-611, 1979.

Kahn, R. L. "Organizational Development: Some Problems and Proposals." *Journal of Applied Behavioral Science*, 10:484-502, 1974.

Kaplan, A. *Conduct of Inquiry.* Scranton, Penn.: Chandler, 1964.

Katz, D., and Kahn, R. L. *The Social Psychology of Organizations.* New York: John Wiley, 1978.

Kerlinger, F. N. *Behavioral Research: A Conceptual Approach.* New York: John Wiley, 1979.

Klein, D. "Some Notes on the Dynamics of Resistance to Change: The Defender Role."
Reprinted in W. G. Bennis, K. D. Benne and R. Chin, (eds.), *The Planning of Change*. New York: Holt, Rinehart and Winston, 1969.

Kotter, J. P., and Schlesinger, L. A. "Choosing Strategies for Change." In J. B. Ritchie and P. Thompson, (eds.), *Organization and People: Readings, Cases, and Exercises in Organizational Behavior*. New York: West Publishing Company, 1984.

Krippendorf, K. *Content Analysis: An Introduction to its Methodology*. Beverly Hills, Calif.: Sage Publications, 1980.

Kuhn, T. S. *The Structure of Scientific Revolutions*. 2nd ed. Chicago: University of Chicago Press, 1970.

Lawler, E. E., Mohrman, Jr., A. M., Mohrman, S. A., Ledford, Jr., G. E., and Cummings T. G. and Associates. *Doing Research That Is Useful for Theory and Practice*. San Francisco: Jossey-Bass, 1985.

Lewin, K. "Action Research and Minority Problems." *Journal of Social Issues*. 2:34-46, 1946.

Lewin, K. "Group Decision and Social Change." In T. M. Newcombe and E. L. Hartley, (eds.), *Readings in Social Psychology*. New York: Holt, Rinehart and Winston, 1947.

Lewin, K. *Field Theory and Social Science*. New York: Harper and Brothers, 1951.

Lewin, K. "Quasi-stationary Social Equilibria and the Problem of Permanent Change." In W. G. Bennis, K. D. Benne, and R. Chin (eds.), *The Planning of Change*. New York: Holt, Rinehart and Winston, 1969.

Lincoln, Y. and Guba, E. *Naturalistic Inquiry*. Beverly Hills, Calif.: Sage Publications, 1985.

MacNamara, M., and Weekes, W. H. "The Action Learning Model of Experiential Learning for Developing Managers." *Human Relations*, 35:819-902, 1982.

Maier, N. R. F. *Principles of Human Relations*. New York: John Wiley, 1952.

Marrow, A. J. *The Action Theorist*. New York: Basic Books, 1958.

Marrow, A. J. *The Practical Theorist* New York: Basic Books, 1969.

Marshall, C., and Rossman, G. B. *Designing Qualitative Research*. Newbury Park, Calif.: Sage Publications, 1989.

Martinko, M. J., and Gardner, W. L. "Beyond Structured Observation: Methodological Issues and New Directions." *Academy of Management Review,* 10:676-695, 1985.

Maruyama, M. "Endogenous Research: Rationale." In P. Reason and J. Rowan (eds.), *Human Inquiry: A Source Book of New Paradigm Research*. Chichester, England: Wiley, 1981.

Menzies, I. E. P. "A Case Study in the Functioning of Social Systems as a Defence Against Anxiety: A Report of a Study of the Nursing Services of a General Hospital." *Human Relations*, 13:95-121, 1960.

Micceris, T. "The Unicorn, the Normal Curve, and Other Improbable Creatures." *Psychological Bulletin*, 105:156-166, 1989.

Miles, M. B., and Huberman, A. M. *Qualitative Data Analysis*. Beverley Hills: Sage Publications, 1984.

Miller, E. J., and Rice, A. K. *Systems of Organization*. London: Tavistock, 1967.

Miner, J. B. "The Validity and Usefulness of Theories in an Emerging Organizational Science." *Academy of Management Review*, 9:296-306, 1984.

Mintzberg, H. *The Nature of Managerial Work*. New York: Harper and Row, 1973.

Mitroff, I. I., and Kilmann, R. H. *Methodological Approaches to Social Science: Integrating Divergent Concepts and Theories*. San Francisco: Jossey-Bass, 1978.

Mohr, L. B. *Explaining Organizational Behavior: The Limits and Possibilities of Theory and Research*. San Fancisco:Jossey-Bass, 1982.

Morgan, G. *Images of Organization*. Beverly Hills, Calif.: Sage Publications, 1986.

Morgan, G., and Smircich, L."The Case for Qualitative Research." *Academy of Management Review*, 5:491-500, 1980.

Nicholas, J. M., and Katz, M. "Research Methods and Reporting Practices in Organizational Development: A Review and Some Guidelines." *Academy of Management Review*, 10:737-749, 1985.

Nutt, P. C. "Tactics of Implementation." *Academy of Management Journal*, 29:230-261, 1986.

Passow, A. H., Miles, B. M., Corey, S. M., and Draper, D. C. *Training Curriculum Leaders for Cooperative Research*. New York: Teachers' College, Columbia University, 1955.

Patton, M. Q. *Qualitative Evaluation Methods*. Beverly Hills, Calif.: Sage Publications, 1980.

Payne, S. L. *The Art of Asking Questions*. Princeton, N. J.: Princeton University Press. 1951.

Pfeffer, J., and Salancik, G. R. *The External Control of Organizations: A Resource Dependence Perspective*. New York: Harper and Row, 1978.

Quinn, R. E. *Beyond Rational Management: Mastering the Paradoxes and Competing Demands of High Performance*. San Francisco, Calif.: Jossey-Bass, 1988.

Rapoport, R. N. "Three Dilemmas in Action Research." *Human Relations*. 23:499-513, 1970.

Reason, R., and Rowan, J. *Issues of Validity in New Paradigm Research*. Chichester England: Wiley, 1981.

Revans, R. "Action Learning: Its Origins and Nature." In Mike Pedler, (ed.), *Action Learning in Practice*. Aldershot. England: Gower, 1983.

Roberts, R. M. *Serendipity: Accidental Discoveries in Science*. New York: John Wiley, 1989.

Rogers, C. R. *Client-centered Therapy*. New York: Houghton Mifflin, 1951.

Rothenberg, A. *The Emerging Goddess: The Creative Process in Art, Science, and Other Fields*. Chicago: University of Chicago Press, 1979.

Sanford, N. "Whatever Happened to Action Research." *Journal of Social Issues*, 26:3-23, 1970.

Schatzman, L., and Strauss, A. L. *Field Research: Strategies for a Natural Sociology*. Englewood Cliffs, N. J.: Prentice Hall, 1973.

Schwab, D. P. "Reviewing Empirically Based Manuscripts: Perspectives on Process." In L. L. Cummings and P. J. Frost (eds.), *Publishing in Organizational Sciences*. Homewood, Ill.: Richard D. Irwin, 1985.

Seashore, S. E. "Field Experiments with Formal Organizations." *Human Organization*, 23:164- 170, 1964.

Shrivastava, P., and Mitroff, I. I. "Enhancing Organizational Research Utilization: The Role of Decision-makers' Assumptions." *Academy of Management Review*, 9:18-26, 1984.

Smith, M. L., and Glass, G. V. *Research and Evaluation in Education and the Social*

Sciences. Englewood Cliffs, N. J.: Prentice Hall, 1987.

Sofer, C. *The Organization from Within: A Comparative Study of Social Institutions Based on a Socio-therapeutic Approach*. London: Tavistock, 1961.

Spender, S. "The Making of a Poem." In B. Ghiselin, *The Creative Process*. New York: Mentor, 1952.

Strauss, A. and Corbin, J. *Basics of Qualitative Research, Grounded Theory Procedures and Techniques*. Calif.: Sage, 1990.

Sudman, S., and Bradburn, S. S. *Asking Questions*. San Francisco: Jossey-Bass, 1982.

Susman, G. I. and Evered, R. D. "An Assessment of the Scientific Merits of Action Research." *Administrative Science Quarterly*, 23:582-603, 1978.

Torbert, W. R. "Why Educational Research has Been so Uneducational; The Case of a New Model of Social Science Based on Collaborative Inquiry." In P. Reason and J. Rowan (eds.), *Human Inquiry: A Sourcebook of New Paradigm Research*. Chichester, England: Wiley, 1981.

Trist, E. L. *The Evolution of Sociotechnical Systems*. Toronto, Ontario: Ontario Quality of Working Life Centre, 1981.

Trist, E. L. "Action Research and Adaptive Planning" In A. Clark, (ed.), *Experimenting with Organizational Life*. New York: Plenum, 1976.

Trist, E. L. and Bamforth, K. W. "Some Social and Psychological Consequences of the Longwall Method of Coal-Getting." *Human Relations*, 4:3-38, 1951.

Tsoukas, H. "The Validity of Ideologic Research Explanations." *Academy of Management Review*, 14:551-561, 1989.

Van de Vall, E., Bolas, M., Bolas, C., and Kang, T. S. "Applied Social Research in Industrial Organizations: An Evaluation of Functions, Theory, and Methods." *Journal of Applied Behavioral Science*, 12:158-177, 1976.

Van Maanen, J. "Making Things Visible." In J. Van Maanen, J. M. Dabbs, and R. R. Faulker, (eds.), *Varieties of Qualitative Research*. Beverly Hills, Calif.: Sage, 1982.

Webb, E., and Weick, K. E. "Unobtrusive Measures in Organizational Theory: A Reminder." *Administrative Science Quarterly,* vol. 24, 1979, pp. 650-659.

Weber, R. P. *Basic Content Analysis*. Beverly Hills, Calif.: Sage, 1985.

Weick, D. K. *The Social Psychology of Organizing*. Reading, Mass: Addison Wesley, 1979.

Weigl, E. "On the Psychology of So Called Processes of Abstraction," translated by M. J. Rioch. *Journal of Abnormal Psychology*, 36:3-33, 1941.

Weiss, R. S. "Issues in Holistic Research." In H. S. Becker, B. Geer, D. Riesman, and R. Weiss (eds.), *Institutions and the Person. Papers presented to Everett C. Hughes*. Chicago: Aldine, 1968.

Whyte, W. F. "Models for Building and Changing Organizations." *Human Organizations*, 26:22- 31, 1967.

Yin, R. K. *Case Study Research Design and Methods, Applied Social Research Methods Series*. vol. 5. Beverly Hills, Calif.: Sage, 1989, 1984.

Index

About the Author

J. BARTON CUNNINGHAM is a Professor in the School of Public Administration at the University of Victoria in British Columbia, Canada. He also has an appointment in the School of Accountancy and Business at Nanyang Technological University, Singapore.